The
Garland Library
of
War and Peace

The
Garland Library
of
War and Peace

Under the General Editorship of

Blanche Wiesen Cook, *John Jay College, C.U.N.Y.*

Sandi E. Cooper, *Richmond College, C.U.N.Y.*

Charles Chatfield, *Wittenberg University*

Discourses on War

by
William Ellery Channing

with an introduction by
Edwin D. Mead

with a new introduction
for the Garland Edition by
Ralph E. Weber

Garland Publishing, Inc., New York & London
1972

The new introduction for this
Garland Library Edition is Copyright © 1972, by
Garland Publishing Inc.

———

All Rights Reserved

———

Library of Congress Cataloging in Publication Data

Channing, William Ellery, 1780-1842.
    Discourses on war.

    (The Garland library of war and peace)
    1. War. 2. Peace. I. Title. II. Series.
JX1949.C5 1972   327'.172   77-149545
ISBN 0-8240-0508-2

Printed in the United States of America

Introduction

I know of no safe depository of the ultimate powers of society but the people themselves; and if we think them not enlightened enough to exercise their control with a wholesome discretion, the remedy is not to take it from them, but to inform their discretion by education.

— *Thomas Jefferson 1821*

The one passion next to the passion of gain in the American heart is the passion for extended empire.... They want to stand at the head of the Anglo-Saxon race, and to allow no gun to be fired in any part of the civilized world without their consent.

— The Times *(London) 1863*

Among the nineteenth century American Christian advocates for peace, William Ellery Channing deserves singular recognition for his relentless pursuit of an objective deemed illusory or perhaps utopian by most of his fellow citizens. From the pulpit and with pamphlets he described the ugly barbarism of warfare: more than this, he reminded his select audiences that Christ required brotherhood, demanded love, promised martyrdom, and provoked discontent among His followers.

INTRODUCTION

Channing provided respectability, status, and leadership for the American peace movement and the anti-slavery societies during the first four decades of the nineteenth century. With remarkable insight and unremitting optimism, he hammered on the theme of the peaceful man, the peaceful society, and in time, an international community in which non-violence may prevail. One of the best-known Americans of his era, Channing recognized the complexity of man and society, of power and its tendency towards corruption, and he taught the Christian virtues of charity, of faith, and certainly hope. In an era of reform, during a time when James Russell Lowell said that reformers believed everything should be held in common except common sense, Channing maintained a rational view of society, spoke of man's individual responsibilities, and kept faith with Christian brotherhood.

Born in Newport, Rhode Island, in 1780, Channing began his life in a war-torn society as Americans sought their independence from Great Britain. As a grandson of William Ellery, a signer of the Declaration of Independence, Channing followed the customs of his class and region. He attended school at Newport until the age of twelve, and then received private tutoring in New London, Connecticut, prior to admission to Harvard from which he graduated in 1798 with highest honors. For the next eighteen months he served as tutor in the David Meade Randolph family in Richmond, Virginia. While there

6

he faced a severe personal crisis: he reacted to the luxury of Richmond society by adopting an ascetic life of sleeping on the cold floor, fasting, and embracing a relentless pursuit of knowledge, particularly that of history. Shy and uncomfortable, he reflected on the meaning of power and international relationships. His hatred of war was already strong as evidenced in a remark to one of his associates: ". . . I am not for enlarging our standing army. I wish there was nothing of the kind." [1] Weakened in health, he returned to Newport and the further study of theology, and in June 1803 he became pastor of the Federal Street Church in Boston.

Through careful preparation and a characteristically relentless dedication, he attracted large audiences to the church services as his sermons gained him city-wide fame and a larger church building. For a brief time in 1813 he also served as Dexter Lecturer in the divinity school at Harvard before ill health forced his resignation. In 1814, he married Ruth Gibbs and her wealth freed him from the often difficult financial problems he had known since his father's death in 1793. Continuing his liberal ministry in the Federal Street Church, Channing became by 1819 the acknowledged leader of the Unitarian movement in America. The next year, Harvard granted him a D.D. degree.

In December 1815, the Massachusetts Peace Society was established in Channing's Boston home where twenty-one others, including Noah Worcester, the New England Unitarian minister and pacifist, signed the charter of the Society and pledged themselves to promote peace "by exhibiting with all clearness and distinctness the pacific nature of the gospel, and by turning the attention of the community to the nature, spirit, causes, and effects of war." [2] *The Society included those who believed, as did Channing, that the Scriptures permitted war in some cases.*

Already in the 1790s, Benjamin Rush, a brilliant physician and reformer, had sought to shift American public opinion against the institution of war through the establishment of a federal Peace Office to counterbalance the War Office. [3] *His remarkable design was not funded and instead wars, real and threatened, stirred the anxieties of Americans living on the western frontier and near the sea. Other hopeful signs of pacifism, however, surfaced in America. For example, shortly after the United States declared war against Great Britain in 1812, a Canadian newspaper reported:*

> *We understand, upon good authority, that the British Settlers in the townships bordering on the Lines of Vermont and New Hampshire have solemnly agreed not to make any aggression upon each other. In the event of individuals committing any outrage by plundering and so forth, the offenders are to be delivered over to either party as prisoners.* [4]

Among Americans, the War of 1812 became

INTRODUCTION

increasingly unpopular, particularly in New England
where it threatened to bring about the dissolution of
the federal union. The conflict forced Worcester to
adopt the position that wars were both barbarous and
unjust methods for settling disputes.[5] His pamphlet,
A Solemn Review of the Custom of War showing that
war is the effect of popular delusion, and Proposing a
Remedy, was published in 1814 under the
pseudonym, Philo Pacificus, and at his own expense
since a publisher could not be found who was willing
to risk public censure.

Other individuals who initiated peace organizations
in these troubled years were William Ladd in New
Hampshire and Maine, Elihu Burritt in Massachusetts
and David Low Dodge in New York City.[6] Channing,
though he could not accept the absolute pacifist
position which Worcester quietly adopted, fostered
the pioneering peace movement and spoke out against
the horrors of warfare. The Massachusetts Peace
Society came to include many of the more
respectable members of Boston and Massachusetts
society. The governor and lieutenant governor, several
judges, the president of Harvard and several
professors together with leading merchants followed
the leadership of Channing and Worcester. Many
other influential citizens, however, opposed the
Society and agreed with John Adams who declined an
invitation to membership in 1816 with the comment:

Experience has convinced me, that wars are as necessary

9

and as inevitable, in our system, as hurricanes, earthquakes and volcanoes. . . . Instead of discouraging a martial spirit, in my opinion it ought to be excited. We have not enough of it to defend us by sea or land. Universal and perpetual peace, appears to me, no more or less than everlastingly passive obedience and non-resistance. The human flock would soon be fleeced and butchered by one or a few. I cannot therefore, Sir, be a subscriber or a member of your society. [7]

Membership in the Society peaked at about 1,000 members and then declined during the 1820s until it merged in 1828 with the newly founded American Peace Society.

The fledgling peace crusade, basically a middle class movement of clergymen, teachers, and professional men, centered around New England: members found themselves labeled unpatriotic, unrealistic and impractical. Most members belonged to one of the following religions: Unitarian, Presbyterian, Baptist, Methodist or Congregational. The Society of Friends in America rarely collaborated with the peace societies because they believed that all wars must be condemned, selective resistance was insufficient. On the other hand, the peace societies often judged that the Quakers had failed in their protests against war because they had cut themselves off from the surrounding community and therefore exerted no real influence on their fellow men.

Channing could not bring himself to condemn all wars. As he wrote in his essay, "War and Human Brotherhood,"

INTRODUCTION

If, indeed, my country were invaded by hostile armies, threatening without disguise its rights, liberties, and dearest interests, I should strive to repel them, just as I should repel a criminal who should enter my house to slay what I hold most dear, and what is intrusted to my care.[8]

In another essay, "First Discourse on War," he took a similar position:

War, as it is commonly waged, is indeed a tremendous evil; but national subjugation is a greater evil than a war of defense; and a community seems to me to possess an indisputable right to resort to such a war when all other means have failed for the security of its existence or freedom.[9]

Oftentimes, Channing found this middle position uncomfortable, for it left him open to criticism from both extremes; nevertheless, he maintained this belief.

Like Worcester, Channing found the causes of war to be rooted in a passion for power, false patriotism, ignorance, and a hunger for physical superiority. In addition, he recognized the powerful instinct for aggression when he wrote:

War is of all games the deepest, awakening most powerfully the soul, and, of course, presenting powerful attraction to those restless and adventurous minds which pant for scenes of greater experiment and exposure than peace affords.[10]

INTRODUCTION

As Worcester wrote before him, and Charles Sumner (whom Channing greatly influenced) would describe more forcefully in the "True Grandeur of Nations" in 1845, Channing depicted the evils of warfare, the suffering and desolation on the battlefields, the utter brutality and immorality of conquest by force. Nevertheless, he continued to believe, like Sumner would, that people may engage in war, that force may be necessary: that the welfare, dignity and honor of a nation may require it to meet force with invincible resolution.[11]

Charged with optimism, Channing wrote that old motives for war were losing power, that peaceful progress because of better communication promised real progress. Moreover, he added that as the poor and middle classes of society increased in intelligence, they would be unwilling to serve in war.[12] And he then propounded a theme not often found in the peace literature of his era:

> One of the fruits of civilization is the increasing expensiveness of war, so that when the voice of humanity cannot be heard, the hollow sound of an empty treasury is a warning which cannot be silenced.[13]

Again and again, Channing appealed to the Christian conscience. In common with other American peace pamphlets and appeals, the author's frame of reference was the Christian world. The Christian, he said, must not serve in war simply because his ruler demands service: let the Christian

12

bear witness against unholy wars, as his country's greatest crimes. If called to take part in them, let him deliberately refuse. If martial law seize on him, let him submit. If hurried to prison, let him submit. If brought thence to be shot, let him submit. There must be martyrs to peace as truly to other principles of our religion.[14]

The power and example of individual effort impressed him as he called for a future world based upon Christian brotherhood.

In 1831, Channing attacked the institution of American slavery from his pulpit. Having returned shortly before from a vacation in St. Croix in the West Indies where brutal slave conditions brought back faded memories of his earlier introduction to slavery in Virginia, he appealed to his audience to eliminate the degrading practice. His condemnation of slavery offended many businessmen in his congregation who feared his attack on slavery could harm their textile businesses. Consequently, though he remained the nominal minister of the Federal Street Church, he lived in partial retirement in Rhode Island and continued also his leadership of the American Unitarian Movement. Channing believed that the abolitionists were too willing to employ violence and invective to achieve their objectives; thus, Garrison and his associates charged Channing with being too patient with slavery, while the Federal Street Church congregation thought him the opposite.[15] His moderate stance irritated many of his *more vocal critics and he spoke out less frequently on slavery for several years.*

In 1834, he became more vocal as an anti-slavery advocate and published a pamphlet entitled, Slavery. *As his confidence grew, so did his concern for the elimination of slavery. In 1836, he published "The Abolitionists," an open letter to James G. Birney in which he defended with a few qualifications the abolitionist position.*[16] *The next year, he wrote another open letter, this time to Henry Clay, entitled, "The Annexation of Texas." Parts of this letter form the last chapter in this volume and reveal the wisdom of Channing as he analyzed the priorities of the United States. His review of the relations between the United States and Mexico provided the sharpest contemporary evaluation of the grave dangers confronting both countries. He believed that greed and misunderstandings threatened to destroy friendly relations between the neighboring republics. He concluded this remarkable essay with a call for internal reform:*

> We are destined *(that is the word)* [sic] to overspread North America, and, intoxicated with the idea, it matters little to us how we accomplish our fate. To spread, to supplant others, to cover a boundless space, this seems our ambition, no matter what influence we spread with us. Why cannot we rise to noble conceptions of our destiny? Why do we feel that our work as a nation is to carry freedom, religion, science, and a nobler form of human nature over this continent? and why do

14

we not remember that to diffuse these blessings we must first cherish them in our own borders, and that whatever deeply and permanently corrupts us will make our spreading influence a curse, not a blessing, to this New World? [17]

Channing's plea for internal reform went unheeded and thus, as noted above, the Times *(London) could later condemn the American passion for extended empire.*

In October 1842, William Channing died and thus escaped the wars he fearfully anticipated as the United States raced down the road of Manifest Destiny. The violence he spoke against brought a brutal war with Mexico, and a Civil War to the United States. His reflections on war and peace, his earnest concern for mankind and internal reform set wholesome priorities, and like Thomas Jefferson, he sought to inform the peoples' discretion by education. Channing provided respectability for the anti-war movement when wars were popular; he spoke common sense to the anti-slavery movement when slavery prevailed; and he inspired his contemporaries and descendents when pessimism threatened to wrap them in its web.

Peace, if it ever exists, will not be based on the fear of war but on the love of peace. It will not be the abstaining from an act, but the coming of a state of mind. In this sense the most insignificant writer can serve peace where the most powerful tribunals can do nothing.

> — *Julien Benda*

Ralph E. Weber

INTRODUCTION

NOTES

[1] *David P. Edgell*, William Ellery Channing *(Boston, 1955), p. 17. This biography together with Arthur W. Brown's books, Always Young for Liberty: A Biography of* William Ellery Channing *(Syracuse, 1956) and* William Ellery Channing *(New Haven, 1961), are the most recent portrayals. Martin E. Marty's book,* Righteous Empire: The Protestant Experience in America *(New York, 1970), notes only Channing's leadership in the Unitarian movement. The author wishes to thank the Marquette University Committee on Research for financial assistance during his study of war protest prior to the coming of the war with Mexico.*

[2] *As quoted in Merle Curti,* The American Peace Crusade, 1815-1860 *(Durham, 1929), p. 11.*

[3] *For a detailed description of Rush's plan, see this author's introduction to Charles Sumner's* Addresses on War *(New York: Garland Publishing, 1971).*

[4] The Quebec Gazette, *July 16, 1812.*

[5] *Cf. Peter Brock,* Pacifism in the United States: From the Colonial Era to the First World War *(Princeton, 1968), pp. 468 ff.*

[6] *Cf. Curti,* American Peace Crusade, *and Brock,* Pacifism in the United States, *for a detailed analysis of these men.*

[7] *As quoted in Devere Allen,* The Fight for Peace *(New York, 1930), and reprinted in Brock,* Pacifism, *p. 473.*

[8] *William Ellery Channing,* Discourses on War *(Boston, 1903), p. 13.*

[9] Ibid., *p. 32.*

[10] Ibid., *p. 27.*

[11] Ibid., *p. 65.*

[12] Ibid., *p. 59.*

[13] Ibid., *p. 90.*

[14] Ibid., *pp. 106-107.*

NOTES

[15] *William Lloyd Garrison became frustrated with Channing's qualifications about abolishing slavery immediately, while others judged the minister to be cowardly. Arthur M. Schlesinger, Jr., believed Channing sabotaged liberal movements by insisting upon internal reform while being indifferent to external social change. Cf.* The Age of Jackson *(Boston, 1946), p. 146 and Edgell,* Channing, *pp. 45 ff.*

[16] *The problem of slavery continued to occupy his main interest during his last years. In 1840, he defended emancipation in the West Indies and in 1842 he wrote on the moral implications of freeing the slaves from the slave ship,* Creole, *which had been seized by the slaves and put in at a British port.*

[17] *Channing,* Discourses, *p. 227. Charles Shackford in a lecture delivered at Lyceum Hall, in Lynn, Massachusetts, on January 16, 1846, quoted from Channing's open letter to Henry Clay by repeating Channing's prediction that the American eagle "will whet, not gorge its appetite on its first victim; and will snuff a more tempting quarry, more alluring blood, in every new region which opens southward. To annex Texas is to declare perpetual war with Mexico. Texas is the first step to Mexico." Charles Shackford,* A Citizen's Appeal in Regard to the War with Mexico *(Boston, 1848), p. 6.*

18

DISCOURSES ON WAR

BY

WILLIAM ELLERY CHANNING

WITH AN INTRODUCTION BY

EDWIN D. MEAD

PUBLISHED FOR THE INTERNATIONAL UNION
GINN & COMPANY, BOSTON
1903

CONTENTS

INTRODUCTION

RUSKIN, in one of his eloquent passages, declares that war would quickly vanish from among the civilized nations if the great body of women could once appreciate its enormity and unite in effort against it. The same thing may be said of the Christian Church and its ministers. With a common high resolve upon their part to be true to the principles of the Church's great founder, the Prince of Peace, war and the military system could not endure for a decade as a regular feature in the life of the commonwealth of nations. There is nothing so melancholy, nothing so discouraging to the worker for the peace and order of the world, as the easy readiness of multitudes of Christian churches and ministers to follow the multitude to do evil; to abdicate their ideals and high functions when their nation is once embarked or once bent on unjust war and turn with the crowd from the harp and organ to the drum and fife. The hard, severe, and unpopular but ennobling and commanding duties of moral leadership are forgotten, and the selfish motives and passions of the people are condoned and whitewashed, and mid prayer and song the worse is made to seem the better reason. No other single thing could do more for the promotion of the cause of peace and international reason, in its conflict with the hoary methods of violence and war, than the conversion of the Christian Church to Christian principles; and nothing, surely, can help more efficiently to this end than the contemplation and careful study of one who in the pulpit from the beginning to the end of life applied those principles heroically and luminously to this great issue, as the exigencies of national life from time to time commanded it. Among all men who have stood in pulpits there is none to whom we can more fitly turn as an example here, and none who can better render the religious world this great and needed service; and the present time, when we are emerging from a period in which, in England and America, we have seen in churches a relinquishment of the prophetic function and a time-serving spirit more general and more disastrous than in any period since that of the antislavery struggle in which he played so strong a part, is an opportune time for us to turn back and listen once again to Channing's noble and lofty discourses upon war.

Christianity, Christian principles, the Christian Church, — these were what Channing loved and believed in. To regenerate the nation and the world by a church of practical Christianity, — this was his dream and his effort. A Christian minister, — this is what he always was and wished to be in dealing with every question of social and political reform. The function of the religious teacher, the spiritual molder and inspirer of thought, he felt to be the most important function in a free state. The highest power, he said, does not belong to him who is clothed with office, but with him who does most to guide the public mind. The true sovereigns of a country are those who determine its modes of thinking and its

principles; and here the primary place should be held by
the minister of religion. " The noblest work on earth
or in heaven," he said to a young minister, " is to act
on the soul; to inspire it with wisdom and magnanimity,
with reverence for God and love towards man. This
is the highest function of sages and inspired poets, and
also of statesmen worthy of the name, who comprehend
that a nation's greatness is to be laid in its soul. Glory
in your office. Feel that it associates you with the elect
of past ages, with Jesus Christ, and apostles, and con-
fessors, and martyrs, and reformers; with all who have
toiled and suffered to raise men to intelligence and moral
greatness." But if the function of the preacher is to
be properly performed, he must preach plainly and earnestly and bravely. " Preach with moral courage," he
said in his charge at the ordination of John S. Dwight.
" Fear no man, high or low, rich or poor, taught or
untaught. Honor all men; love all men; but fear
none. Speak what you account great truths frankly,
strongly, boldly. Do not spoil them of life to avoid
offense. Do not seek to propitiate passion and prejudice by compromise and concession. Beware of the
sophistry which reconciles the conscience to the suppression or vague, lifeless utterance of unpopular truth. Do
not wink at wrong deeds or unholy prejudices because
sheltered by custom or respected names. Let your
words breathe a heroic valor. You are bound indeed to
listen candidly and respectfully to whatever objections
may be urged against your views of truth and duty.
You must also take heed lest you baptize your rash,
crude notions, your hereditary or sectarian opinions,

with the name of Christian doctrine. But having deliberately, conscientiously sought the truth, abide by your
conviction at all hazards. Never shrink from speaking
your mind through dread of reproach. Wait not to
be backed by numbers. Wait not till you are sure of
an echo from a crowd. The fewer the voices on the
side of truth, the more distinct and strong must be your
own. Put faith in truth as mightier than error, prejudice, or passion, and be ready to take a place among its
martyrs. Feel that truth is not a local, temporary influence, but immutable, everlasting, the same in all worlds,
one with God, and armed with his omnipotence."

Moral courage, he felt, was what the Protestant minister was peculiarly called to cherish. Mixing freely
with society and depending upon public opinion for
bread, he had strong inducements to make a compromise with the world. There was great danger that
while condemning sin in a mass he would touch gently
the prejudices and wrongs which the community had
taken under its wing. Preaching was often disarmed,
he felt, by this silent, almost unconscious concession to
the world. If the minister ever felt himself in danger,
through any social complications, of compromise and
recreancy to the truth, he should shake himself free at
any cost. "Better earn your bread with the sweat of
your brow," said Channing to such, "than part with
moral freedom." The minister who regarded his office
as meant simply to perpetuate what exists, instead of
to introduce a higher condition of the church and the
world, was, above all, the man for whom Channing had
rebuke and scorn. "Christ," he said, "was eminently

the reformer, and reform is the spirit of the ministry. Without this spirit our churches are painted sepulchers, and the preaching in them but sounding brass or a tinkling cymbal." The truth with which the Christian minister is intrusted is a truth "that is to create a new heaven and a new earth, to prostrate the abuses and corruptions of ages, to unite men by new ties to God and to one another."

Instead of being faithful to this truth and this imperative, Channing, in the midst of the great political conflict of his own time, the conflict with slavery, had to contemplate a church and pulpit which in the main were faithless to them. This was true alike of the South and the North. "At the South," he asked, "what is the Christian ministry doing for the slave? Teaching the rightfulness of his yoke, joining in the cry against the men who plead for his freedom, giving the sanction of God's name to the greatest offense against his children. This is the saddest view presented by the conflict with slavery. The very men whose office it is to plead against all wrong, to enforce the obligation of impartial, inflexible justice, to breathe the spirit of universal brotherly love, to resist at all hazards the spirit and evil customs of the world, to live and to die under the banner of Christian truth, have enlisted under the standard of slavery." Had these ministers chosen to be silent on account of the furious prejudices surrounding them, that might have been approved or pardoned by many; although, says Channing, "it is wise for the minister to resign his office when it can be exercised only under menace and unrighteous restraint, and to go where, with unsealed lips, he may teach and enforce human duty in its full extent." But the ministers at the South had not been content with silence; they had given their support to slavery and thrown their weight into the scale of the master. Channing was slow to believe that in doing this they had preached known falsehood and what their deliberate judgments condemned. But in such cases, he said, "how common is it for the judgment to receive a shape and hue from self-interest, from private affection, from the tyranny of opinion and the passions of the multitude! How common is it for the mind to waver and to be obscured in regard to scorned and persecuted truth! Can we help saying that the loud, menacing popular voice has proved too strong for the servants of Christ?"

This, however, was not chiefly a southern question. "What have the Christians of the North done?" Channing asked. He paid warm tribute to the testimonies against slavery from individual ministers and conventions; but he was forced to declare that "the churches and congregations of the free states have, in the main, looked coldly on the subject, and discouraged, too effectually, the free expression of thought and feeling in regard to it by the religious teacher. Under that legislation of public opinion which, without courts or offices, sways more despotically than czars or sultans, the pulpit and the press have in no small degree been reduced to silence as to slavery, especially in cities, the chief seats of this invisible power." He continued, with deeper feeling: " As a general rule, the Christianity of this day falls fearfully short of the Christianity of the

immediate followers of our Lord. Then the meaning
of a Christian was that he took the cross and followed
Christ, that he counted not his life dear to him in the
service of God and man, that he trod the world under his
feet. Now we ask leave of the world how far we shall
follow Christ. What wrong or abuse is there, which
the bulk of the people may think essential to their prosperity, and may defend with outcry and menace, before
which the Christianity of this age will not bow? We
need a new John who, with the untamed and solemn
energy of the wilderness, shall cry out among us, Repent!
We need that the Crucified should speak to us with a
more startling voice, 'He that forsaketh not all things
and followeth me cannot be my disciple.' We need that
the all-sacrificing, all-sympathizing spirit of Christianity
should cease to bow to the spirit of the world. We
need that, under a deep sense of want and woe, the
church should cry out, 'Thy kingdom come!' and with
holy importunity should bring down new strength and
life and love from heaven."

It was not the pulpit only which he condemned for its
subserviency to popular prejudice and party opinion. He
spoke with equal plainness and severity, in that strenuous antislavery time, of the nervelessness and compliance
of the press. Such a revolution, he said, as would result
from the establishment by good and true men, of whom
there are always enough to turn the balance on all great
questions, of newspapers " in which men and measures
of all parties would be tried without fear or favor by
the moral Christian law," would do more than all things
else for the political regeneration of the country. " I

cannot easily conceive of a greater good to a city," he
wrote to James G. Birney, at a time when freedom of
the press in many of our cities was almost lost, "than the
establishment of a newspaper by men of superior ability
and moral independence, who should judge all parties
and public measures by the standard of the Christian
law, who should uncompromisingly speak the truth and
adhere to the right, who should make it their steady
aim to form a just and lofty public sentiment, and who
should at the same time give to upright and honorable
men an opportunity of making known their opinions
on matters of general interest, however opposed to the
opinions and passions of the day. In the present stage
of society, when newspapers form the reading of all
classes and the chief reading of multitudes, the importance of the daily press cannot be overrated. It is one
of the mightiest instruments at work among us. It is
a power which should be wielded by the best minds in
the community. The office of editor is one of solemn
responsibility, and the community should encourage the
most gifted and virtuous men to assume it, by according
to them that freedom of thought and speech without
which no mind puts forth all its vigor, and which the
highest minds rank among their dearest rights."

The present time, like that of sixty years ago, is peculiarly one when the press and pulpit and people of
England and America need to heed the lessons which
Channing taught. In his new life of Channing, Mr.
Chadwick says with seriousness, discerning well our
danger points: "While on certain lines the thought
and purpose of our time are approximating Channing's

and should enjoy a livelier sympathy with him, on other lines they are departing from him to their hurt and shame, and making themselves amenable to his deprecation and rebuke. The right of the strong nations to subject the weak to their good pleasure; the conviction that 'the black, brown, yellow, and dirty-white people *will have to go*,' and with these the population of the slums; a certain hard complacency in the presence of infernal cruelty, whether at home or in our insular possessions; the flouting of our traditional ideals of popular rights as sentimental constructions for which we have no longer any use, — these are so many aspects of our time that do not so much indicate our response to Channing's spirit as the need of our return to him for guidance in the doubtful way. Never at any time have we been more plainly called to hold up our social, political, and individual life to the searching light of his clear eyes than in this immediate present, when a certain skepticism of human brotherhood has not only entered into minds naturally inclined to such skepticism, but has infected many whom we imagined born for other things."

The wrongs which Mr. Chadwick here specifies, wrongs such as those into which England and America have in these last years been betrayed, the wrongs of unjust war and the subjugation of weaker peoples, were the wrongs peculiarly abhorrent to Channing's humane and chivalric spirit. They were opposed to the first principles of the teaching of Christ as he understood that teaching. Of his lifelong opposition to national greed, aggression, and passion for dominion, to unjust and unnecessary war, to war altogether as a proper means to-day for the arbitrament of the differences between civilized nations, the discourses brought together in the present volume are in a measure the record. "The man of the twentieth century who cares to equip himself with moral weapons and ammunition for use in the 'war against war,'" said Rev. Charles G. Ames in his noble address on "Channing's Testimony against War" before the Free Religious Association in 1902, "may find in Channing's writings a quite adequate outfit. Indeed, like so many other so-called back numbers, these papers contain so much matter that is fresh and up to date, such a network of live wires along which the lightning still plays, that if any one of them were just now printed anonymously it would touch the quick. . . . In reading these discourses of Channing I am impressed by his masterly combination of clear, luminous intelligence and breadth of view with a vast weight of moral passion, — of outspeaking truthfulness, honest hatred of cruelty, and love of mankind. In his reverence for the least of his human brethren there was something almost like worship. The humblest being endowed with the awful gift of reason appeared to him a more sacred object than the whole outward universe. Out of this profound conviction of the dignity and divinity of human nature came his testimony against war, with his sturdy demand for equal laws, for justice to working-men, for the abolition of slavery, for universal education, and for the breaking of every fetter from body or soul. . . . As he traces the origin of war in the lower passions of mankind, so he finds the remedy,

not alone in those provisions for arbitration which he
urges should be adopted, but chiefly in the development
and diffusion of the spirit and principles of Christianity,
by which he always means the love of God translated
into the love of man, as illustrated in the great Prince
of Peace, whose leadership he lovingly acknowledged.
The nations will never beat their swords into plowshares
till they reverence their brotherhood through recognition of their kinship to a common Father. . . . He
feels called to speak all the more freely," adds Mr.
Ames, "because his peace principles are unpopular;
because the people idolize military heroes and are blind
to the wickedness of war; because the war spirit rages
like an intermittent fever in the veins of his countrymen; and because the churches of Christ are asleep and
allow themselves to be made accessories before and after
the bloody fact."

In the first sermon which Channing ever wrote he
declared that all Christian morals may be reduced to
the one principle of love. The aim of the gospel is to
transform our spirits into love. All men lean upon
one another; no man is unnecessary, no man stands
alone. Mutual dependencies unite all creatures, and
only through fraternity can man reflect the goodness
of God. In 1809 he preached a sermon upon "Peace
on Earth." Jesus Christ came, he said, to convert
men into real friends; to give them a common feeling
and a common interest; to implant a principle of love ;
to strip human character of everything fierce and repul-
sive; to take from men's hands the implements of war;
to dispel distrust, suspicion, and jealousy; to win

them to objects in which all may combine and which will form the means of affectionate intercourse. The next year, moved by the military despotism of France and the wars which devastated Europe, he preached a solemn sermon upon the waste and wickedness of the military system. Two years later, and again two years after that, he devoted further sermons to the evils of war. He directed his rebukes especially, as they still need to be directed to-day, to "the proud, vaunting, irritable, contentious, aspiring temper, more disposed to honor courage than humanity, more restless the more it is successful, more devoted to party than to public weal, more open to the influence of parasites and intriguers than of wise and impartial men." In the spring of 1816 he preached a discourse on war before the Convention of Congregational ministers of Massachusetts, which was immediately printed and widely circulated. This discourse, which is included in the present volume, deepened convictions which were already being formed in many minds, in a time in which wars had brought such terrible sufferings to the world. Two years before this, in 1814, Rev. Noah Worcester, the father of the peace movement in America, had published his "Solemn Review of the Custom of War," and in 1815 had begun the regular publication of the *Friend of Peace* and founded the Massachusetts Peace Society — the first influential peace society in the world.[1] Channing was Worcester's colaborer and

[1] A society, the first peace society which ever existed, had been formed in New York in August, 1815 ; and another in Warren County, Ohio, Dec. 2, 1815, the same month that the Massachusetts society

an officer of the new society from the beginning. Indeed, the first meeting of the society was held in his study, in the parsonage house of the parish. It was on the day after Christmas, 1815, that the society was formed; and at the Christmas time for many years its public meetings were held. Its original twenty-two members included the governor of Massachusetts, the president of Harvard College, and several of the professors. The membership rose within four years to a thousand. In 1828, the society, with nearly fifty others in different states, was merged in the American Peace Society. Channing's " Discourse on War " became at once one of the Massachusetts society's most efficient tracts; the first annual report gives account of the circulation of two thousand copies. Channing's close friendship with Worcester finds expression in the noble tribute paid after Worcester's death, included in the present volume; and of the Peace Society itself Dr. Pierce tells us that Channing was " its life and soul." He condemned with special indignation the privateer, the " legalized plunderer," as he called it, in a day when privateering was regular, as the seizure of defenseless private merchantmen in war has remained until our own day. " This pursuit is indeed allowed by the law of nations; but Christians and the friends to public morals must dread and abhor it." In a letter to Mr. Worcester concerning the war against the Seminoles he urges considerations of a character which recent events

was organized. These three societies were formed without any knowledge of one another. The Massachusetts society at once took the lead. The first society in England was formed June 14, 1816.

have made imperative for ourselves. The public had not been given the facts, and he wished to utilize the society's publication for a connected recital of the transactions of that "justifiable war!" with comments upon it. "Let us allow, for the sake of the argument," he said, "that the majority are right in construing the laws of war. Let us then state distinctly, and without any exaggeration, the acts of General Jackson, which they say were justified by these laws. May we not then bring home to men's minds the question whether the time has not come for repealing such horrible laws? If war demands such regulations or outrages to accomplish its end, can war too soon be abolished? Is it not time to exert ourselves to prevent the recurrence of this infernal state of things?"

Shortly after the formation of the Peace Society, Channing prepared in its behalf a remarkable memorial to Congress, urging that our government should unite with the governments of Europe in distinct acknowledgment of the principles of peace and institute a deliberate inquiry to ascertain the methods by which the various governments might coöperate to make the reference of national controversies to impartial judges the regular law of nations, and also to reduce the world's enormous and ruinous military establishments. It was to be fourscore years before, at the call of the Czar of Russia, the official representatives of the world's governments were to gather at The Hague to confer responsibly upon these great issues. But let it not be forgotten that this proposition was made thus early in Boston by an American democrat and Christian minister. The memorial is of such historical significance, as well as intrinsic worth, that it is here given place in its entirety; and there was never so interesting a time to turn back to it as the present, when the American Peace Society has just secured the passage by the Massachusetts Legislature of a memorial to the President and Congress in behalf of the establishment of a stated International Congress, which shall ultimately perform for the organized world a legislative service corresponding to the judicial service performed by the Hague Tribunal.

To the Honorable the Senate and House of Representatives of the United States in Congress assembled. The memorial of the members of the Peace Society of Massachusetts respectfully represents, —

That the society which now solicits the attention of our national rulers was instituted for the single purpose of diffusing pacific and benevolent sentiments through this country and through the world. Impressed with a deep and sorrowful conviction that the spirit of Christianity, which is a spirit of mercy, peace, and kind affection, is imperfectly understood; afflicted by the accumulated miseries and extensive desolations which war has lately spread over the fairest, most fruitful, and most enlightened regions of the earth; and at the same time encouraged by many decisive proofs of the revival of purer and more benevolent principles among Christian nations, your memorialists have formed this association with the solemn and deliberate purpose of coöperating with the philanthropists of every country in promoting the cause of peace and charity, in stripping war of its false glory, and in uniting different communities in the bonds of amity and mutual good will. We are sensible that from the nature of our object it is chiefly to be accomplished by a silent and gradual influence on the minds of men, and accordingly we have limited our operations to the circulation of useful treatises in which the pacific spirit of our religion has been exhibited with clearness and we hope with success. We believe, however, that the present moment demands a departure from our usual course, and we cherish the hope that by an application to the government under which we live, important service may be rendered to the cause of humanity in which we are engaged.

The present memorial is founded on two occurrences which we hail as auspicious to the pacification of the world. The first occurrence to which we refer is the well-known and unprecedented union of several of the most illustrious powers of Europe in declaring before " the universe their unwavering determination to adopt for the only rule of their conduct, both in the administration of their respective states and in their political relations with every other government, the precepts of Christianity, the precepts of justice, of charity, and of peace."

The second occurrence to which we refer is the decided expression of pacific sentiments and anticipations in the conclusion of the late message of the President of the United States, in which his parting wishes for his country are expressed with tenderness and power. In this remarkable passage, worthy the chief magistrate of a Christian community, he expresses his conviction that the " destined career of his country will exhibit a government which, whilst it refines its domestic code from every ingredient not congenial with the precepts of an enlightened age and the sentiments of a virtuous people, will seek by appeals to reason and by its liberal examples to infuse into the law which governs the civilized world a spirit which may diminish the frequency or circumscribe the calamities of war, and meliorate the social and benevolent relations of peace; a government, in a word, which may bespeak the noblest of all ambitions, that of promoting peace on earth and good will to man."

On the occurrences now stated your memorialists respectfully beg leave to found the following suggestions and solicitations.

First. We respectfully solicit, if it be consistent with the principles of the constitution, that the solemn profession of pacific principles lately made by several distinguished sovereigns of Europe may be met by corresponding professions on the part of our own government. Whilst we are sensible that a melancholy discordance has often existed between the language and the conduct of rulers, we still believe that the solemn assertion of great and important principles by men of distinguished rank and influence has a beneficial operation on society by giving to these principles an increased authority over the consciences of those by whom they are professed; by reviving and diffusing a reverence for them in the community; and by thus exalting the standard of *public opinion*, that invisible sovereign to whose power the most absolute prince is often compelled to bow, and to which the measures of a free government are entirely subjected. When we consider the support which is now derived to war from the perversion of public sentiment, we are desirous that our government should unite with the governments of Europe in a distinct and religious acknowledgment of those principles of peace and charity on which the prosperity of states and the happiness of families and individuals are alike suspended.

Secondly. We respectfully solicit that Congress will institute a deliberate inquiry for the purpose of ascertaining the methods by which this government may exert on human affairs that happy influence which is anticipated by the President of the United States, the methods by which it " may infuse into the law which governs the civilized world a pacific spirit," " may diminish the frequency or circumscribe the calamities of war," and may express the " most noble of all ambitions, that of promoting peace on earth and good will to man." We are persuaded that a government sincerely disposed to sustain the august and sublime character which is here described, of the pacificator of the world, will not want means of promoting its ends. We trust that, under the persevering and well-directed efforts of such a government, milder principles would be introduced into the conduct of national hostilities; that the reference of national controversies to an impartial umpire would gradually be established as the law of the Christian world; and that national compacts would be formed for the express purpose of reducing the enormous and ruinous extent of military establishments and of abolishing that outward splendor which has so long been thrown around war, and which has contributed so largely to corrupt the moral sentiments of mankind.

When we represent to ourselves a Christian government sustaining this beneficent relation to the world, mediating between contending states, recommending peaceful methods of deciding the jarring claims of nations, laboring to strip war of its pernicious glare and to diminish the number of those who are interested in its support, diffusing new and generous sentiments in regard to the mutual duties and obligations of different communities, and inculcating by its own example a frank and benevolent policy and a sincere regard to the interests of the world, — when we represent to ourselves such a government we want language to express our conceptions of the happy and magnificent results of its operations. It would form a new and illustrious era in human affairs, whilst, by the blessings which it would spread and by the honor and confidence which it would enjoy, it would obtain a moral empire more enviable than the widest dominion ever founded on violence and crime.

Loving our country with tenderness and zeal, accustomed to regard her as destined to an exalted rank and to great purposes, and desirous to behold in her institutions and policy increasing claims to our reverence and affection, we are solicitous that she should enter first on the career of glory which has now been described, and that all her connections with foreign states should be employed to diffuse the spirit of philanthropy and to diminish the occasions and miseries of war. Of such a country we shall exult to be the children, and we pledge to it an attachment, veneration, and support which can be accorded only to a virtuous community.

Channing's two papers upon the life and character of Napoleon Bonaparte were written for the *Christian Examiner* in 1827–1828, and made a profound impression. They were a powerful expression of his deep distrust and dread of the militant spirit in the world, the spirit of conquest and aggression. He never wrote anything into which he put greater care or more conscience. He wrote, as he said, from a sincere interest in the cause of freedom and mankind. If he had erred, he would thank any friend of truth, he said, to expose his errors. Many friends of truth, as sincere lovers of freedom and humanity as himself, might take issue with him as to many things in the first paper regarding Napoleon's personality, the primary responsibility for the various wars in which he was engaged, and the complex social and political problems in Europe which he confronted; but no lover of freedom and humanity can read the second paper, which is here reprinted almost in its entirety, and which is one great sermon, without saying Amen to every warning and every exhortation.

In 1835, when the President of the United States himself favored war with France and many voices in Congress were violent, Channing delivered before his people the discourse here reprinted, in which he rebuked with solemn earnestness the national indifference to the claims of humanity and pointed out wherein the true honor of states consisted. The lecture on war, prepared three years later and also included in this volume, was similarly prompted by the reckless talk in political and commercial circles about a war with England. "The whole system of war," Channing said, "as it now exists, is abominable. Most actual wars are unjust; so that a philanthropist and Christian should die sooner than engage in them." To Francis Wayland he wrote, in 1835: "You have borne your testimony against war very strongly. Ought not Christians to speak on this subject as they have never done before? At the present moment we are threatened with war for a punctilio, a matter of etiquette. All the crimes and miseries of war are to be encountered for nothing, and yet the public press utters not a word on our obligations as a Christian community. The politicians have the whole affair in their hands. The Christians among us sit still and silent, and leave worldly, self-seeking politicians to decide whether they shall imbrue their hands in the blood of their brethren. Is Christianity always to remain a dead letter in the determination of national concerns, and especially of peace and war?" "Can we wonder," he exclaims in another place, " that when the spirit of war is cherished in the very bosom of the church, it has continued to rage among the nations?"

The school and social usage, he clearly saw, were as culpable as the church in this matter — more responsible for the false definitions of patriotism and national duty and honor which work so much mischief. Our public education is disproportionate and deficient. We have not put the emphasis in the right place. We do not cultivate the habit of honoring the things which civilized and democratic men ought chiefly to honor. Our most popular festivals are not worthy of us and do not educate us in the ways of peace and progress. Our statues are seldom of the men who most deserve them. The crowd pays tribute to the admiral and general as it does not pay tribute to the poet, the artist, the scholar, or the captain of industry, the representative of constructive activity and of intellect. "I should be pleased," said Channing, "to see the members of an important trade setting apart an anniversary for the commemoration of those who have shed luster on it by their virtues, their discoveries, their genius. It is time that honor should

be awarded on higher principles than have governed
the judgment of past ages. Surely the inventor of the
press, the discoverer of the compass, the men who have
applied the power of steam to machinery, have brought
the human race more largely into their debt than the
bloody race of conquerors, and even than many beneficent princes. Antiquity exalted into divinities the first
cultivators of wheat and the useful plants and the first
forgers of metals; and we, in these maturer ages of the
world, have still greater names to boast in the records
of useful art. Let their memory be preserved to kindle
a generous emulation in those who have entered into
their labors."

Channing was not a non-resistant — he often takes
pains to tell us that, and to tell us why. But he
always felt an anxious concern as to any melioration
which was accomplished through violence and bloodshed. As a Christian, he said, "I feel a misgiving,
when I rejoice in any good, however great, for which
this fearful price has been paid. In truth, a good so
won is necessarily imperfect and generally transient.
War may subvert a despotism, but seldom builds up
better institutions. Even when joined, as in our own
history, with high principles, it inflames and leaves
behind it passions which make liberty a feverish conflict of jealous parties, and which expose a people to
the tyranny of faction under the forms of freedom.
Few things impair men's reverence for human nature
more than war; and did I not see other and holier
influences than the sword working out the regeneration
of the race, I should indeed despair."

That the regeneration of the race must be worked
out through earnest and desperate struggle, that life
is an eternal battle between right and wrong, no one,
surely, knew better than Channing. But he felt that
the time had come in Christendom when men's struggles should not be like the struggles of the brutes, but
struggles in the realm of ideas, with ideas themselves
as the only respectable weapons. His own life was a
long warfare with superstition, selfishness, and sin. It
was no life of quietism and serenity, but valiant and
heroic, and none ever paid warmer tribute than he to
the heroic quality in man. Milton was especially the
object of his admiration and enthusiasm ; and in such
terms as these he defends him from the tender folk
who criticise his sharp and wrathful words:

There is constantly going on in our world a conflict between
good and evil. The cause of human nature has always to wrestle
with foes. All improvement is a victory won by struggles. It
is especially true of those great periods which have been distinguished by revolutions in government and religion, and from
which we date the most rapid movements of the human mind,
that they have been signalized by conflict. Thus Christianity
convulsed the world and grew up amidst storms; and the Reformation of Luther was a signal to universal war; and liberty
in both worlds has encountered opposition over which she has
triumphed only through her own immortal energies. At such
periods, men gifted with great power of thought and loftiness
of sentiment are especially summoned to the conflict with evil.
They hear, as it were, in their own magnanimity and generous
aspirations, the voice of a divinity; and thus commissioned, and
burning with a passionate devotion to truth and freedom, they
must and will speak with an indignant energy, and they ought
not to be measured by the standard of ordinary minds in ordinary

times. Men of natural softness and timidity, of a sincere but effeminate virtue, will be apt to look on these bolder, hardier spirits as violent, perturbed, and uncharitable; and the charge will not be wholly groundless. But that deep feeling of evils which is necessary to effectual conflict with them, and which marks God's most powerful messengers to mankind, cannot breathe itself in soft and tender accents. The deeply moved soul will speak strongly, and ought to speak so as to move and shake nations.

Channing's open letter to Henry Clay on the annexation of Texas, a portion of which, to which we have given the title of "National Destiny in National Character," appears almost unaltered in the following pages, was published in 1837. Five years later, in 1842, appeared his burning pamphlet upon "The Duty of the Free States." This was the year of Channing's death; and the strong passage in the pamphlet upon the imminent war with Mexico, upon the war threatened also with England, and upon the obligations of a generous settlement with England of the northeast boundary question are therefore Channing's last public utterances upon war, unless we except the inspired closing passage of his address at Lenox, on the first of August in the same year, two months before his death, which was his last public word. It is interesting to learn that Channing read his pamphlet before its publication to Charles Sumner, who was back from his long European journey and in the very month of his arrival had joined the American Peace Society, being at once placed on the executive committee, on motion of Channing's colleague, Dr. Gannett. A warm intimacy had sprung up between him and Channing,

to whom alike the two great evils of the world were
slavery and war; and when on the Fourth of July,
three years later, Sumner gave in Tremont Temple, in
Boston, his great oration on "The True Grandeur of
Nations," there surely were still ringing in his ears the
solemn words which Channing had read to him and the
proofs of which, in its pamphlet form, he had read
for Channing when the latter had gone away for rest.
Only a month before Channing's death, Sumner wrote
to his brother George: "With the moral elevation of
Channing, Webster would become a prophet. Webster
wants sympathy with the mass — with humanity —
with truth. Without Webster's massive argumentation,
Channing sways the world with a stronger influence.
Thanks to God, who has made the hearts of men to
respond to what is elevated, noble, true! Whose
position do you prefer, — that of Webster or that of
Channing?"

In his discussion of the boundary question in his
pamphlet, Channing makes this wise general statement
of a principle which the world has until now so sadly
neglected, to its cost: "It is the interest of a nation to
establish, on all sides, boundaries which will be satis-
factory alike to itself and its neighbors. This is almost
essential to enduring peace. Wars have been waged
without number for the purpose of uniting the scattered
provinces of a country, of giving it compactness, unity,
and the means of communication. A nation prizing peace
should remove the irritations growing out of unnatural
boundaries." His words upon the war cry against England are so impressive, both in their particular and

general application, that — with the double reason that they are Channing's last words to us on war — we give them here almost without abridgment.

I proceed to offer a few remarks on the duties of the free states as to a subject of infinite importance, — the subject of war. To add to the distresses of the country, a war cry is raised; and a person unaccustomed to the recklessness with which the passions of the moment break out among us in conversation and the newspapers would imagine that we were on the brink of a conflict with the most powerful nation on earth. That we are indeed to fight cannot easily be believed. That two nations of a common origin, having so many common interests, united by so many bonds, speaking one language, breathing the same free spirit, holding the same faith, to whom war can bring no good, and on whom it must inflict terrible evils; that such nations should expose themselves and the civilized world to the chances, crimes, and miseries of war, for the settlement of questions which may be adjusted honorably and speedily by arbitration; this implies such an absence of common sense, as well as of moral and religious principle, that, bad as the world is, one can hardly believe, without actual vision, that such a result can take place. Yet the history of the world, made up of war, teaches us that we may be too secure; and no excitement of warlike feeling should pass without a word of warning.

In speaking of our duties on this subject I can use but one language, that of Christianity. I do believe that Christianity was meant to be a law for society, — meant to act on nations; and, however I may be smiled at for my ignorance of men and things, I can propose no standard of action to individuals or communities but the law of Christ, the law of eternal rectitude, the law not only of this nation but of all worlds.

The great duty of God's children is to love one another. This duty on earth takes the name and form of the law of humanity. We are to recognize all men as brethren, no matter where born or under what sky or institution or religion they may live.

Every man belongs to the race and owes a duty to mankind. Every nation belongs to the family of nations and is to desire the good of all. Nations are to love one another. It is true that they usually adopt towards one another principles of undisguised selfishness, and glory in successful violence or fraud. But the great law of humanity is unrepealed. Men cannot vote this out of the universe by acclamation. The Christian precepts, "Do to others as you would they should do to you," "Love your neighbor as yourself," "Love your enemies," apply to nations as well as individuals. A nation renouncing them is a heathen, not a Christian nation. . . . I know that these principles will receive little hearty assent. Multitudes who profess to believe in Christ have no faith in the efficacy of his spirit or in the accomplishment of that regenerating work which he came to accomplish. There is a worse skepticism than what passes under the name of infidelity, a skepticism as to the reality and the power of moral and Christian truth; and accordingly a man who calls on a nation to love the great family of which it is a part, to desire the weal and the progress of the race, to blend its own interests with the interests of all, to wish well to its foes, must pass for a visionary, — perhaps in war would be called a traitor. The first teacher of universal love was nailed to the cross for withstanding the national spirit, hopes, and prejudices of Judea. His followers, in these better days, escape with silent derision or neglect.

It is a painful thought that our relations to foreign countries are determined chiefly by men who are signally wanting in reverence for the law of Christ, the law of humanity. Should we repair to the seat of government and listen to the debates of Congress, we should learn that the ascendant influence belongs to men who have no comprehension of the mild and generous spirit of our religion; who exult in what they are pleased to call a quick sense of honor, which means a promptness to resent and a spirit of vengeance. And shall Christians imbrue their hands in the blood of their brethren at the bidding of such men? At this moment our chief exposure to war arises from sensibility to what is called the honor of the nation. A nation cannot, indeed, be too jealous of its honor. But, unhappily, few communities

know what this means.   There is but one true honor for men or
nations.   This consists in impartial justice and generosity; in
acting up fearlessly to a high standard of right.   Were the spirit
of justice and humanity to pervade this country, we could not be
easily driven into war.

Channing was the most confident of optimists.   There
might be unjust and unnecessary wars with England and
with Mexico; governments and peoples might harden
their hearts and do wrong to-day, to-morrow and to-morrow; greedy and aggressive policies might succeed this
year and next.   But Channing knew well that " no good
thing is ever failure and no evil thing success," and
that sooner or later the eternal scales should register
redress.   The very last word, therefore, of his pamphlet
on the annexation of Texas, most burning perhaps of
all his condemnations of violence and fraud, is a word
of cheer.   " I place a cheerful trust in Providence.
The triumphs in evil, which men call great, are but
clouds passing over the serene and everlasting heavens.
Public men may, in craft or passion, decree violence
and oppression.   But silently, irresistibly, they and
their works are swept away.   A voice of encouragement comes to us from the ruins of the past, from the
humiliations of the proud, from the prostrate thrones of
conquerors, from the baffled schemes of statesmen, from
the reprobation with which the present age looks back
on the unrighteous policy of former times.   Such sentence the future will pass on present wrongs.   Men,
measures, and all earthly interests pass away; but principles are eternal."   He knew well that a nemesis waits
for nations as for men ; he knew well that the theory

of one morality for men in their corporate capacity and another for men as individuals was a devil's theory; and he knew that a republic may become a tyrant as truly as an emperor. "That government is most perfect in which policy is most entirely subjected to justice, or in which the supreme and constant aim is to secure the rights of every human being. This is the beautiful idea of a free government, and no government is free but in proportion as it realizes this. Liberty must not be confounded with popular institutions. A representative government may be as despotic as an absolute monarchy. In as far as it tramples on the rights, whether of many or one, it is a despotism. The sovereign power, whether wielded by a single hand or several hands, by a king or a congress, which spoils one human being of the immunities and privileges bestowed on him by God, is so far a tyranny. The great argument in favor of representative institutions is that a people's rights are safest in their own hands, and should never be surrendered to an irresponsible power. Rights, rights, lie at the foundation of a popular government; and when this betrays them, the wrong is more aggravated than when they are crushed by despotism."

Channing lived at a time, as we live at a time, in America, when "prosperity" was a god and when multitudes, if they felt that injustice was somehow identified with that prosperity, were willing that the injustice should go on rather than the prosperity be jeopardized. "The people at large are swallowed up in gain, are intoxicated with promises of boundless wealth, are worshiping what they call prosperity. It concerns them little who is slave and who is free, or how the battles of liberty and truth are fought at home and abroad, provided they can drive some enormously profitable bargain, or bring some vast speculation to a successful issue." There are no passages in Channing more necessary for us to-day than those in which he discusses the national wealth which is not derived from national virtue; which is accumulated by conquest and rapacity, or concentrated in the hands of the few whom it strengthens to crush the many. "No greater calamity," he says,

can befall a people than to prosper by crime. No success can be a compensation for the wound inflicted on a nation's mind by renouncing right as its supreme law. Let a people exalt prosperity above rectitude, and a more dangerous end cannot be proposed. Public prosperity, general good, regarded by itself or apart from the moral law, is something vague, unsettled, and uncertain, and will infallibly be so construed by the selfish and grasping as to secure their own aggrandizement. It may be made to wear a thousand forms, according to men's interests and passions. This is illustrated by every day's history. Not a party springs up which does not sanctify all its projects for monopolizing power by the plea of general good. Not a measure, however ruinous, can be proposed which cannot be shown to favor one or another national interest. The truth is that in the uncertainty of human affairs — an uncertainty growing out of the infinite and very subtile causes which are acting on communities — the consequences of no measure can be foretold with certainty. The best concerted schemes of policy often fail; whilst a rash and profligate administration may, by unexpected concurrences of events, seem to advance a nation's glory. In regard to the means of national prosperity the wisest are weak judges. We are too shortsighted to find our law in outward interests. To states, as to individuals, rectitude is the supreme law. It was never

designed that the public good, as disjoined from this, as distinct
from justice and reverence for all rights, should be comprehended
and made our end. Statesmen work in the dark until the idea
of right towers above expediency or wealth. Woe to that people
which would found its prosperity in wrong! It is time that the
low maxims of policy which have ruled for ages should fall. It
is time that public interest should no longer hallow injustice and
fortify government in making the weak their prey.

No shame was so great to Channing as that which he
felt when his own America was recreant to her high
ideals of freedom and humanity; when encouragement
to wrong came "from that country whose Declaration
of Independence was an era in human history." "O
my country!" he exclaims in one place, "hailed once as
the asylum of the oppressed, once consecrated to liberty,
once a name pronounced with tears of joy and hope,
. . . is the sword which wrought out our liberties to
be unsheathed now to enforce the claims of slavery on
foreign states? Can we bear this burning shame?" He
was unwilling to believe that the American democracy
would ultimately be recreant to its duties. "The cant
of indifference or despair" was, of all American cants,
that which was to him least tolerable. "It is, indeed,
possible that this country may sink beneath the work
imposed on it by Providence, and, instead of bringing
the world into its debt, may throw new darkness over
human hope. But great ideas once brought to light do
not die. The multitude of men through the civilized
world are catching some glimpses, however indistinct,
of a higher lot. . . . Thank God! it is natural for man
to aspire; and this aspiration ceases to be dangerous
just in proportion as the intelligent members of society

interpret it aright and respond to it and give themselves to the work of raising their brethren.   If, through
self-indulgence or pride, they decline this work, the
aspiration will not cease ; but, growing up under resistance or contempt, it may become a spirit of hostility,
conflict, revenge.   The fate of this country depends on
nothing so much as on the growth or decline of the great
idea which lies at the foundation of all our institutions,
— the idea of the sacredness of every man's right, the
respect due to every human being."   Even when the
republic was faithless to this great ideal, as she was so
long in his day and has been again in ours, when she
stood before the world "branded with the crime of resisting the progress of freedom on the earth," he still clung
to her in faithful confidence in the persistency and the
resiliency of that ideal, through whatsoever obscurations
or suppressions.   America stood for human rights; for
the principle of self-government.

Every country is characterized by certain great ideas which
pervade the people and the government, and by these chiefly its
rank is determined.   When one idea predominates strongly above
all others, it is a key to a nation's history.   The great idea of
Rome — that which the child drank in with his mother's milk —
was dominion.   The great idea of France is glory.   In despotisms, the idea of the king or the church possesses itself of the
minds of the people, and a superstitious loyalty or piety becomes
the badge of the inhabitants.   The most interesting view of this
country is the grandeur of the idea which has determined its history and which is expressed in all its institutions.   Take away
this, and we have nothing to distinguish us.   A great idea from
the beginning has been working in the minds of this people, and
it broke forth with peculiar energy in our Revolution.   We
believed that the rights of the people were safest, and alone safe,

in their own keeping; under this freedom men's powers would expand and secure immeasurably greater good than could be conferred by a government intermeddling perpetually with the subject. In all other countries the man has been obscured, over-powered by rulers, merged in the state, made a means or tool. Here every man has been recognized as having rights on which no one can trench without crime. The nation has recognized something greater than the nation's prosperity, than outward, material interests; and that is, individual right. In our Revolution a dignity was seen in human nature; a generous confidence was placed in men. It was believed that they would attain to greater nobleness by being left to govern themselves; that they would attain to greater piety by being left to worship God according to their own convictions; that they would attain to greater energy of intellect and to higher truths by being left to freedom of thought and utterance, than by the wisest forms of arbitrary rule. It was believed that a universal expansion of the higher faculties was to be secured by increasing men's responsibilities, by giving them higher interests to watch over, by throwing them very much on themselves. Such is the grand idea which lies at the root of our institutions; such the fundamental doctrine of the political creed into which we have all been baptized.

Channing's consciousness of his American citizenship was a constant and proud consciousness. He was eminently a patriot, at the same time that he was the true citizen of the world and measured his own country and her policies always by universal moral principles. "Few men," says his biographer, "have lived more profoundly moved by patriotism — if that much abused word may be redeemed to signify a devotedness to the essential principles and real prosperity of a people. With his whole soul he longed to realize that ideal of a 'Christian commonwealth' which heralded our forefathers to this

virgin land. No storms, no frosts, could dim the beacon
fire of this great hope."   America to him represented
new things in the world; she had a sublime new vocation
and must obey great new imperatives.   He would have
her self-reliant, would have her break boldly away from
everything which in the Old World had been inimical
to the progress and freedom of man.   His address upon
" National Literature," in 1823, was one of the strongest
words which had until then been spoken in behalf of a
spirit of independence, originality, and national ambition
in the field of American culture and literary life.   He
believed that as a people we occupied a position from
which the great subjects of literature might be viewed
more justly than elsewhere.   He recognized our lack
of a thousand associations and traditions, and of the
literary apparatus of Europe, her libraries, her learned
institutions, and the rest; but he said:

Man is the great subject of literature, and juster and profounder views of man may be expected here than elsewhere.
In Europe, political and artificial distinctions have more or less
triumphed over and obscured our common nature.   In Europe
we meet kings, nobles, priests, peasants.   How much rarer is
it to meet *men :* by which we mean human beings conscious of
their own nature and conscious of the utter worthlessness of
all outward distinctions compared with what is treasured up in
their own souls.   Man does not value himself as man.   It is
for his blood, his rank, or some artificial distinction, and not
for the attributes of humanity, that he holds himself in respect.
The institutions of the Old World all tend to throw obscurity
over what we most need to know, and that is the worth and
claims of a human being.   We know that great improvements
in this respect are going on abroad.   Still the many are too
often postponed to the few.   The mass of men are regarded as

instruments to work with, as materials to be shaped for the use of their superiors. We conceive that our position favors a juster and profounder estimate of human nature. We mean not to boast, but there are fewer obstructions to that moral consciousness, that consciousness of humanity, of which we have spoken. Man is not hidden from us by so many disguises as in the Old World. The essential equality of all human beings, founded on the possession of a spiritual, progressive, immortal nature, is, we hope, better understood; and nothing more than this single conviction is needed to work the mightiest changes in every province of human life and of human thought.

The distinctions between American and European social conditions have lessened much in sixty years; but it is useful to refresh ourselves with Channing's fundamental thought. He believed that all existing literature ought to pass under rigorous review in the light of this democratic principle. The history of the human race must be rewritten. The great men and great events of past ages must undergo a new trial. " The most interesting questions to mankind are yet in debate. Great principles are yet to be settled in criticism, in morals, in politics; and, above all, the true character of religion is to be rescued from the disguises and corruptions of ages. We want a literature in which genius will pay supreme if not undivided homage to truth and virtue; in which the childish admiration of what has been called greatness will give place to a wise moral judgment. The part which this country is to bear in this great intellectual reform we presume not to predict. We feel, however, that, if true to itself, it will have the glory and happiness of giving new impulses to the human mind. We cannot admit the thought that this country is to be only a repetition of the Old World. We delight to believe that God in the fullness of time has brought a new continent to light in order that the human mind should move here with a new freedom, should frame new social institutions, should explore new paths, and reap new harvests."

Patriotism with Channing never degenerated into boasting or complacency, and never made him forget that before he was an American he was a man. The question which he most solicitously asked was what race of men America is likely to produce. He considered our liberty of value only as far as it favored the growth of men. "Our attachment to our country must be very much proportioned to what we deem its tendency to form a generous race of men. We pretend not to have thrown off national feeling; but we have some stronger feelings. We love our country much, but mankind more. As men and Christians our first desire is to see the improvement of human nature. In our survey of our own and other countries the great question which comes to us is this, Where and under what institutions are men most likely to advance? Where are the soundest minds and the purest hearts formed? What nation possesses in its history, its traditions, its government, its religion, its manners, its pursuits, its relations to other communities, and especially in its private and public means of education, the instruments and pledges of a more resolute virtue and devotion to truth? America to him was always to be viewed as a member of the great family of nations; and the advance of all nations together in peace, sympathy, and coöperation was to his thought the supreme task of history.

A nation blessed as we are with free institutions should feel that it holds these not for itself only, but for mankind, and that all oppressive establishments must fall before their influence, if it will but give proof of their tendency and power to exalt a people in spirit, in virtue, and in condition. In truth, this close connection of different communities should lead us as individuals, as well as in our associated character, to interest ourselves in the cause of humanity through the whole earth. The present is an age of great movements, of great perils, and still of glorious prospects, and one in which there is a power of sympathy as well as means of coöperation and extensive agency never known before. In such an age we should not shut up ourselves in ourselves, or look on the struggles of nations with a vain curiosity, but should watch the changes of the world with profound concern, and respond to great principles and cheer philanthropic efforts wherever manifested. We should feel, I think, that the time is approaching in which Christian philanthropy is to act a new part on the theater of human affairs, is to unite men of different countries in the same great work of rolling away abuses, of staying widespread evils, vindicating private rights, establishing public peace, and exalting the condition of the ignorant. We should do what we can to hasten on this era. Our children should be educated on more generous principles, and taught to make new sacrifices to the cause of their fellow-creatures. Every age teaches its own lesson. The lesson of this age is that of sympathy with the suffering and of devotion to the progress of the whole human race.

This larger patriotism, the politics which embraces in its view the whole family of nations, is a part of the more universal and fraternal view of man in his various relations which has resulted from Christianity, and especially from modern democracy. Here we touch a

principle which is omnipresent with Channing as a political reformer. War will cease and the federation of the
world will come because man everywhere is slowly coming to his full stature, to a realization of his rights, and
the consciousness that other men are his brothers; that
he has claims on them and they have claims on him. It
is the same thought which inspired Immanuel Kant
when he said that universal peace would come with
the universal republic. Says Channing:

In looking at our age I am struck immediately with one
commanding characteristic, and that is the tendency in all its
movements to expansion, to diffusion, to universality. This tendency is directly opposed to the spirit of exclusiveness, restriction,
narrowness, monopoly, which has prevailed in past ages. Human
action is now freer, more unconfined. All goods, advantages, helps,
are more open to all. The privileged, petted individual is becoming less, and the human race is becoming more. The multitude
is rising from the dust. Once we heard of the few, now we hear
of the many; once of the prerogatives of a part, now of the rights
of all. We are looking as never before through the disguises,
envelopments of ranks and classes to the common nature which
lies below them, and are beginning to learn that every being who
partakes of it has noble powers to cultivate, solemn duties to perform, inalienable rights to assert, a vast destiny to accomplish.
The grand idea of humanity, of the importance of man as man,
is spreading silently but surely. Not that the worth of the human
being is at all understood as it should be; but the truth is glim-
mering through the darkness. A faint consciousness of it has
seized on the public mind. Even the most abject portions of
society are visited by some dreams of a better condition for which
they were designed. The grand doctrine that every human being
should have the means of self-culture, — of progress in knowledge
and virtue, of health, comfort, and happiness, of exercising the
powers and affections of a man, — this is slowly taking its place

as the highest social truth. That the world was made for all
and not for a few; that society is to care for all; that no human
being shall perish but through his own fault; that the great end
of government is to spread a shield over the rights of all, — these
propositions are growing into axioms, and the spirit of them is
coming forth in all the departments of life.

This thought echoes in a hundred passages of Channing. "The words of the genius of our age breathe a
spirit of universal sympathy. The great poet of our
times, Wordsworth, has gone to common life, to the feelings of our universal nature." "To what is the civilized world tending? To popular institutions, to the
influence of the people, of the mass of men, over public affairs. A little while ago and the people were
unknown as a power in the state. Now they are get-
ting all power into their hands. Even in despotisms,
where they cannot act through institutions, they act
through public opinion. Intelligence is stronger, and
in proportion as the many grow intelligent they must
guide the world. Once history did not know that the
multitude existed, except when they were gathered
together on the field of battle, to be sabered and shot
down for the glory of their masters; now they are coming forward into the foreground of her picture."

Some one has said that Channing's tribute to Fénelon
is a tribute to his own characteristic virtues. Of his
tribute to Worcester, the founder of the Peace Society,
the same might be said; and so of his tribute to John
Gallison, who was a devoted member of the Peace
Society. "Accustomed as he was to believe that every
principle which a man adopts is to be carried into life,

he was shocked with the repugnance between the Christian code and the practice of its professed followers on the subject of war; and he believed that Christianity, seconded as it is by the progress of society, was a power adequate to the production of a great revolution of opinion on this point, if its plain principles and the plain interests of men were earnestly unfolded." Similarly, in his memorial discourse upon Dr. Follen, we find that his tribute to that noble philanthropist's commanding sense of the dignity of man is a burning statement of the principle which informed and inspired all his own aims and methods as a social reformer. "Tender and affectionate as his nature was, his sense of justice, his reverence for right, was stronger than his affections; and this was the chief basis and element of his heroic character. Accordingly the love of freedom glowed as a central, inextinguishable fire in his soul; not the schoolboy's passion for liberty, caught from the blood-stained pages of Greece and Rome, but a love of freedom resting on and blended with the calmest knowledge, growing from clear, profound perceptions of the nature and destiny and inalienable rights of man. He felt to the very depth of his soul that man, God's rational, immortal creature, was worth living for and dying for. To him the most grievous sight on earth was not misery in its most agonizing forms, but the sight of man oppressed, trodden down by his brother. To lift him up, to make him free, to restore him to the dignity of a man, to restore him to the holy hope of a Christian, — this seemed to him the grandest work on earth, and he consecrated himself to it with his whole soul."

This ever-present, all-pervading sense of the dignity
and divinity of human nature was what made Channing
the powerful champion which he was of the unprivileged
and poor, of the struggling working classes, and of a
more democratic politics and industry. His words here
are always solemn and prophetic. He was a century
ahead of his time in his demands for a regenerated
society. He could not tolerate injustice, inequality, or
undeserved and unearned privilege. As a minister of
Jesus Christ he could not sanction these, and he felt
that no minister of Christ was to be pardoned who did
sanction them. "The spirit of Christianity," he said,
"is distinguished by universality. It is universal justice. It respects all the rights of all beings. It suffers
no being, however obscure, to be wronged without condemning the wrong-doer. Impartial, uncompromising,
fearless, it screens no favorites, is dazzled by no power,
spreads its shield over the weakest, summons the mightiest to its bar, and speaks to the conscience in tones under
which the mightiest have quailed. It is also universal
love, comprehending those that are near and those that
are far off, the high and the low, the rich and poor,
descending to the fallen, and especially binding itself
to those in whom human nature is trampled under foot."
His fundamental theory of human nature, of man as a
social and political being, was precisely that which lay
at the foundation of Grotius's great work on "The
Rights of War and Peace," in which international law as
we know it had its birth. "Man has rights by nature.
The disposition of some to deride abstract rights, as if
all rights were uncertain, mutable, and conceded by

society, shows a lamentable ignorance of human nature. Whoever understands this must see in it an immovable foundation of rights. These are gifts of the Creator, bound up indissolubly with our moral constitution. In the order of things they precede society, lie at its foundation, constitute man's capacity for it, and are the great objects of social institutions. The consciousness of rights is not a creation of human art, a conventional sentiment, but essential to and inseparable from the human soul."

Contemplating man's brutality to man and the flagrant wrongs which still in our time, as in his, pervade society, he trembled often lest the new order was destined to come in through fearful social cataclysms.

When we look back on the mysterious history of the human race we see that Providence has made use of fearful revolutions as the means of sweeping away the abuses of ages and of bringing forward mankind to their present improvement. Whether such revolutions may not be in store for our own times I know not. The present civilization of the Christian world presents much to awaken doubt and apprehension. It stands in direct hostility to the great ideas of Christianity. It is selfish, mercenary, sensual. Such a civilization can not, must not, endure forever. How it is to be supplanted I know not. I hope, however, that it is not doomed, like the old Roman civilization, to be quenched in blood. I trust that the works of ages are not to be laid low by violence, rapine, and the all-devouring sword. I trust that the existing social state contains in its bosom something better than it has yet unfolded. I trust that a brighter future is to come, not from the desolation but from gradual, meliorating changes of the present. Among the changes to which I look for the salvation of the modern world one of the chief is the intellectual and moral elevation of the laboring class. The impulses which are to reform and quicken society are probably to come not from its more conspicuous but from its obscurer divisions; and among these I see with joy new wants, principles, and aspirations beginning to unfold themselves.

He found far more ground for hope among the struggling working classes than " among what are called the better classes." " These," he said, " are always selfishly timid, and never originate improvements worthy of the name." He found " the great features of society hard and selfish," and Christianity " so at war with the present conditions of society that it can hardly be spoken and acted out without giving great offense." His hopes for the improvement of society centered steadily more and more in the poorer classes. " As Paul turned to the Gentiles," writes Mr. Chadwick truly, " so he to the wage-earners, when he found the rich and cultured unable or unwilling to translate his spiritual message into terms of social justice." What he saw in connection with the antislavery movement is what the reformer sees always in his struggle with convention and all vested rights, with the military system or with whatever has got itself intrenched in popularity, fashion, passion, and prejudice. " Another fact which struck me at this meeting was the absence of what is called the influential part of the community. Men of standing, as they are called, were not there. Abolitionism seems to make no progress in this class, nor will it unless it should gain a party large enough in the middle and laboring ranks to be worth the notice of politicians, and then it will be amply repaid by courtesy and attention for the neglect it now receives. The harvest of abolitionism is to be reaped among what are called the middle classes, and an engine of immense power has been put into their hands for this purpose by southern politicians, who have taught that we, the rich and educated of the free states, can keep our property and our political institutions only by making the great laboring portion of the community our slaves. This new southern doctrine is as yet but imperfectly understood by the mass of our farmers, mechanics, and other workingmen. But the abolitionists are wielding this weapon with zeal and effect, and are linking themselves more and more with the mass of the people."

With joy indeed he would have seen, could he have lived till now, the new aspirations and resolutions of the workingmen of the world touching the appalling waste and wrong of war. Could he have entered at this time the parliaments of Germany and France, he would have found the representatives of the working classes the eloquent and chief protestants there against the military system and the monstrous armaments which are exhausting the resources of the nations and ever menacing the world's peace. Nowhere is international organization so complete as in the realm of industry and labor; and the federation of the workingmen in the great family of nations seems likely to precede and pioneer the federation of the world.

The temptations to war in our own time spring chiefly from commercial rivalry and from the arrogance of the so-called superior races toward weaker and less civilized men. A false interpretation of the doctrine of evolution has strengthened among us, in the last generation, a social and political philosophy which appeals so naturally and strongly to all the selfish instincts of men and nations that the vicious alliance has counteracted in melancholy measure the humane and democratic tendencies which in the nineteenth century were gaining such hopeful and inspiring headway. The last decade has shown Christendom acting, in lamentable degree, upon the principle that the weak have no rights which the strong are bound to respect; and Anglo-Saxondom, we are forced to confess, has shown itself the most conspicuous sinner. Channing said, sixty years ago: " I have great faith in our Anglo-Saxon blood. We Anglo-Saxons have much that is bad in us. I doubt whether through this race the world is to be saved; but for practical energy, for skill in surmounting difficulties, for richness of resources, we are unrivaled." We must believe, we will not doubt, that through this race as much as through any other, we will hope more than through any other, the world is to be redeemed from darkness, despotism, and disorder. If the race does not subserve this high purpose, then all its practical energy will prove no benediction; and it cannot subserve this purpose unless it learns to respect sacredly the humblest people, however backward in the long struggle toward political enlightenment and capacity, and throttles in itself those instincts of the dominator and the spoiler, the condemnation of which in all the world has been the noblest expression of its own political genius.

Kossuth in Faneuil Hall fifty years ago begged us not to speak of " American liberty." We might speak of liberty in America; but liberty was not American —

it should have no geographical adjective — it was the right of man. This Channing too asked America, whose honor it was to make the most historic assertion of the principle, never to forget. " It was the glory of the American people that in their Declaration of Independence they took the ground of the indestructible rights of every human being. They declared all men to be essentially equal, and each born to be free. They did not, like the Greek or Roman, assert for themselves a liberty which they burned to wrest from other states. They spoke in the name of humanity, as the representatives of the rights of the feeblest as well as mightiest of their race. They published universal, everlasting principles which are to work out the deliverance of every human being. Such was their glory. Let not the idea of rights be erased from their children's minds by false ideas of public good. Let not the sacredness of individual man be forgotten in the feverish pursuit of property. It is more important that the individual should respect himself and be respected by others than that the wealth of both worlds should be accumulated on our shores. National wealth is not the end of society. It may exist where large classes are depressed and wronged. It may undermine a nation's spirit, institutions, and independence."

To the tyrannous commercialism which above all else to-day tempts England and America to infidelity to their best traditions, Channing's voice especially comes.

Allow me to express an earnest desire and hope that the merchants of this country will carry on their calling with these generous views. Let them not pursue it for themselves alone.

Let them rejoice to spread improvements far and wide and to unite men in more friendly ties. Let them adopt maxims of trade which will establish general confidence. Especially in their intercourse with less civilized tribes let them feel themselves bound to be harbingers of civilization. Let their voyages be missions of humanity, useful arts, science, and religion. It is a painful thought that commerce, instead of enlightening and purifying less privileged communities, has too often made the name of Christian hateful to them, has carried to the savage not our useful arts and mild faith but weapons of war and the intoxicating draught. I call not on God to smite with his lightnings, to overwhelm with his storms, the accursed ship which goes to the ignorant, rude native freighted with poison and death ; which goes to add new ferocity to savage life, new licentiousness to savage sensuality. I have learned not to call down fire from heaven. But in the name of humanity, of religion, of God, I implore the merchants of this country not to use the light of a higher civilization to corrupt, to destroy our uncivilized brethren. Establish with them an intercourse of usefulness, justice, and charity. Before they can understand the name of Christ, let them see his spirit in those by whom it is borne.

He believed that the artificial commercial regulations and protective policies of nations were a fruitful source of enmity and conflicts and that the worker for internationalism and the world's peace should be the worker for the freest possible commercial intercourse. "Free trade!" he exclaimed; "this is the plain duty and plain interest of the human race. To level all barriers to free exchange; to cut up the system of restriction, root and branch; to open every port on earth to every product, — this is the office of enlightened humanity. To this a free nation should especially pledge itself. Freedom of the seas, freedom of harbors, an intercourse of nations free as the winds, — this is not a dream of philanthropists. We are tending towards it, and let us hasten it. Under a wiser and more Christian civilization we shall look back on our present restrictions as we do on the swaddling bands by which in darker times the human body was compressed."

In his very last public address, the address at Lenox, in 1842, occurs a passage which we Americans sixty years later may take to heart: " When I am told that society can only subsist by robbing men of their dearest rights, my reason is as much insulted as if I were gravely taught that effects require no cause, or that it is the nature of yonder beautiful stream to ascend these mountains or to return to its source. The doctrine that violence, oppression, inhumanity, is an essential element of society, is so revolting that, did I believe it, I would say, let society perish, let man and his works be swept away, and the earth be abandoned to the brutes. Better that the globe should be tenanted by brutes than brutalized men. No! it is safe to be just, to respect men's rights, to treat our neighbors as ourselves; and any doctrine hostile to this is born of the Evil One. Men do not need to be crushed. A wise kindness avails with them more than force. Treat men as men, and they will not prove wild beasts."

It was an echo of this thought which we had in the word of that noble English administrator, Sir Andrew Clarke, describing his work among the Malays of the Straits Settlements, among whom he sought to " restore order from chaos without curtailing their sovereignty."

"They were willing," he said, "to listen to reason, as the vast majority of persons, whether wearing a silk hat or a turban, usually are." "Not by wars involving the slaughter of native races," he added, "not by the agency of chartered companies, which necessarily seek first their own interests, has the development of the Malay States been attained. Their present peace and marvelous advance in prosperity have been due to a sympathetic administration which has dealt tenderly with native prejudices and sought to lead upward a free people instead of forcibly driving a subject race."

"It is no excuse for taking possession of a man," said Channing, "that we can make him happier. We are poor judges of another's happiness. He was made to work it out for himself. Our opinion of his best interests is particularly to be distrusted when our own interest is to be advanced by making him our tool. Especially if to make him happy we must drive him as a brute, subject him to the lash, it is plainly time to give up our philanthropic efforts and to let him seek his good in his own way." Channing counted civilization "a doubtful good when it is promoted by establishing the dominion of one man or people over another." He pronounced it "the crime of crimes to use power against liberty; to crush and subdue and subjugate mankind; to rob men of the free use of their nature; to take them out of their own hands and compel them to bend to another's will." Every man must live under law, yet it were "better for him to be lawless than to live under lawless sway." "Whoever holds one human being in bondage," said Channing again, almost in the

words of Lincoln, "invites others to plant the foot on
his own neck. Thanks to God, not one human being
can be wronged with impunity. The foundation of the
liberties of a people is impartial justice, is respect for
human nature, is respect for the rights of every human
being." Few passages in Channing are more powerful
or persuasive than those in which he shows how in a
republic it is impossible to be tyrannous in one place
without menacing freedom in another. "It is instructive to observe how soon and naturally retribution
follows crime. We uphold slavery in the District of
Columbia, and this is beginning to intrench on our own
freedom; it is making of no effect the right of petition
— a right founded not on convention and charters but
on nature, and granted even by despots to their subjects. By sanctioning an acknowledged wrong at the
seat of government we have provoked a blow at our
own privileges."

The danger which always threatens a democracy is
the coercion of public opinion by majorities and multitudes, and especially the feeling that in great crises the
government of a country must be unquestioningly supported—the feeling against which Chatham, Burke, and
Fox protested so righteously in our behalf in 1775.
"The feeling of individual responsibility," said Channing, "is very much lost in consequence of the deference of the private man to the government under which
he lives. The private conscience is merged in the
public. What the government determines the multitude
of men are apt to think right. We are members of a
community, and this relation triumphs over all others.

We do not exercise our moral judgment." "Multitudes," he says again, "know no higher authority than human government. They think that a number of men, perhaps little honored as individuals for intelligence and virtue, are yet competent, when collected into a legislature, to create right and wrong. The most immoral institutions thus gain a sanctity from law. Is conscience to stoop from its supremacy and to become an echo of the human magistrate? Is the law written by God's finger on the heart placed at the mercy of interested statesmen? Is it not one of the chief marks of social progress that men are coming to recognize immutable principles, to understand the independence of truth and duty on the human will, on the sovereignty of the state, whether lodged in one or many hands?" Channing's supreme effort as a citizen was to keep the communal mind moral. "My great aim in what I have written on matters of public interest is to reunite politics and morality, to bring into harmony the law of the land and the law of God. Among the chief causes of the miseries of nations is the divorce which has taken place between politics and morality; nor can we hope for a better day till this breach be healed. Men intrusted with government have always been disposed to regard themselves as absolved from the laws of justice and humanity. Falsehoods and frauds are allowed them for their country or their party. To maintain themselves against their opponents they may even involve nations in war; and the murders and robberies which follow this crime are not visited on their heads by human justice. In all times government has been the grand

robber, the grand murderer, and has yet escaped the deep
reprobation which breaks forth against private guilt."
"The human soul," said Channing, "is greater, more
sacred than the state, and must never be sacrificed to
it." "There are grand, fundamental, moral principles
which shine with their own light, which approve themselves to the reason, conscience, and heart, and which
have gathered strength and sanctity from the experience
of nations and individuals through all ages. These are
never to be surrendered to the urgency of the moment,
however pressing, or to imagined interests of individuals
or states. Let these be sacrificed to hope or fear, and
our foundation is gone."

To the vulgar notion that might makes right, that
majorities have sacred credentials, and that patriotism
prescribes the support of the policies of the governments
which majorities create, Channing, from the standpoint
of his principle of justice as natural right, urges one
rejoinder which cannot fail to make even the most
conservative listen.

I always hear with pain the doctrine too common among
lawyers, that property is the creature of the law; as if it had no
natural foundation, as if it were not a natural right, as if it did
not precede all laws and were not their ground instead of being
their effect. Government is ordained not to create so much as
to protect and regulate property ; and the chief strength of government lies in the sanction which the moral sense, the natural
idea of right, gives to honestly earned possessions. The notion
which I am combating is essentially revolutionary and destructive. We hear much of radicalism, of agrarianism, at the present
day. But of all radicals the most dangerous perhaps is he who
makes property the "creature of law" ; because what law creates

it can destroy. If we of this Commonwealth have no right in our persons, houses, ships, farms, but what a vote of the legislature or the majority confers, then a vote of the same masses may strip us of them all and transfer them to others; and the right will go with the law. According to this doctrine I see not why the majority, who are always comparatively poor, may not step into the mansions and estates of the rich. I see not why the law cannot make some idle neighbor the rightful owner of your fortune or mine. What better support can radicalism ask than this?

Channing was not the spokesman for the rich man; but he would have the rich man and the rich nation understand what the principles are upon which alone their just rights rest. He was the spokesman for the poor man, the arraigner of social inequity, the prophet of sweeping social changes; and he never failed to see that the problem of ringing war itself out of the world was the problem of ringing in a better political economy. It was his firm belief " that our present low civilization, the central idea of which is wealth, cannot last forever; that the mass of men are not doomed hopelessly and irresistibly to the degradation of mind and heart in which they are now sunk; that a new comprehension of the end and dignity of a human being is to remodel social institutions and manners; that in Christianity and in the powers and principles of human nature we have the promise of something holier and happier than now exists." In the same year, 1835, in which he gave his Second Discourse on War he wrote: " The cry is, ' Property is insecure, law a rope of sand, and the mob sovereign.' The actual, present evil, — the evil of that worship of property which stifles all the nobler sentiments and makes man property, — this nobody sees; but appearances of approaching convulsions of property, these shake the nerves of men, who are willing that our moral evils should be perpetuated to the end of time, provided their treasures be untouched. I have no fear of revolutions. We have conservative principles enough at work here. What exists troubles me more than what is to come." St. Simonism, Owen's doctrines, the coöperative system, and all the new manifestations which began to swarm in his own time satisfied him "that the old principles of property are to undergo a fiery trial; that the monstrous inequalities of condition must be redressed, and that greater revolutions than the majority have dreamed of, whether for good or evil, are to be anticipated." These revolutions could be for good, he held, substantial social improvement and the world's peace and order could be promoted, only through the connection of social duty with religion, the connection of man with God, and through each man's viewing all other men as his brothers and in deed and truth sons of God.

This is what it always comes to with Channing. This was his politics and this his religion. The maintenance of this democratic sentiment and its embodiment in public policy was the imperative laid upon the republic. Channing was joyful when this democratic sentiment was strong, and sad when it was weak. He had occasions enough for sadness in the last twenty years of his life. "The old enthusiasm of liberty seems to be dying among us. The spirit of aristocracy, which always grows with the growth of population and wealth, and still more the crimes and errors which have dishonored the cause of constitutional freedom in both continents, have chilled the old republican ardor. The faith of many in the capacity of men for self-government is shaken. Little interest is felt in the struggles of other nations for emancipation from old abuses and for securing better institutions. This is not to be wondered at, but it is much to be deplored. Despair of improvement is the symptom of spiritual death. Freedom is departing when faith in it is lost." The simple old American faith, he knew well, would be exposed to many shocks as America grew rich and strong, came into closer touch with the older nations, and approached more nearly their conditions. "I suppose there will be an increase of the aristocratic spirit and feeling in our cities, which are already too much disposed to sympathize with the exclusives abroad. The natural development of our institutions and national character will be more interfered with; spiritual objects will for a time be more lost sight of; but I trust freedom is a mightier and more contagious principle than the opposite and that in the long run its influence will be more felt. The present stage of civilization is a necessary one and will follow its own course. The child grows strong in mind as well as body by acting on matter and seeking physical good, and the race may need the same discipline. We must try that the Old World may hear some generous, inspiring tones from the New."

Too often in his day, as in ours, the friends of freedom, peace, and honor in the Old World had to hear tones from the New which were not generous and inspiring but faithless and reactionary.   Yet his own faith never wavered, and he was ever ready to champion America when criticisms, however warranted and just, came over the ocean, in the strength and light of the long view which he took of the course and fortune of the republic. In the same spirit in which he wrote the following words to Sismondi, the Swiss historian, in 1841, would he write were he with us to-day.

The late untoward events to which you refer do not discourage me as much as they do you.   I expect the people to make a great many mistakes.   It seems the order of Providence that we should grow wise by failures.   Sometimes we learn the true way by having first tried every wrong one.   I see vast obstacles to be overcome.   To reconcile freedom and order, popular legislation and an efficient executive power, manual labor and intellectual culture, general suffrage and a stable administration, equality and mutual deference, the law of population and a comfortable subsistence for all, — this is the work of ages.   It is to undo almost the whole past, to create society anew.   Can we expect it to be done in a day?   I see hostile forces on every side.   In this country I see false and pernicious notions about democracy, and much unfaithfulness to free institutions.   I shut my eyes on none of its dangers, though these seem to me much exaggerated by the friends as well as foes of freedom in Europe.   A dark cloud hangs over the reputation of our country at this moment, and I care not how loud the reproaches are which come to us from your side the ocean.   But I who live here see that the people after this storm are much as they were before.   The great mass are unharmed in character.   I trust in those around me as before.

Channing was writing specifically of a business crisis, in which financial turpitude could fairly be charged not against the body politic but only against individuals and corporations, although indeed large numbers of these.

None knew better than he that a state, a nation, could not corporately decree any unjust policy, or condone it, without suffering in its corporate character. If the great mass remained morally unharmed, it could only be because the great mass did not clearly grasp the facts and comprehend the issues, and therefore did not sin deliberately against the light. Even were the great mass in the republic, betrayed by pride and passion, recreant again and again to the republic's best ideals, a faith like Channing's in the better nature which sooner or later will bring the better mind is the saving faith; and if the general knowledge and the general thought are not yet commensurate with the claims of civilization and international duty, it is the office of the teachers of the people, of the churches and the schools, to push patiently on the work of education that shall make them so. There is no field in which such education is so imperatively demanded to-day as in that which concerns the great questions of war and peace, true and false patriotism, the real honor of nations, and constructive internal policies that shall supersede the present methods of destruction, waste, and wrong.

In such education Channing was a great pioneer. " Truly he was the morning star of a better day for man made one around our globe, by universal equity and brotherly kindness, by heroic works of beneficence and beauty, above all by living communion with the living God." It was the reward and benediction of this lifelong communion that his last words could be, " I have received many messages from the spirit." Of all these messages he transmitted to us none nobler or diviner than those which continue to remind churches and ministers of religion that the founder of Christianity was the Prince of Peace, and that the first Christmas greeting and command was "Peace on earth, good will toward men."

EDWIN D. MEAD.

BOSTON, 1903.

DISCOURSES ON WAR

Mighty powers are at work in the world. Who can stay them? God's word has gone forth, and " it cannot return to him void." A new comprehension of the Christian spirit, — a new reverence for humanity, a new feeling of brotherhood, and of all men's relation to the common Father, — this is among the signs of our times. We see it; do we not feel it? Before this all oppressions are to fall. Society, silently pervaded by this, is to change its aspect of universal warfare for peace. The power of selfishness, all-grasping and seemingly invincible, is to yield to this diviner energy. The song of angels, " On earth peace," will not always sound as fiction. O come, thou kingdom of heaven, for which we daily pray! Come, Friend and Saviour of the race, who didst shed thy blood on the cross to reconcile man to man, and earth to heaven! Come, ye predicted ages of righteousness and love, for which the faithful have so long yearned! Come, Father Almighty, and crown with thine omnipotence the humble strivings of thy children to subvert oppression and wrong, to spread light and freedom, peace and joy, the truth and spirit of thy Son, through the whole earth! — CHANNING'S LAST PUBLIC WORDS.

2

WAR AND HUMAN BROTHERHOOD[1]

I HAVE felt and continually insisted that a new reverence for man was essential to the cause of social reform. As long as men regard one another as they now do, that is, as little better than the brutes, they will continue to treat one another brutally. Each will strive, by craft or skill, to make others his tools. There can be no spirit of brotherhood, no true peace, any farther than men come to understand their affinity with and relation to God and the infinite purpose for which he gave them life. As yet these ideas are treated as a kind of spiritual romance; and the teacher who really expects men to see in themselves and one another the children of God is smiled at as a visionary. The reception of this plainest truth of Christianity would revolutionize society and create relations among men not dreamed of at the present day. A union would spring up, compared with which our present friendships would seem estrangements. Men would know the import of the word Brother, as yet nothing but a word to multitudes. None of us can conceive the change of manners, the new courtesy and sweetness, the mutual kindness, deference, and sympathy, the life and energy of efforts for social melioration, which are to spring up, in proportion as man shall penetrate beneath the body to the spirit, and shall learn what the lowest human

[1] From Channing's Introduction to his published Works.

3

being is. Then insults, wrongs, and oppressions, now
hardly thought of, will give a deeper shock than we
receive from crimes which the laws punish with death.
Then man will be sacred in man's sight; and to injure
him will be regarded as open hostility towards God.
It has been under a deep feeling of the intimate connection of better and juster views of human nature with
all social and religious progress that I have insisted on
it so much in the following pages; and I hope that the
reader will not think that I have given it disproportionate importance.

I proceed to another sentiment, which is expressed
so habitually in these writings as to constitute one of
their characteristics, and which is intimately connected
with the preceding topic. It is reverence for liberty,
for human rights, — a sentiment which has grown with
my growth, which is striking deeper root in my age,
which seems to me a chief element of true love for
mankind, and which alone fits a man for intercourse
with his fellow-creatures. I have lost no occasion for
expressing my deep attachment to liberty in all its
forms, civil, political, religious, to liberty of thought,
speech, and the press, and of giving utterance to my
abhorrence of all the forms of oppression. This love
of freedom I have not borrowed from Greece or Rome.
It is not the classical enthusiasm of youth, which, by
some singular good fortune, has escaped the blighting
influences of intercourse with the world. Greece and
Rome are names of little weight to a Christian. They
are warnings rather than inspirers and guides. My
reverence for human liberty and rights has grown up

in a different school, under milder and holier discipline. Christianity has taught me to respect my race and to reprobate its oppressors. It is because I have learned to regard man under the light of this religion that I cannot bear to see him treated as a brute, insulted, wronged, enslaved, made to wear a yoke, to tremble before his brother, to serve him as a tool, to hold property and life at his will, to surrender intellect and conscience to the priest, or to seal his lips or belie his thoughts through dread of the civil power. It is because I have learned the essential equality of men before the common Father that I cannot endure to see one man establishing his arbitrary will over another by fraud, or force, or wealth, or rank, or superstitious claims. It is because the human being has moral powers, because he carries a law in his own breast, and was made to govern himself, that I cannot endure to see him taken out of his own hands and fashioned into a tool by another's avarice or pride. It is because I see in him a great nature, the divine image, the vast capacities, that I demand for him means of self-development, spheres for free action; that I call society not to fetter but to aid his growth. Without intending to disparage the outward, temporal advantages of liberty, I have habitually regarded it in a higher light, — as the birthright of the soul, as the element in which men are to put themselves forth, to become conscious of what they are, and to fulfill the end of their being.

Christianity has joined with all history in inspiring me with a peculiar dread and abhorrence of the passion for power, for dominion over men. There is nothing

in the view of our divine teacher so hostile to his divine
spirit as the lust of domination. This we are accustomed to regard as eminently the sin of the arch-fiend.
" By this sin fell the angels." It is the most satanic
of all human passions, and it has inflicted more terrible
evils on the human family than all others. It has
made the names of king and priest the most appalling
in history. There is no crime which has not been perpetrated for the strange pleasure of treading men under
foot, of fastening chains on the body or mind. The
strongest ties of nature have been rent asunder, her
holiest feelings smothered, parents, children, brothers
murdered, to secure dominion over man. The people
have now been robbed of the necessaries of life, and
now driven to the field of slaughter like flocks of sheep,
to make one man the master of millions. Through
this passion, government, ordained by God to defend
the weak against the strong, to exalt right above might,
has up to this time been the great wrong-doer. Its
crimes throw those of private men into the shade. Its
murders reduce to insignificance those of the bandits,
pirates, highwaymen, assassins, against whom it undertakes to protect society. How harmless at this moment
are all the criminals of Europe compared with the
Russian power in Poland! This passion for power,
which in a thousand forms, with a thousand weapons,
is warring against human liberty, and which Christianity condemns as its worst foe, I have never ceased
to reprobate with whatever strength of utterance God
has given me. Power trampling on right, whether in the
person of king or priest, or in the shape of democracies,

majorities, and republican slaveholders, is the saddest
sight to him who honors human nature and desires its
enlargement and happiness.

So fearful is the principle of which I have spoken
that I have thought it right to recommend restrictions
on power and a simplicity in government beyond what
most approve. Power, I apprehend, should not be suffered to run into great masses. No more of it should
be confided to rulers than is absolutely necessary to
repress crime and preserve public order. A purer age
may warrant larger trusts; but the less of government
now the better, if society be kept in peace. There
should exist, if possible, no office to madden ambition.
There should be no public prize tempting enough to
convulse a nation. One of the tremendous evils of the
world is the monstrous accumulation of power in a few
hands. Half a dozen men may, at this moment, light
the fires of war through the world, may convulse all
civilized nations, sweep earth and sea with armed hosts,
spread desolation through the fields and bankruptcy
through cities, and make themselves felt by some form
of suffering through every household in Christendom.
Has not one politician recently caused a large part of
Europe to bristle with bayonets? And ought this
tremendous power to be lodged in the hands of any
human being? Is any man pure enough to be trusted
with it? Ought such a prize as this to be held out
to ambition? Can we wonder at the shameless profligacy, intrigue, and the base sacrifices of public interests
by which it is sought and when gained held fast?
Undoubtedly great social changes are required to heal

this evil, to diminish this accumulation of power. National spirit, which is virtual hostility to all countries but our own, must yield to a growing humanity, to a new knowledge of the spirit of Christ. Another important step is a better comprehension by communities that government is at best a rude machinery, which can accomplish but very limited good, and which, when strained to accomplish what individuals should do for themselves, is sure to be perverted by selfishness to narrow purposes, or to defeat through ignorance its own ends. Man is too ignorant to govern much, to form vast plans for states and empires. Human policy has almost always been in conflict with the great laws of social well-being, and the less we rely on it the better. The less of power given to man over man the better. I speak, of course, of physical, political force. There is a power which cannot be accumulated to excess, — I mean moral power, that of truth and virtue, the royalty of wisdom and love, of magnanimity and true religion. This is the guardian of all right. It makes those whom it acts on free. It is mightiest when most gentle. In the progress of society this is more and more to supersede the coarse workings of government. Force is to fall before it.

It must not be inferred from these remarks that I am an enemy to all restraint. Restraint in some form or other is an essential law of our nature, a necessary discipline running through life, and not to be escaped by any art or violence. Where can we go and not meet it? The powers of nature are all of them limits to human power. A never-ceasing force of gravity chains us to the earth. Mountains, rocks, precipices, and seas forbid our advances. If we come to society, restraints multiply on us. Our neighbor's rights limit our own. His property is forbidden ground. Usage restricts our free action, fixes our manners, the language we must speak, and the modes of pursuing our ends. Business is a restraint, setting us wearisome tasks and driving us through the same mechanical routine day after day. Duty is a restraint, imposing curbs on passion, enjoining one course and forbidding another, with stern voice, with uncompromising authority. Study is a restraint, compelling us, if we would learn anything, to concentrate the forces of thought and to bridle the caprices of fancy. All law, divine or human, is, as the name imports, restraint. No one feels more than I do the need of this element of human life. He who would fly from it must live in perpetual conflict with nature, society, and himself.

But all this does not prove that liberty, free action, is not an infinite good, and that we should seek and guard it with sleepless jealousy. For if we look at the various restraints of which I have spoken, we shall see that liberty is the end and purpose of all. Nature's powers around us hem us in, only to rouse a free power within us. It acts that we should react. Burdens press on us that the soul's elastic force should come forth. Bounds are set that we should clear them. The weight which gravitation fastens to our limbs incites us to borrow speed from winds and steam, and we fly where we seemed doomed to creep. The sea, which first stopped us, becomes the path to a new hemisphere.

The sharp necessities of life, cold, hunger, pain, which chain man to toil, wake up his faculties and fit him for wider action. Duty restrains the passions only that the nobler faculties and affections may have freer play, may ascend to God, and embrace all his works. Parents impose restraint that the child may learn to go alone, may outgrow authority. Government is ordained that the rights and freedom of each and all may be inviolate. In study thought is confined that it may penetrate the depths of truth, may seize on the great laws of nature, and take a bolder range. Thus freedom, ever-expanding action, is the end of all just restraint. Restraint without this end is a slavish yoke. How often has it broken the young spirit, tamed the heart and the intellect, and made social life a standing pool. We were made for free action. This alone is life, and enters into all that is good and great. Virtue is free choice of the right; love, the free embrace of the heart; grace, the free motion of the limbs; genius, the free, bold flight of thought; eloquence, its free and fervent utterance. Let me add that social order is better preserved by liberty than by restraint. The latter, unless most wisely and justly employed, frets, exasperates, and provokes secret resistance; and, still more, it is rendered needful very much by that unhappy constitution of society which denies to multitudes the opportunities of free activity. A community which should open a great variety of spheres to its members, so that all might find free scope for their powers, would need little array of force for restraint. Liberty would prove the best peace officer. The social order of our country, without a soldier and almost without a police, bears loud witness to this truth. These views may suffice to explain the frequent recurrence of this topic in the following pages.

I have written once and again on war, — a hackneyed subject, as it is called, yet one would think too terrible ever to become a commonplace. Is this insanity never to cease? At this moment, whilst I write, two of the freest and most enlightened nations, having one origin, bound together above all others by mutual dependence, by the interweaving of interests, are thought by some to be on the brink of war. False notions of national honor, as false and unholy as those of the duelist, do most towards fanning this fire. Great nations, like great boys, place their honor in resisting insult and in fighting well. One would think the time had gone by in which nations needed to rush to arms to prove that they were not cowards. If there is one truth which history has taught, it is that communities in all stages of society, from the most barbarous to the most civilized, have sufficient courage. No people can charge upon its conscience that it has not shed blood enough in proof of its valor. Almost any man, under the usual stimulants of the camp, can stand fire. The poor wretch enlisted from a dramshop and turned into the ranks soon fights like a "hero." Must France and England and America, after so many hard-fought fields, go to war to disprove the charge of wanting spirit? Is it not time that the point of honor should undergo some change, that some glimpses at least of the true glory of a nation should be caught by rulers and people? "It is the honor of a man to pass over a transgression,"

and so it is of states. To be wronged is no disgrace.
To bear wrong generously, till every means of concilia-
tion is exhausted; to recoil with manly dread from the
slaughter of our fellow-creatures; to put confidence in
the justice which other nations will do to our motives;
to have that consciousness of courage which will make
us scorn the reproach of cowardice; to feel that there
is something grander than the virtue of savages; to
desire peace for the world as well as ourselves; and to
shrink from kindling a flame which may involve the
world, — these are the principles and feelings which do
honor to a people. Has not the time come when a
nation professing these may cast itself on the candor of
mankind? Must fresh blood flow forever, to keep
clean the escutcheon of a nation's glory? For one, I
look on war with a horror which no words can express.
I have long wanted patience to read of battles. Were
the world of my mind, no man would fight for glory;
for the name of a commander, who has no other claim
to respect, seldom passes my lips, and the want of sympathy drives him from my mind. The thought of man,
God's immortal child, butchered by his brother; the
thought of sea and land stained with human blood by
human hands, of women and children buried under the
ruins of besieged cities, of the resources of empires
and the mighty powers of nature all turned by man's
malignity into engines of torture and destruction, — this
thought gives to earth the semblance of hell. I shudder
as among demons. I cannot now, as I once did, talk
lightly, thoughtlessly, of fighting with this or that
nation. That nation is no longer an abstraction to me.

It is no longer a vague mass. It spreads out before me into individuals, in a thousand interesting forms and relations. It consists of husbands and wives, parents and children, who love one another as I love my own home. It consists of affectionate women and sweet children. It consists of Christians, united with me to the common Saviour, and in whose spirit I reverence the likeness of his divine virtue. It consists of a vast multitude of laborers at the plow and in the workshop, whose toils I sympathize with, whose burden I should rejoice to lighten, and for whose elevation I have pleaded. It consists of men of science, taste, genius, whose writings have beguiled my solitary hours and given life to my intellect and best affections. Here is the nation which I am called to fight with, into whose families I must send mourning, whose fall or humiliation I must seek through blood. I cannot do it without a clear commission from God. I love this nation. Its men and women are my brothers and sisters. I could not without unutterable pain thrust a sword into their hearts. If, indeed, my country were invaded by hostile armies, threatening without disguise its rights, liberties, and dearest interests, I should strive to repel them, just as I should repel a criminal who should enter my house to slay what I hold most dear, and what is intrusted to my care. But I cannot confound with such a case the common instances of war. In general, war is the work of ambitious men, whose principles have gained no strength from the experience of public life, whose policy is colored if not swayed by personal views or party interests, who do not seek peace

with a single heart, who to secure doubtful rights per-
plex the foreign relations of the state, spread jealousies
at home and abroad, enlist popular passions on the side
of strife, commit themselves too far for retreat, and are
then forced to leave to the arbitration of the sword
what an impartial umpire could easily have arranged.
The question of peace and war is too often settled for
a country by men in whom a Christian, a lover of his
race, can put little or no trust; and, at the bidding of
such men, is he to steep his hands in human blood?
But this insanity is passing away. This savageness
cannot endure, however hardened to it men are by
long use. The hope of waking up some from their
lethargy has induced me to recur to this topic so often
in my writings.

FIRST DISCOURSE ON WAR

BEFORE THE CONGREGATIONAL MINISTERS OF
MASSACHUSETTS, BOSTON, 1816

Nation shall not lift up sword against nation, neither shall they
learn war any more. — *Isaiah* ii. 4.

I HAVE chosen a subject which may seem at first
view not altogether appropriate to the present occasion,
— the subject of WAR. It may be thought that an
address to an assembly composed chiefly of the ministers of religion should be confined to the duties, dangers, encouragements of the sacred office. But I have
been induced to select this topic because, after the slumber of ages, Christians seem to be awakening to a sense
of the pacific character of their religion, and because I
understood that this convention were at this anniversary to consider the interesting question whether no
method could be devised for enlightening the public
mind on the nature and guilt of war. I was unwilling
that this subject should be approached and dismissed
as an ordinary affair. I feared that, in the pressure
of business, we might be satisfied with the expression
of customary disapprobation; and that, having in this
way relieved our consciences, we should relapse into
our former indifference, and continue to hear the howl-
ings of this dreadful storm of human passions with as
much unconcern as before. I resolved to urge on you

the duty, and I hoped to excite in you the purpose, of making some new and persevering efforts for the abolition of this worst vestige of barbarism, this grossest outrage on the principles of Christianity. The day, I trust, is coming when Christians will look back with gratitude and affection on those men who, in ages of conflict and bloodshed, cherished generous hopes of human improvement, withstood the violence of corrupt opinion, held forth, amidst the general darkness, the pure and mild light of Christianity, and thus ushered in a new and peaceful era in the history of mankind. May you, my brethren, be included in the grateful recollection of that day!

The *miseries* and *crimes* of war, its *sources*, its *remedies*, will be the subjects of our present attention.

In detailing its miseries and crimes there is no temptation to recur to unreal or exaggerated horrors. No depth of coloring can approach reality. It is lamentable that we need a delineation of the calamities of war to rouse us to exertion. The mere idea of human beings employing every power and faculty in the work of mutual destruction ought to send a shuddering through the frame. But on this subject our sensibilities are dreadfully sluggish and dead. Our ordinary sympathies seem to forsake us when war is named. The sufferings and death of a single fellow-being often excite a tender and active compassion ; but we hear without emotion of thousands enduring every variety of woe in war. A single murder in peace thrills through our frames. The countless murders of war are heard as an amusing tale. The execution of a criminal depresses the mind, and philanthropy is laboring to substitute milder punishments for death. But benevolence has hardly made an effort to snatch from sudden and untimely death the innumerable victims immolated on the altar of war. This insensibility demands that the miseries and crimes of war should be placed before us with minuteness, with energy, with strong and indignant feeling.

The miseries of war may be easily conceived from its very nature. By war we understand the resort of nations to force, violence, and the most dreaded methods of destruction and devastation. In war the strength, skill, courage, energy, and resources of a whole people are concentrated for the infliction of pain and death. The bowels of the earth are explored, the most active elements combined, the resources of art and nature exhausted, to increase the power of man in destroying his fellow-creatures.

Would you learn what destruction man, when thus aided, can spread around him? Look, then, at that extensive region, desolate and overspread with ruins; its forests rent as if blasted by lightning; its villages prostrated as by an earthquake; its fields barren as if swept by storms. Not long ago the sun shone on no happier spot. But ravaging armies prowled over it; war frowned on it; and its fruitfulness and happiness are fled. Here thousands and ten thousands were gathered from distant provinces, not to embrace as brethren, but to renounce the tie of brotherhood; and thousands in the vigor of life, when least prepared for death, were hewn down and scattered like chaff before the whirlwind.

Repair, my friends, in thought, to a field of recent battle. Here are heaps of slain, weltering in their own blood, their bodies mangled, their limbs shattered, and almost every vestige of the human form and countenance destroyed. Here are multitudes trodden under foot, and the war horse has left the trace of his hoof in many a crushed and mutilated frame. Here are severer sufferers; they live, but live without hope or consolation. Justice dispatches the criminal with a single stroke; but the victims of war, falling by casual, undirected blows, often expire in lingering agony, their deep groans moving no compassion, their limbs writhing on the earth with pain, their lips parched with a burning thirst, their wounds open to the chilling air, the memory of home rushing on their minds, but not a voice of friendship or comfort reaching their ears. Amidst this scene of horrors, you see the bird and beast of prey gorging themselves with the dead or dying, and human plunderers rifling the warm and almost palpitating remains of the slain. If you extend your eye beyond the immediate field of battle, and follow the track of the victorious and pursuing army, you see the roads strewed with the dead; you see scattered flocks, and harvests trampled under foot, the smoking ruins of cottages, and the miserable inhabitants flying in want and despair; and even yet the horrors of a single battle are not exhausted. Some of the deepest pangs which it inflicts are silent, retired, enduring, to be read in the widow's countenance, in the unprotected orphan, in the aged parent, in affection cherishing the memory of the slain, and weeping that it could not minister to their last pangs.

I have asked you to traverse in thought a field of
battle. There is another scene often presented in war,
perhaps more terrible. I refer to a besieged city. The
most horrible pages in history are those which record
the reduction of strongly fortified places. In a besieged
city are collected all descriptions and ages of mankind,
—women, children, the old, the infirm. Day and night
the weapons of death and conflagration fly around them.
They see the approaches of the foe, the trembling bulwark, and the fainting strength of their defenders.
They are worn with famine, and on famine presses
pestilence. At length the assault is made, every bar-
rier is broken down, and a lawless soldiery, exasperated
by resistance, and burning with lust and cruelty, are
scattered through the streets. The domestic retreat is
violated; and even the house of God is no longer a sanc-
tuary. Venerable age is no protection, female purity
no defense. Is woman spared amidst the slaughter of
father, brother, husband, and son? She is spared for a
fate which makes death in comparison a merciful doom.
With such heartrending scenes history abounds; and
what better fruits can you expect from war?

These views are the most obvious and striking which
war presents. There are more secret influences, appealing less powerfully to the senses and imagination, but
deeply affecting to a reflecting and benevolent mind.
Consider, first, the condition of those who are immediately engaged in war. The sufferings of soldiers from
battle we have seen, but their sufferings are not limited
to the period of conflict. The whole of war is a succession of exposures too severe for human nature. Death

employs other weapons than the sword. It is computed that in ordinary wars greater numbers perish by sickness than in battle. Exhausted by long and rapid marches, by unwholesome food, by exposure to storms, by excessive labor under a burning sky through the day, and by interrupted and restless sleep on the damp ground and in the chilling atmosphere of night, thousands after thousands of the young pine away and die. They anticipated that they should fall, if to fall should be their lot, on what they called the field of honor; but they perish in the inglorious and crowded hospital, surrounded with sights and sounds of woe, far from home and every friend, and denied those tender offices which sickness and expiring nature require.

Consider, next, the influence of war on the character of those who make it their trade. They let themselves for slaughter, place themselves servile instruments, passive machines, in the hands of rulers, to execute the bloodiest mandates, without a thought on the justice of the cause in which they are engaged. What a school is this for the human character! From men trained in battle to ferocity, accustomed to the perpetration of cruel deeds, accustomed to take human life without sorrow or remorse, habituated to esteem an unthinking courage a substitute for every virtue, encouraged by plunder to prodigality, taught improvidence by perpetual hazard and exposure, restrained only by an iron discipline which is withdrawn in peace, and unfitted by the restless and irregular career of war for the calm and uniform pursuits of ordinary life; from such men what ought to be expected but contempt of human

rights and of the laws of God? From the nature of
his calling, the soldier is almost driven to sport with the
thought of death, to defy and deride it, and, of course,
to banish the thought of that retribution to which it
leads; and though of all men the most exposed to sudden death, he is too often of all men most unprepared
to appear before his Judge.

The influence of war on the community at large, on
its prosperity, its morals, and its political institutions,
though less striking than on the soldiery, is yet baleful.
How often is a community impoverished to sustain a war
in which it has no interest? Public burdens are aggravated, whilst the means of sustaining them are reduced.
Internal improvements are neglected. The revenue of
the state is exhausted in military establishments, or
flows through secret channels into the coffers of corrupt
men, whom war exalts to power and office. The regular
employments of peace are disturbed. Industry in many
of its branches is suspended. The laborer, ground with
want and driven to despair by the clamor of his suffering
family, becomes a soldier in a cause which he condemns,
and thus the country is drained of its most effective
population. The people are stripped and reduced,
whilst the authors of war retrench not a comfort, and
often fatten on the spoils and woes of their country.

The influence of war on the morals of society is also
to be deprecated. The suspension of industry multiplies
want, and criminal modes of subsistence are the resource
of the suffering. Commerce, shackled and endangered,
loses its upright and honorable character, and becomes
a system of stratagem and collusion. In war the moral

sentiments of a community are perverted by the admiration of military exploits. The milder virtues of Christianity are eclipsed by the baleful luster thrown round a ferocious courage. The disinterested, the benignant, the merciful, the forgiving, those whom Jesus has pronounced blessed and honorable, must give place to the hero, whose character is stained not only with blood, but sometimes with the foulest vices, but all whose stains are washed away by victory. War especially injures the moral feelings of a people by making human nature cheap in their estimation, and human life of as little worth as that of an insect or a brute.

War diffuses through a community unfriendly and malignant passions. Nations, exasperated by mutual injuries, burn for each other's humiliation and ruin. They delight to hear that famine, pestilence, want, defeat, and the most dreadful scourges which Providence sends on a guilty world are desolating a hostile community. The slaughter of thousands of fellow-beings, instead of awakening pity, flushes them with delirious joy, illuminates the city, and dissolves the whole country in revelry and riot. Thus the heart of man is hardened. His worst passions are nourished. He renounces the bonds and sympathies of humanity. Were the prayers, or rather the curses, of warring nations prevalent in heaven, the whole earth would long since have become a desert. The human race, with all its labors and improvements, would have perished under the sentence of universal extermination.

But war not only assails the prosperity and morals of a community; its influence on the political condition is threatening. It arms government with a dangerous patronage, multiplies dependents and instruments of oppression, and generates a power which, in the hands of the energetic and aspiring, endangers a free constitution. War organizes a body of men who lose the feelings of the citizen in the soldier; whose habits detach them from the community; whose ruling passion is devotion to a chief; who are inured in the camp to despotic sway; who are accustomed to accomplish their ends by force, and to sport with the rights and happiness of their fellow-beings; who delight in tumult, adventure, and peril, and turn with disgust and scorn from the quiet labors of peace. Is it wonderful that such protectors of a state should look with contempt on the weakness of the protected, and should lend themselves base instruments to the subversion of that freedom which they do not themselves enjoy? In a community in which precedence is given to the military profession freedom cannot long endure. The encroachments of power at home are expiated by foreign triumphs. The essential interests and rights of the state are sacrificed to a false and fatal glory. Its intelligence and vigor, instead of presenting a bulwark to domestic usurpation, are expended in military achievements. Its most active and aspiring citizens rush to the army, and become subservient to the power which dispenses honor. The nation is victorious, but the recompense of its toils is a yoke as galling as that which it imposes on other communities.

Thus war is to be ranked among the most dreadful calamities which fall on a guilty world; and, what

deserves consideration, it tends to multiply and perpetuate itself without end.   It feeds and grows on the
blood which it sheds.   The passions from which it
springs gain strength and fury from indulgence.   The
successful nation, flushed by victory, pants for new
laurels; whilst the humbled nation, irritated by defeat,
is impatient to redeem its honor and repair its losses.
Peace becomes a truce, a feverish repose, a respite to
sharpen anew the sword and to prepare for future
struggles.   Under professions of friendship lurk hatred
and distrust, and a spark suffices to renew the mighty
conflagration.   When from these causes large military
establishments are formed and a military spirit kindled,
war becomes a necessary part of policy.   A foreign field
must be found for the energies and passions of a martial
people.   To disband a numerous and veteran soldiery
would be to let loose a dangerous horde on society.
The bloodhounds must be sent forth on other communities lest they rend the bosom of their own country.
Thus war extends and multiplies itself.   No sooner is
one storm scattered than the sky is darkened with the
gathering horrors of another.   Accordingly, war has
been the mournful legacy of every generation to that
which succeeds it.   Every age has had its conflicts.
Every country has in turn been the seat of devastation
and slaughter.   The dearest interests and rights of
every nation have been again and again committed to
the hazards of a game of all others the most uncertain, and in which, from its very nature, success too
often attends on the fiercest courage and the basest
fraud.

Such, my friends, is an unexaggerated and, I will add, a faint delineation of the miseries of war; and to all these miseries and crimes the human race have been continually exposed, for no worthier cause than to enlarge an empire already tottering under its unwieldy weight, to extend an iron despotism, to support some idle pretension, to repel some unreal or exaggerated injury. For no worthier cause human blood has been poured out as water, and millions of rational and immortal beings have been driven like sheep to the field of slaughter.

Having considered the crimes and miseries of war, I proceed, as I proposed, to inquire into its sources, — an important branch of our subject, for it is only by a knowledge of the sources that we can be guided to the remedies of war. And here, I doubt not, many will imagine that the first place ought to be given to malignity and hatred. But justice to human nature requires that we ascribe to national animosities a more limited operation than is usually assigned to them in the production of this calamity. It is indeed true that ambitious men who have an interest in war too often accomplish their views by appealing to the malignant feelings of a community, by exaggerating its wrongs, ridiculing its forbearance, and reviving ancient jealousies and resentments. But it is believed that, were not malignity and revenge aided by the concurrence of higher principles, the false splendor of this barbarous custom might easily be obscured and its ravages stayed.

One of the great springs of war may be found in a very strong and general propensity of human nature,

in the love of excitement, of emotion, of strong interest,
— a propensity which gives a charm to those bold and
hazardous enterprises which call forth all the energies
of our nature. No state of mind, not even positive suffering, is more painful than the want of interesting
objects. The vacant soul preys on itself, and often
rushes with impatience from the security which demands
no effort to the brink of peril. This part of human
nature is seen in the kind of pleasures which have
always been preferred. Why has the first rank among
sports been given to the chase? Because its difficulties,
hardships, hazards, tumults awaken the mind and give
to it a new consciousness of existence and a deep feeling of its powers. What is the charm which attaches
the statesman to an office which almost weighs him
down with labor and an appalling responsibility? He
finds much of his compensation in the powerful emotion
and interest awakened by the very hardships of his lot,
by conflict with vigorous minds, by the opposition of
rivals, and by the alternations of success and defeat.
What hurries to the gaming table the man of prosperous fortune and ample resource? The dread of apathy,
the love of strong feeling and of mental agitation. A
deeper interest is felt in hazarding than in securing
wealth, and the temptation is irresistible. One more
example of this propensity may be seen in the attachment of pirates and highwaymen to their dreadful
employment. Its excess of peril has given it a terrible
interest; and to a man who has long conversed with its
dangers the ordinary pursuits of life are vapid, taste-
less, and disgusting. We have here one spring of war.

War is of all games the deepest, awakening most powerfully the soul, and, of course, presenting powerful attraction to those restless and adventurous minds which pant for scenes of greater experiment and exposure than peace affords. The savage, finding in his uncultivated modes of life few objects of interest, few sources of emotion, burns for war as a field for his restless energy. Civilized men, too, find a pleasure in war, as an excitement of the mind. They follow with an eager concern the movements of armies, and wait the issue of battles with a deep suspense, an alternation of hope and fear, inconceivably more interesting than the unvaried uniformity of peaceful pursuits.

Another powerful principle of our nature, which is the spring of war, is the passion for superiority, for triumph, for power. The human mind is aspiring, impatient of inferiority, and eager for preëminence and control. I need not enlarge on the predominance of this passion in rulers whose love of power is influenced by the possession, and who are ever restless to extend their sway. It is more important to observe that, were this desire restrained to the breasts of rulers, war would move with a sluggish pace. But the passion for power and superiority is universal; and as every individual, from his intimate union with the community, is accustomed to appropriate its triumphs to himself, there is a general promptness to engage in any contest by which the community may obtain an ascendency over other nations. The desire that our country should surpass all others would not be criminal did we understand in what respects it is most honorable for a nation to excel;

did we feel that the glory of a state consists in intellectual and moral superiority, in preëminence of knowledge,
freedom, and purity. But to the mass of a people this
form of preëminence is too refined and unsubstantial.
There is another kind of triumph which they better
understand, — the triumph of physical power, triumph
in battle, triumph not over the minds, but the territory
of another state.   Here is a palpable, visible superiority;
and for this a people are willing to submit to severe
privations. A victory blots out the memory of their
sufferings, and in boasting of their extended power
they find a compensation for many woes.

I now proceed to another powerful spring of war;
and it is the admiration of the brilliant qualities displayed in war.   These qualities, more than all things,
have prevented an impression of the crimes and miseries
of this savage custom.   Many delight in war not for
its carnage and woes, but for its valor and apparent
magnanimity, for the self-command of the hero, the
fortitude which despises suffering, the resolution which
courts danger, the superiority of the mind to the body,
to sensation, to fear.   Let us be just to human nature
even in its errors and excesses.   Men seldom delight in
war considered merely as a source of misery.   When
they hear of battles, the picture which rises to their
view is not what it should be, a picture of extreme
wretchedness, of the wounded, the mangled, the slain.
These horrors are hidden under the splendor of those
mighty energies which break forth amidst the perils of
conflict, and which human nature contemplates with an
intense and heart-thrilling delight.   Attention hurries

from the heaps of the slaughtered to the victorious
chief, whose single mind pervades and animates a host
and directs with stern composure the storm of battle;
and the ruin which he spreads is forgotten in admiration
of his power. This admiration has in all ages been
expressed by the most unequivocal signs. Why that
garland woven? that arch erected? that festive board
spread? These are tributes to the warrior. Whilst
the peaceful sovereign, who scatters blessings with the
silence and constancy of Providence, is received with a
faint applause, men assemble in crowds to hail the conqueror, perhaps a monster in human form, whose private
life is blackened with lust and crime, and whose greatness is built on perfidy and usurpation. Thus war is
the surest and speediest road to renown; and war will
never cease while the field of battle is the field of glory,
and the most luxuriant laurels grow from a root nourished
with blood.

Another cause of war is a false patriotism. It is
a natural and generous impulse of nature to love the
country which gave us birth, by whose institutions we
have been molded, by whose laws defended, and with
whose soil and scenery innumerable associations of early
years, of domestic affection, and of friendship have been
formed. But this sentiment often degenerates into a
narrow, partial, exclusive attachment, alienating us from
other branches of the human family and instigating to
aggression on other states. In ancient times this principle was developed with wonderful energy, and sometimes absorbed every other sentiment. To the Roman,
Rome was the universe. Other nations were of no value

but to grace her triumphs and illustrate her power; and he who in private life would have disdained injustice and oppression exulted in the successful violence by which other nations were bound to the chariot wheels of this mistress of the world. This spirit still exists. The tie of country is thought to absolve men from the obligations of universal justice and humanity. Statesmen and rulers are expected to build up their own country at the expense of others, and in the false patriotism of the citizen they have a security for any outrages which are sanctioned by success.

Let me mention one other spring of war, — I mean the impressions we receive in early life. In our early years we know war only as it offers itself to us at a review; not arrayed in terror, not stalking over fields of the slain, and desolated regions, its eye flashing with fury and its sword reeking with blood. War, as we first see it, is decked with gay and splendid trappings and wears a countenance of joy. It moves with a measured and graceful step to the sound of the heart-stirring fife and drum. Its instruments of death wound only the air. Such is war; the youthful eye is dazzled with its ornaments; the youthful heart dances to its animated sounds. It seems a pastime full of spirit and activity, the very sport in which youth delights. These false views of war are confirmed by our earliest reading. We are intoxicated with the exploits of the conqueror, as recorded in real history or in glowing fiction. We follow with a sympathetic ardor his rapid and triumphant career in battle, and, unused as we are to suffering and death, forget the fallen and miserable who are crushed under his victorious car. Particularly by the study of the ancient poets and historians, the sentiments of early and barbarous ages on the subject of war are kept alive in the mind. The trumpet which roused the fury of Achilles and of the hordes of Greece still resounds in our ears; and, though Christians by profession, some of our earliest and deepest impressions are received in the school of uncivilized antiquity. Even where these impressions in favor of war are not received in youth, we yet learn from our early familiarity with it to consider it as a necessary evil, an essential part of our condition. We become reconciled to it as to a fixed law of our nature, and consider the thought of its abolition as extravagant as an attempt to chain the winds or arrest the lightning.

I have thus attempted to unfold the principal causes of war. They are, you perceive, of a moral nature. They may be resolved into wrong views of human glory, and into excesses of passions and desires which, by right direction, would promote the best interests of humanity. From these causes we learn that this savage custom is to be repressed by moral means, by salutary influences on the sentiments and principles of mankind. And thus we are led to our last topic, — the remedies of war. In introducing the observations which I have to offer on this branch of the subject, I feel myself bound to suggest an important caution. Let not the cause of peace be injured by the assertion of extreme and indefensible principles. I particularly refer to the principle that war is absolutely and in all possible cases unlawful, and prohibited by Christianity. This doctrine is considered, by a great majority of the judicious and enlightened, as endangering the best interests of society; and it ought not therefore to be connected with our efforts for the diffusion of peace unless it appear to us a clear and indubitable truth. War, as it is commonly waged, is indeed a tremendous evil; but national subjugation is a greater evil than a war of defense; and a community seems to me to possess an indisputable right to resort to such a war when all other means have failed for the security of its existence or freedom. It is universally admitted that a community may employ force to repress the rapacity and violence of its own citizens, to disarm and restrain its internal foes; and on what ground can we deny to it the right of repelling the inroads and aggressions of a foreign power? If a government may not lawfully resist a foreign army, invading its territory to desolate and subdue, on what principles can we justify a resistance of a combination of its own citizens for the same injurious purpose? Government is instituted for the very purpose of protecting the community from all violence, no matter by what hands it may be offered; and rulers would be unfaithful to their trust were they to abandon the rights, interests, and improvements of society to unprincipled rapacity, whether of domestic or foreign foes.

We are indeed told that the language of Scripture is, "Resist not evil." But the Scriptures are given to us as reasonable beings. We must remember that to the renunciation of reason in the interpretation of Scripture we owe those absurdities which have sunk Christianity almost to the level of heathenism. If the precept to "resist not evil" admit no exception, then civil government is prostrated; then the magistrate must in no case resist the injurious; then the subject must in no case employ the aid of the laws to enforce his rights. The very end and office of government is to *resist* evil men. For this the civil magistrate bears the sword; and he should beware of interpretations of the Scriptures which would lead him to bear it in vain. The doctrine of the absolute unlawfulness of war is thought by its advocates to be necessary to a successful opposition to this barbarous custom. But were we employed to restore peace to a contentious neighborhood, we should not consider ourselves as obliged to teach that self-defense is in every possible case a crime; and equally useless is this principle in our labors for the pacification of the world. Without taking this uncertain and dangerous ground, we may and ought to assail war, by assailing the principles and passions which gave it birth, and by improving and exalting the moral sentiments of mankind.

For example, important service may be rendered to the cause of peace by communicating and enforcing just and elevated sentiments in relation to the true honor of rulers. Let us teach that the prosperity, and not the extent, of a state is the measure of a ruler's glory; that the brute force and crooked policy which annex a conquest are infinitely inferior to the wisdom, justice, and beneficence which make a country happy; and that the earth holds not a more abandoned monster than the sovereign who, intrusted with the dearest interests of a people, commits them to the dreadful hazards

of war, that he may extend his prostituted power
and fill the earth with his worthless name. Let us
exhibit to the honor and veneration of mankind the
character of the Christian ruler, who, disdaining the
cheap and vulgar honor of a conqueror, aspires to a
new and more enduring glory; who, casting away the
long-tried weapons of intrigue and violence, adheres
with a holy and unshaken confidence to justice and
philanthropy, as a nation's best defense; and who
considers himself as exalted by God only that he may
shed down blessings and be as a beneficent deity to
the world.

To these instructions, in relation to the true glory of
rulers, should be added just sentiments as to the glory
of nations. Let us teach that the honor of a nation
consists not in the forced and reluctant submission of
other states, but in equal laws and free institutions, in
cultivated fields and prosperous cities; in the development of intellectual and moral power, in the diffusion of
knowledge, in magnanimity and justice, in the virtues
and blessings of peace. Let us never be weary in
reprobating that infernal spirit of conquest by which a
nation becomes the terror and abhorrence of the world,
and inevitably prepares a tomb — at best a splendid
tomb — for its own liberties and prosperity. Nothing
has been more common than for nations to imagine
themselves great and glorious on the ground of foreign
conquest, when at home they have been loaded with
chains. Cannot these gross and monstrous delusions be
scattered? Can nothing be done to persuade Christian
nations to engage in a new and untried race of glory, in

generous competitions, in a noble contest for superiority
in wise legislation and internal improvements, in the
spirit of liberty and humanity?

Another most important method of promoting the
cause of peace is to turn men's admiration from military
courage to qualities of real nobleness and dignity.   It
is time that the childish admiration of courage should
give place to more manly sentiments; and in proportion
as we effect this change we shall shake the main pillar
of war, we shall rob military life of its chief attraction.
Courage is a very doubtful quality, springing from very
different sources, and possessing a corresponding variety
of character.   Courage sometimes results from mental
weakness.   Peril is confronted, because the mind wants
comprehension to discern its extent.   This is often the
courage of youth, the courage of unreflecting ignorance,
— a contempt of peril because peril is but dimly seen.
Courage still more frequently springs from physical
temperament, from a rigid fiber and iron nerves, and
deserves as little praise as the proportion of the form or
the beauty of the countenance.   Again, every passion
which is strong enough to overcome the passion of fear,
and to exclude by its vehemence the idea of danger,
communicates at least a temporary courage.   Thus
revenge, when it burns with great fury, gives a terrible
energy to the mind, and has sometimes impelled men to
meet certain death, that they might inflict the same fate
on an enemy.   You see the doubtful nature of courage.
It is often associated with the worst vices.   The most
wonderful examples of it may be found in the history
of pirates and robbers, whose fearlessness is generally

proportioned to the insensibility of their consciences and to the enormity of their crimes . . . Let the tribute of honor be freely and liberally given to the soldier of principle, who exposes his life for a cause which his conscience approves, and who mingles clemency and mercy with the joy of triumph. But as for the multitude of military men who regard war as a trade by which to thrive, who destroy their fellow-beings with as little concern as the husbandman does the vermin that infest his fields, I know no class of men on whom admiration can more unjustly and more injuriously be bestowed. Let us labor, my brethren, to direct the admiration and love of mankind to another and infinitely higher kind of greatness, to that true magnanimity which is prodigal of ease and life in the service of God and mankind, and which proves its courage by unshaken adherence, amidst scorn and danger, to truth and virtue. Let the records of past ages be explored, to rescue from oblivion not the wasteful conqueror, whose path was as the whirlwind, but the benefactors of the human race, martyrs to the interests of freedom and religion, men who have broken the chain of the slave, who have traversed the earth to shed consolation into the cell of the prisoner, or whose sublime faculties have explored and revealed useful and ennobling truths. Can nothing be done to hasten the time when to such men eloquence and poetry shall offer their glowing homage, — when for these the statue and monument shall be erected, the canvas be animated, and the laurel entwined, — and when to these the admiration of the young shall be directed as their guides and forerunners to glory and immortality?

I proceed to another method of promoting the cause of peace. Let Christian ministers exhibit, with greater clearness and distinctness than ever they have done, the pacific and benevolent spirit of Christianity. My brethren, this spirit ought to hold the same place in our preaching which it holds in the gospel of our Lord. Instead of being crowded and lost among other subjects, it should stand in the front of Christian graces ; it should be inculcated as the life and essence of our religion. We should teach men that charity is greater than faith and hope; that God is love, or benevolence; and that love is the brightest communication of divinity to the human soul. We should exhibit Jesus in all the amiableness of his character, now shedding tears over Jerusalem, and now his blood on Calvary, and in his last hours recommending his own sublime love as the badge and distinction of his followers. We should teach men that it is the property of the benevolence of Christianity to diffuse itself like the light and rain of heaven, to disdain the limits of rivers, mountains, or oceans, by which nations are divided, and to embrace every human being as a brother. Let us never forget that our preaching is evangelical just in proportion as it inculcates and awakens this disinterested and unbounded charity; and that our hearers are Christians just as far as and no farther than they delight in peace and beneficence.

It is a painful truth, which ought not to be suppressed, that the pacific influence of the gospel has been greatly obstructed by the disposition which has prevailed in all ages, and especially among Christian ministers, to give importance to the peculiarities of sects and to rear walls of partition between different denominations. Shame ought to cover the face of the believer when he remembers that under no religion have intolerance and persecution raged more fiercely than under the gospel of the meek and forbearing Saviour. Christians have made the earth to reek with blood and to resound with denunciation. Can we wonder that, while the spirit of war has been cherished in the very bosom of the church, it has continued to ravage among the nations? Were the true spirit of Christianity to be inculcated with but half the zeal which has been wasted on doubtful and disputed doctrines, a sympathy, a coöperation might in a very short time be produced among Christians of every nation, most propitious to the pacification of the world. In consequence of the progress of knowledge and the extension of commerce, Christians of both hemispheres are at this moment brought nearer to one another than at any former period; and an intercourse, founded on religious sympathies, is gradually connecting the most distant regions. What a powerful weapon is furnished by this new bond of union to the ministers and friends of peace! Should not the auspicious moment be seized to inculcate on all Christians, in all regions, that they owe their first allegiance to their common Lord in heaven, whose first and last and great command is love? Should they not be taught to look with a shuddering abhorrence on war, which continually summons to the field of battle, under opposing standards, the followers of the same Saviour, and commands them to imbrue their hands in each other's blood? Once let Christians of every

nation be brought to espouse the cause of peace with
one heart and one voice, and their labor will not be in
vain in the Lord.   Human affairs will rapidly assume a
new and milder aspect.   The predicted ages of peace
will dawn on the world.   Public opinion will be purified.   The false luster of the hero will grow dim.   A
nobler order of character will be admired and diffused.
The kingdoms of the world will gradually become the
kingdoms of God and of his Christ.

My friends, I did intend, but I have not time, to
notice the arguments which are urged in support of
war.   Let me only say that the common argument,
that war is necessary to awaken the boldness, energy,
and noblest qualities of human nature, will, I hope,
receive a practical refutation in the friends of philanthropy and peace.   Let it appear in your lives that you
need not this spark from hell to kindle a heroic resolution in your breasts.   Let it appear that a pacific spirit
has no affinity with a tame and feeble character.   Let
us prove that courage, the virtue which has been
thought to flourish most in the rough field of war, may
be reared to a more generous height and to a firmer
texture in the bosom of peace.   Let it be seen that it
is not fear, but principle, which has made us the enemies of war.   In every enterprise of philanthropy which
demands daring and sacrifice and exposure to hardship
and toil, let us embark with serenity and joy.   Be it
our part to exhibit an undaunted, unshaken, unwearied
resolution, not in spreading ruin, but in serving God
and mankind, in alleviating human misery, in diffusing
truth and virtue, and especially in opposing war.   The

doctrines of Christianity have had many martyrs. Let us be willing, if God shall require it, to be martyrs to its spirit, — the neglected, insulted spirit of peace and love. In a better service we cannot live; in a nobler cause we cannot die. It is the cause of Jesus Christ, supported by Almighty Goodness, and appointed to triumph over the passions and delusions of men, the customs of ages, and the fallen monuments of the forgotten conqueror.

NOTE TO THE FIRST DISCOURSE ON WAR

I have deferred to this place a few remarks on the arguments which are usually adduced in support of war.

War, it is said, kindles patriotism; by fighting for our country, we learn to love it. But the patriotism which is cherished by war is ordinarily false and spurious, a vice and not a virtue, a scourge to the world, a narrow, unjust passion, which aims to exalt a particular state on the humiliation and destruction of other nations. A genuine, enlightened patriot discerns that the welfare of his own country is involved in the general progress of society; and in the character of a patriot, as well as of a Christian, he rejoices in the liberty and prosperity of other communities, and is anxious to maintain with them the relations of peace and amity.

It is said that a military spirit is the defense of a country. But it more frequently endangers the vital interests of a nation by embroiling it with other states. This spirit, like every other passion, is impatient for gratification, and often precipitates a country into unnecessary war. A people have no need of a military spirit.

Let them be attached to their government and institutions by habit, by early associations, and especially by experimental conviction of their excellence, and they will never want means or spirit to defend them.

War is recommended as a method of redressing national grievances. But unhappily the weapons of war, from their very nature, are often wielded most successfully by the unprincipled. Justice and force have little congeniality. Should not Christians everywhere strive to promote the reference of national as well as of individual disputes to an impartial umpire? Is a project of this nature more extravagant than the idea of reducing savage hordes to a state of regular society? The last has been accomplished. Is the first to be abandoned in despair?

It is said that war sweeps off the idle, dissolute, and vicious members of the community. Monstrous argument! If a government may for this end plunge a nation into war, it may with equal justice consign to the executioner any number of its subjects whom it may deem a burden on the state. The fact is, that war commonly generates as many profligates as it destroys. A disbanded army fills the community with at least as many abandoned members as at first it absorbed. There is another method, not quite so summary as war, of ridding a country of unprofitable and injurious citizens, but vastly more effectual; and a method which will be applied with spirit and success just in proportion as war shall yield to the light and spirit of Christianity. I refer to the exertions which Christians have commenced for the reformation and improvement of the ignorant

and poor, and especially for the instruction and moral
culture of indigent children.   Christians are entreated
to persevere and abound in these godlike efforts.   By
diffusing moral and religious principles and sober and
industrious habits through the laboring classes of society,
they will dry up one important source of war.   They
will destroy in a considerable degree the materials of
armies.   In proportion as these classes become well
principled and industrious, poverty will disappear, the
population of a country will be more and more proportioned to its resources, and of course the number will be
diminished of those who have no alternative but beg-
gary or a camp.   The moral care which is at the present day extended to the poor is one of the most honorable features of our age.   Christians! remember that
your proper warfare is with ignorance and vice, and
exhibit here the same unwearied and inventive energy
which has marked the warriors of the world.

It is sometimes said that a military spirit favors
liberty.   But how is it that nations, after fighting for
ages, are so generally enslaved?   The truth is, that
liberty has no foundation but in private and public
virtue; and virtue, as we have seen, is not the common
growth of war.

But the great argument remains to be discussed.   It
is said that without war to excite and invigorate the
human mind, some of its noblest energies will slumber,
and its highest qualities — courage, magnanimity, fortitude — will perish.   To this I answer that if war is to be
encouraged among nations because it nourishes energy
and heroism, on the same principle war in our families,

and war between neighborhoods, villages, and cities ought to be encouraged; for such contests would equally tend to promote heroic daring and contempt of death. Why shall not different provinces of the same empire annually meet with the weapons of death, to keep alive their courage? We shrink at this suggestion with horror; but why shall contests of nations, rather than of provinces or families, find shelter under this barbarous argument?

I observe, again, if war be a blessing because it awakens energy and courage, then the savage state is peculiarly privileged; for every savage is a soldier, and his whole modes of life tend to form him to invincible resolution. On the same principle, those early periods of society were happy, when men were called to contend not only with one another but with beasts of prey; for to these excitèments we owe the heroism of Hercules and Theseus. On the same principle, the feudal ages were more favored than the present; for then every baron was a military chief, every castle frowned defiance, and every vassal was trained to arms. And do we really wish that the earth should again be overrun with monsters, or abandoned to savage or feudal violence, in order that heroes may be multiplied? If not, let us cease to vindicate war as affording excitement to energy and courage.

I repeat, what I have observed in the preceding discourse, we need not war to awaken human energy. There is at least equal scope for courage and magnanimity in blessing as in destroying mankind. The condition of the human race offers inexhaustible objects for enterprise and fortitude and magnanimity. In relieving the countless wants and sorrows of the world, in exploring unknown regions, in carrying the arts and virtues of civilization to unimproved communities, in extending the bounds of knowledge, in diffusing the spirit of freedom, and especially in spreading the light and influence of Christianity, how much may be dared, how much endured! Philanthropy invites us to services which demand the most intense, and elevated, and resolute, and adventurous activity. Let it not be imagined that, were nations imbued with the spirit of Christianity, they would slumber in ignoble ease; that, instead of the high-minded murderers who are formed on the present system of war, we should have effeminate and timid slaves. Christian benevolence is as active as it is forbearing. Let it once form the character of a people, and it will attach them to every important interest of society. It will call forth sympathy in behalf of the suffering in every region under heaven. It will give a new extension to the heart, open a wider sphere to enterprise, inspire a courage of exhaustless resource, and prompt to every sacrifice and exposure for the improvement and happiness of the human race. The energy of this principle has been tried and displayed in the fortitude of the martyr and in the patient labors of those who have carried the gospel into the dreary abodes of idolatry. Away, then, with the argument that war is needed as a nursery of heroism. The school of the peaceful Redeemer is infinitely more adapted to teach the nobler as well as the milder virtues which adorn humanity.

SECOND DISCOURSE ON WAR

Delivered January 25, 1835

Whence come wars and fightings among you? — *James* v. 1.

I ASK your attention to the subject of public war. I am aware that to some this topic may seem to have political bearings which render it unfit for the pulpit; but to me it is eminently a moral and religious subject. In approaching it political parties and interest vanish from my mind. They are forgotten amidst the numerous miseries and crimes of war. To bring war to an end was one of the purposes of Christ, and his ministers are bound to concur with him in the work. The great difficulty on the present occasion is to select some point of view from the vast field which opens before us. After some general remarks, I shall confine myself to a single topic, which at present demands peculiar attention.

Public war is not an evil which stands alone, or has nothing in common with other evils. It belongs, as the text intimates, to a great family. It may be said that society, through its whole extent, is deformed by war. Even in families we see jarring interests and passions, invasions of rights, resistance of authority, violence, force; and in common life, how continually do we see men struggling with one another for property or distinction, injuring one another in word or deed, exasperated against one another by jealousies,

neglects, and mutual reproach.   All this is essentially
war, but war restrained, hemmed in, disarmed by the
opinions and institutions of society.   To limit its ravages, to guard reputation, property, and life, society has
instituted government, erected the tribunal of justice,
clothed the legislator with the power of enacting equal
laws, put the sword into the hand of the magistrate, and
pledged its whole force to his support.   Human wisdom
has been manifested in nothing more conspicuously than
in civil institutions for repressing war, retaliation, and
passionate resort to force, among the citizens of the
same state.   But here it has stopped.   Government,
which is ever at work to restrain the citizen at home,
often lets him loose and arms him with fire and sword
against other communities, sends out hosts for desolation and slaughter, and concentrates the whole energies
of a people in the work of spreading misery and death.
Government, the peace officer at home, breathes war
abroad, organizes it into a science, reduces it to a system, makes it a trade, and applauds it as if it were
the most honorable work of nations.   Strange that the
wisdom which has so successfully put down the wars
of individuals has never been inspired and emboldened
to engage in the task of bringing to an end the more
gigantic crimes and miseries of public war!   But this
universal pacification, until of late, has hardly been
thought of; and in reading history we are almost
tempted to believe that the chief end of government in
promoting internal quiet has been to accumulate greater
resources for foreign hostilities.   Bloodshed is the staple
of history, and men have been butchered and countries

ravaged, as if the human frame had been constructed
with such exquisite skill only to be mangled, and the
earth covered with fertility only to attract the spoiler.

These reflections, however, it is not my intention to
pursue. The miseries of war are not my present subject. One remark will be sufficient to place them in
their true light. What gives these miseries preëminence among human woes — what should compel us to
look on them with peculiar horror — is not their awful
amount, but their origin, their source. They are miseries
inflicted by man on man. They spring from depravity
of will. They bear the impress of cruelty, of hardness
of heart. The distorted features, writhing frames, and
shrieks of the wounded and dying, — these are not the
chief horrors of war: they sink into unimportance compared with the infernal passions which work this woe.
Death is a light evil when not joined with crime. Had
the countless millions destroyed by war been swallowed
up by floods or yawning earthquakes, we should look
back, awe-struck but submissive, on the mysterious
providence which had thus fulfilled the mortal sentence
originally passed on the human race. But that man,
born of woman, bound by ties of brotherhood to man,
and commanded by an inward law and the voice of God
to love and do good, should, through selfishness, pride,
revenge, inflict these agonies, shed these torrents of
human blood, — here is an evil which combines with
exquisite suffering fiendish guilt. All other evils fade
before it.

Such are the dark features of war. I have spoken of
them strongly, because humanity and religion demand

from us all a new and sterner tone on this master evil.
But it is due to human nature to observe, that whilst
war is, in the main, the offspring and riot of the worst
passions, better principles often mix with it and throw
a veil over its deformity.   Nations fight not merely for
revenge or booty.   Glory is often the stirring word;
and glory, though often misinterpreted and madly pursued by crime, is still an impulse of great minds, and
shows a nature made to burn with high thoughts and
to pour itself forth in noble deeds.   Many have girded
themselves for battle from pure motives; and, as if to
teach us that unmingled evil cannot exist in God's
creation, the most ferocious conflicts have been bright-
ened by examples of magnanimous and patriotic virtue.
In almost all wars there is some infusion of enthusiasm,
and in all enthusiasm there is a generous element.

Still, war is made up essentially of crime and misery,
and to abolish it is one great purpose of Christianity
and should be the earnest labor of philanthropy; nor
is this enterprise to be scoffed at as hopeless.   The
tendencies of civilization are decidedly towards peace.
The influences of progressive knowledge, refinement,
arts, and national wealth are pacific.   The old motives
for war are losing power.   Conquest, which once mad-
dened nations, hardly enters now into the calculation
of statesmen.   The disastrous and disgraceful termina-
tion of the last career of conquest which the world has
known is reading a lesson not soon to be forgotten.   It
is now thoroughly understood that the development of
a nation's resources in peace is the only road to prosperity; that even successful war makes a people poor,

crushing them with taxes and crippling their progress in industry and useful arts. We have another pacific influence at the present moment in the increasing intelligence of the middle and poorer classes of society, who, in proportion as they learn their interests and rights, are unwilling to be used as materials of war, to suffer and bleed in serving the passions and glory of a privileged few. Again, science, commerce, religion, foreign travel, new facilities of intercourse, new exchanges of literature, new friendships, new interests are overcoming the old antipathies of nations, and are silently spreading the sentiment of human brotherhood and the conviction that the welfare of each is the happiness of all. Once more, public opinion is continually gaining strength in the civilized and Christian world; and to this tribunal all states must in a measure bow. Here are pacific influences. Here are encouragements to labor in the cause of peace.

At the present day, one of the chief incitements to war is to be found in false ideas of honor. Military prowess and military success are thought to shed peculiar glory on a people; and many, who are too wise to be intoxicated with these childish delusions, still imagine that the honor of a nation consists peculiarly in the spirit which repels injury, in sensibility to wrongs, and is therefore peculiarly committed to the keeping of the sword. These opinions I shall now examine, beginning with the glory attached to military achievements.

That the idea of glory should be associated strongly with military exploits ought not to be wondered at. From the earliest ages, ambitious sovereigns and states

have sought to spread the military spirit by loading
it with rewards. Badges, ornaments, distinctions, the
most flattering and intoxicating, have been the prizes
of war. The aristocracy of Europe, which commenced
in barbarous ages, was founded on military talent and
success; and the chief education of the young noble
was for a long time little more than a training for battle, — hence the strong connection between war and
honor. All past ages have bequeathed us this prejudice, and the structure of society has given it a fearful
force. Let us consider it with some particularity.

The idea of honor is associated with war. But to
whom does the honor belong? If to any, certainly not
to the mass of the people, but to those who are particularly engaged in it. The mass of a people, who stay at
home, and hire others to fight; who sleep in their warm
beds, and hire others to sleep on the cold and damp
earth; who sit at their well-spread board, and hire
others to take the chance of starving; who nurse the
slightest hurt in their own bodies, and hire others to
expose themselves to mortal wounds, and to linger in
comfortless hospitals, — certainly this mass reap little
honor from war; the honor belongs to those immediately engaged in it. Let me ask, then, what is the
chief business of war? It is to destroy human life; to
mangle the limbs; to gash and hew the body; to plunge
the sword into the heart of a fellow-creature; to strew
the earth with bleeding frames, and to trample them
under foot with horses' hoofs. It is to batter down
and burn cities; to turn fruitful fields into deserts; to
level the cottage of the peasant and the magnificent

abode of opulence; to scourge nations with famine; to multiply widows and orphans. Are these honorable deeds? Were you called to name exploits worthy of demons, would you not naturally select such as these? Grant that a necessity for them may exist; it is a dreadful necessity, such as a good man must recoil from with instinctive horror; and though it may exempt them from guilt, it cannot turn them into glory. We have thought that it was honorable to heal, to save, to mitigate pain, to snatch the sick and sinking from the jaws of death. We have placed among the revered benefactors of the human race the discoverers of arts which alleviate human sufferings, which prolong, comfort, adorn, and cheer human life; and if these arts be honorable, where is the glory of multiplying and aggravating tortures and death?

It will be replied that the honorableness of war consists not in the business which it performs, but in the motives from which it springs, and in the qualities which it indicates. It will be asked, Is it not honorable to serve one's country and to expose one's life in its cause? Yes, our country deserves love and service; and let her faithful friends, her loyal sons, who under the guidance of duty and disinterested zeal have poured out their blood in her cause, live in the hearts of a grateful posterity. But who does not know that this moral heroism is a very different thing from the common military spirit? Who is so simple as to believe that this all-sacrificing patriotism of principle is the motive which fills the ranks of war and leads men to adopt the profession of arms? Does this sentiment reign in the common soldier, who enlists because driven from all other modes of support, and hires himself to be shot at for a few cents a day? Or does it reign in the officer, who, for pay and promotion, from the sense of reputation or dread of disgrace, meets the foe with a fearless front? There is, indeed, a vulgar patriotism nourished by war, — I mean that which burns to humble other nations and to purchase for our own the exultation of triumph and superior force. But as for true patriotism, which has its root in benevolence and which desires the real and enduring happiness of our country, nothing is more adverse to it than war, and no class of men have less of it than those engaged in war. Perhaps in no class is the passion for display and distinction so strong; and in accordance with this infirmity they are apt to regard as the highest interest of the state a career of conquests, which makes a show and dazzles the multitude, however desolating or unjust in regard to foreign nations or however blighting to the prosperity of their own.

The motives which generally lead to the choice of a military life strip it of all claim to peculiar honor. There are employments which from their peculiar character should be undertaken only from high motives. This is peculiarly the case with the profession of arms. Its work is bloodshed, destruction, the infliction of the most dreaded evils not only on wrong-doers, oppressors, usurpers, but on the innocent, weak, defenseless. From this task humanity recoils, and nothing should reconcile us to it but the solemn conviction of duty to God, to our country, to mankind. The man who undertakes this work solely or chiefly to earn money or an epaulet

commits, however unconsciously, a great wrong. Let it
be conceded that he who engages in military life is bound,
as in other professions, to insure from his employers the
means of support, and that he may innocently seek the
honor which is awarded to faithful and successful service.
Still, from the peculiar character of the profession, from
the solemnity and terribleness of its agency, no man
can engage in it innocently or honorably who does
not deplore its necessity, and does not adopt it from
generous motives, from the power of moral and public
considerations. That these are not the motives which
now fill armies is too notorious to need proof. How
common is it for military men to desire war, as giving
rich prizes and as advancing them in their profession.
They are willing to slaughter their fellow-creatures for
money and distinction. . . . That there may be soldiers of principle, men who abhor the thought of shedding human blood, and who consent to the painful office
only because it seems to them imposed by their country
and the best interests of mankind, is freely granted. . . .
More guilt should be attached to society than to the
soldier; but . . . war, as now carried on, is certainly
among the last vocations to be called honorable.

Let not these remarks be misconstrued. I mean not
to deny to military men equal virtue with other classes
of society. All classes are alike culpable in regard to
war, and the burden presses too heavily on all to allow
any to take up reproaches against others. Society has
not only established and exalted the military profession,
but studiously allures men into it by bribes of vanity,
cupidity, and ambition. They who adopt it have on

their side the suffrage of past ages, the sanction of opinion and law, and the applauding voice of nations; so that justice commands us to acquit them of peculiar deviations from duty, or of falling below society in moral worth or private virtue.

Much of the glare thrown over the military profession is to be ascribed to the false estimate of courage which prevails through the Christian world.   Men are dazzled by this quality.   On no point is popular opinion more perverted and more hostile to Christianity, and to this point I would therefore solicit particular attention.   The truth is that the delusion on this subject has come down to us from remote ages and has been from the beginning a chief element of the European character.   Our northern ancestors, who overwhelmed the Roman empire, were fanatical to the last degree in respect to military courage.   They made it the first of virtues.   One of the chief articles of their creed was that a man dying on the field of battle was transported at once to the hall of their god Odin, a terrible paradise, where he was to quaff forever delicious draughts from the skulls of his enemies.   So rooted was this fanaticism that it was thought a calamity to die of disease or old age; and death by violence, even if inflicted by their own hands, was thought more honorable than to expire by the slow, inglorious processes of nature.   This spirit, aided by other causes, broke out at length into chivalry, the strangest mixture of good and evil, of mercy and cruelty, of insanity and generous sentiment, to be found in human history.   This whole institution breathed an extravagant estimation of courage.   To be without fear was the first attribute of a good knight.   Danger was thirsted for, when it might innocently be shunned.   Life was sported with wantonly.   Amusements full of peril, exposing even to mortal wounds, were pursued with passionate eagerness.   The path to honor lay through rash adventures, the chief merit of which was the scorn of suffering and of death which they expressed.   This fanaticism has yielded in a measure to good sense, and still more to the spirit of Christianity.   But still it is rife, and not a few imagine fearless courage to be the height of glory.

That courage is of no worth, I have no disposition to affirm.   It ought to be prized, sought, cherished.   Though not of itself virtuous, it is an important aid to virtue. It gives us the command of our faculties when needed most.   It converts the dangers which palsy the weak into springs of energy.   Its firm look often awes the injurious and silences insult.   All great enterprises demand it, and without it virtue cannot rise into magnanimity.   Whilst it leaves us exposed to many vices, it saves us from one class peculiarly ignominious, — from the servility, deceit, and base compliance which belong to fear.   It is accompanied, too, with an animated consciousness of power, which is one of the high enjoyments of life.   We are bound to cherish it as the safeguard of happiness and rectitude; and when so cherished it takes rank among the virtues.

Still, courage, considered in itself or without reference to its origin and motives, and regarded in its common manifestations, is not virtue, is not moral excellence; and the disposition to exalt it above the spirit of

Christianity is one of the most ruinous delusions which
have been transmitted to us from barbarous times.   In
most men, courage has its origin in a happy organization
of the body.   It belongs to the nerves rather than the
character.   In some it is an instinct bordering on rashness.   In one man it springs from strong passions
obscuring the idea of danger; in another, from the want
of imagination or from the incapacity of bringing future
evils near.   The courage of the uneducated may often
be traced to stupidity, to the absence of thought and
sensibility.   Many are courageous from the dread of
the infamy absurdly attached to cowardice.   One terror
expels another.   A bullet is less formidable than a sneer.
To show the moral worthlessness of mere courage, of
contempt of bodily suffering and pain, one consideration
is sufficient; — the most abandoned have possessed it in
perfection.   The villain often hardens into the thorough
hero, if courage and heroism be one.   The more complete
his success in searing conscience and defying God, the
more dauntless his daring.   Long-continued vice and
exposure naturally generate contempt of life and a reckless encounter of peril.   Courage, considered in itself,
or without reference to its causes, is no virtue, and
deserves no esteem.   It is found in the best and the
worst, and is to be judged according to the qualities
from which it springs and with which it is conjoined.
There is, in truth, a virtuous, glorious courage; but it
happens to be found least in those who are most admired
for bravery.   It is the courage of principle, which dares
to do right in the face of scorn, which puts to hazard
reputation, rank, the prospects of advancement, the

sympathy of friends, the admiration of the world, rather
than violate a conviction of duty. It is the courage
of benevolence and piety, which counts not life dear in
withstanding error, superstition, vice, oppression, injustice, and the mightiest foes of human improvement and
happiness. It is moral energy, that force of will in
adopting duty over which menace and suffering have
no power. It is the courage of a soul which reverences
itself too much to be greatly moved about what befalls
the body; which thirsts so intensely for a pure inward
life that it can yield up the animal life without fear;
in which the idea of moral, spiritual, celestial good has
been unfolded so brightly as to obscure all worldly
interests; which aspires after immortality, and therefore heeds little the pains or pleasures of a day; which
has so concentered its whole power and life in the love
of godlike virtue that it even finds a joy in the perils
and sufferings by which its loyalty to God and virtue
may be approved. This courage may be called the
perfection of humanity, for it is the exercise, result,
and expression of the highest attributes of our nature.
Need I tell you that this courage has hardly anything
in common with what generally bears the name, and
has been lauded by the crowd to the skies? Can any
man not wholly blinded to moral distinctions compare
or confound with this divine energy the bravery derived
from constitution, nourished by ambition, and blazing
out in resentment, which forms the glory of military
men and of men of the world? The courage of military and ordinary life, instead of resting on high and
unchangeable principles, finds its chief motive in the

opinions of the world, and its chief regard in vulgar
praise. Superior to bodily pain, it crouches before censure, and dares not face the scorn which faithfulness to
God and unpopular duty must often incur. It wears
the appearance of energy, because it conquers one strong
passion, fear; but the other passions it leaves unmas-
tered, and thus differs essentially from moral strength
or greatness, which consists in subjecting all appetites
and desires to a pure and high standard of rectitude.
Brilliant courage, as it is called, so far from being a
principle of universal self-control, is often joined with
degrading pleasures, with a lawless spirit, with general
licentiousness of manners, with a hardihood which defies
God as well as man, and which, not satisfied with scorn-
ing death, contemns the judgment that is to follow. So
wanting in moral worth is the bravery which has so long
been praised, sung, courted, adored. It is time that it
should be understood. It is time that the old, barbarous, indiscriminate worship of mere courage should give
place to a wise moral judgment. This fanaticism has
done much to rob Christianity of its due honor. Men
who give their sympathies and homage to the fiery and
destructive valor of the soldier will see little attraction
in the mild and peaceful spirit of Jesus. His unconquerable forbearance, the most genuine and touching
expression of his divine philanthropy, may even seem
to them a weakness. We read of those who, surrounding the cross, derided the meek sufferer. They did it
in their ignorance. More guilty, more insensible are
those who, living under the light of Christianity and
yielding it their assent, do not see in that cross a glory

which pours contempt on the warrior. Will this delusion never cease? Will men never learn to reverence disinterested love? Shall the desolations and woes of ages bear their testimony in vain against the false glory which has so long dazzled the world? Shall Christ, shall moral perfection, shall the spirit of heaven, shall God manifest in his Son, be forever insulted by the worship paid to the spirit of savage hordes? Shall the cross ostentatiously worn on the breast never come to the heart, a touching emblem and teacher of all-suffering love? I do not ask these questions in despair. Whilst we lament the limited triumphs of Christianity over false notions of honor, we see and ought to recognize its progress. War is not now the only or chief path to glory. The greatest names are not now written in blood. The purest fame is the meed of genius, philosophy, philanthropy, and piety, devoting themselves to the best interests of humanity. The passion for military glory is no longer, as once, able of itself to precipitate nations into war. In all this let us rejoice.

In the preceding remarks I aimed to show that the glory awarded to military prowess and success is unfounded, — to show the deceitfulness of the glare which seduces many into the admiration of war. I proceed to another topic, which is necessary to give us a full understanding of the pernicious influence exerted by the idea of honor in exciting nations to hostility. There are many persons who have little admiration of warlike achievements, and are generally inclined to peace, but who still imagine that the honor of a nation consists peculiarly in quickness to feel and repel injury, and who consequently, when their country has been wronged, are too prone to rush into war. Perhaps its interests have been slightly touched. Perhaps its well-being imperiously demands continued peace. Still, its honor is said to call for reparation, and no sacrifice is thought too costly to satisfy the claim. That national honor should be dear, and guarded with jealous care, no man will deny; but in proportion as we exalt it we should be anxious to know precisely what it means, lest we set up for our worship a false, unjust, merciless deity, and instead of glory shall reap shame. I ask, then, in what does the honor of a nation consist? What are its chief elements or constituents? The common views of it are narrow and low. Every people should study it; and in proportion as we understand it we shall learn that it has no tendency to precipitate nations into war. What, I ask again, is this national honor from which no sacrifice must be withheld?

The first element of a nation's honor is undoubtedly justice. A people, to deserve respect, must lay down the maxim, as the foundation of its intercourse with other communities, that justice — a strict regard to the rights of other states — shall take rank of its interests. A nation without reverence for right can never plead in defense of a war that this is needed to maintain its honor, for it has no honor to maintain. It bears a brand of infamy which oceans of human blood cannot wash away. With these views we cannot be too much shocked by the language of a chief magistrate recently addressed to a legislative body in this country.

" No community of men," he says, " in any age or
nation, under any dispensation, political or religious,
has been governed by justice in its negotiations or
conflicts with other states. It is not justice and magnanimity, but interest and ambition, dignified under the
name of state policy, that has governed, and ever will
govern, masses of men acting as political communities.
Individuals may be actuated by a sense of justice; but
what citizen in any country would venture to contend
for justice to a foreign and rival community, in opposition to the prevailing policy of his state, without
forfeiting the character of a patriot? "

Now, if this be true of our country, — and to our
own country it was applied, — then, I say, we have no
honor to fight for. A people systematically sacrificing
justice to its interests is essentially a band of robbers,
and receives but the just punishment of its profligacy
in the assaults of other nations. But it is not true
that nations are so dead to moral principles. The voice
of justice is not always drowned by the importunities of
interest; nor ought we as citizens to acquiesce in an
injurious act on the part of our rulers towards other
states, as if it were a matter of course, a necessary working of human selfishness. It ought to be reprobated as
indignantly as the wrongs of private men. A people
strictly just has an honor independent of opinion, and
to which opinion must pay homage. Its glory is purer
and more enduring than that of a thousand victories.
Let not him who prefers for his country the renown of
military spirit and success to that of justice talk of his
zeal for its honor. He does not know the meaning of

the word. He belongs to a barbarous age, and desires
for his country no higher praise than has been gained
by many a savage horde.

The next great element of a nation's honor is a spirit
of philanthropy. A people ought to regard itself as a
member of the human family, and as bound to bear part
in the work of human improvement and happiness. The
obligation of benevolence, belonging to men as individuals, belongs to them in their associated capacities. We
have, indeed, no right to form an association, of whatever kind, which severs us from the human race. I care
not though men of loose principles scoff at the idea of
a nation respecting the claims of humanity. Duty is
eternal, and too high for human mockery; and this
duty in particular, so far from being a dream, has been
reduced to practice. Our own country, in framing its
first treaties, proposed to insert an article prohibiting
privateering; and this it did in the spirit of humanity,
to diminish the crimes and miseries of war. England,
from philanthropy, abolished the slave trade and slavery.
No nation stands alone; and each is bound to consecrate
its influence to the promotion of equitable, pacific, and
beneficent relations among all countries, and to the
diffusion of more liberal principles of intercourse and
national law. This country is intrusted by God with
a mission for humanity. Its office is to commend to all
nations free institutions, as the sources of public prosperity and personal dignity; and I trust we desire to
earn the thanks and honor of nations by fidelity to our
trust. A people reckless of the interest of the world
and profligately selfish in its policy incurs far deeper

disgrace than by submission to wrongs; and whenever
it is precipitated into war by its cupidity its very victories become monuments of its guilt, and deserve the
execration of present and coming times.

I now come to another essential element of a nation's
honor; and that is, the existence of institutions which
tend and are designed to elevate all classes of its citizens.
As it is the improved character of a people which alone
gives it an honorable place in the world, its dignity is to
be measured chiefly by the extent and efficiency of its
provisions and establishments for national improvement,
— for spreading education far and wide; for purifying
morals and refining manners; for enlightening the ignorant and succoring the miserable; for building up intellectual and moral power, and breathing the spirit of true
religion. The degree of aid given to the individual in
every condition, for unfolding his best powers, determines the rank of a nation. Mere wealth adds nothing
to a people's glory; it is the nation's soul which consti-
tutes its greatness. Nor is it enough for a country to
possess a select class of educated, cultivated men; for
the nation consists of the many, not the few; and where
the mass are sunk in ignorance and sensuality, there you
see a degraded community, even though an aristocracy
of science be lodged in its bosom. It is the moral and
intellectual progress of the people to which the patriot
should devote himself as the only dignity and safeguard
of the state. How needed this truth! In all ages
nations have imagined that they were glorifying themselves by triumphing over foreign foes, whilst at home
they have been denied every ennobling institution; have

been trodden under foot by tyranny, defrauded of the most sacred rights of humanity, enslaved by superstition, buried in ignorance, and cut off from all the means of rising to the dignity of men. They have thought that they were exalting themselves in fighting for the very despots who ground them in the dust. Such has been the common notion of national honor; nor is it yet effaced. How many among ourselves are unable to stifle their zeal for our honor as a people, who never spent a thought on the institutions and improvements which ennoble a community, and whose character and examples degrade and taint their country as far as their influence extends?

I have now given you the chief elements of national honor; and a people cherishing these can hardly be compelled to resort to war. I shall be told, however, that an enlightened and just people, though less exposed to hostilities, may still be wronged, insulted, and endangered; and I shall be asked if in such a case its honor do not require it to repel injury, — if submission be not disgrace? I answer, that a nation which submits to wrong from timidity, or a sordid love of ease or gain, forfeits its claim to respect. A faint-hearted, self-indulgent people, cowering under menace, shrinking from peril, and willing to buy repose by tribute or servile concession, deserves the chains which it cannot escape. But to bear much and long from a principle of humanity, from reverence for the law of love, is noble ; and nothing but moral blindness and degradation induce men to see higher glory in impatience of injury and quickness to resent.

Still I may be asked whether a people, however forbearing, may not sometimes owe it to its own dignity and safety to engage in war? I answer, Yes. When the spirit of justice, humanity, and forbearance, instead of spreading peace, provokes fresh outrage, this outrage must be met and repressed by force. I know that many sincere Christians oppose to this doctrine the precept of Christ, " Resist not evil." But Christianity is wronged, and its truth exposed to strong objections, when these and the like precepts are literally construed. The whole legislation of Christ is intended to teach us the spirit from which we should act, not to lay down rules for outward conduct. The precept, " Resist not evil," if practiced to the letter, would annihilate all government in the family and the state; for it is the great work of government to resist evil passions and evil deeds. It is, indeed, our duty as Christians to love our worst enemy and to desire his true good; but we are to love not only our enemy, but our families, friends, and country, and to take a wise care of our own rights and happiness; and when we abandon to the violence of a wrong-doer these fellow-beings and these rights commended by God to our love and care we are plainly wanting in that expanded benevolence which Christianity demands. A nation, then, may owe it to its welfare and dignity to engage in war; and its honor demands that it should meet the trial with invincible resolution. It ought at such a moment to dismiss all fear, except the fear of its own passions, — the fear of the crimes to which the exasperations and sore temptations of public hostilities expose a state.

I have admitted that a nation's honor may require its citizens to engage in war; but it requires them to engage in it wisely, — with a full consciousness of rectitude and with unfeigned sorrow.   On no other conditions does war comport with national dignity; and these deserve a moment's attention.   A people must engage in war wisely; for rashness is dishonorable, especially in so solemn and tremendous a concern.   A nation must propose a wise end in war; and this remark is the more important because the end or object which, according to common speech, a people is bound by its honor to propose, is generally disowned by wisdom.   How common it is to hear that the honor of a nation requires it to seek redress of grievances, reparation of injuries.   Now, as a general rule, war does not and can not repair injuries. Instead of securing compensation for past evils, it almost always multiplies them.   As a general rule, a nation loses incomparably more by war than it has previously lost by the wrong-doer.   Suppose, for example, a people to have been spoiled by another state of five millions of dollars.   To recover this by war it must expend fifty or a hundred millions more, and will almost certainly come forth from the contest burdened with debt.   Nor is this all.   It loses more than wealth.   It loses many lives.   Now, life and property are not to be balanced against each other.   If a nation, by slaying a single innocent man, could possess itself of the wealth of worlds, it would have no right to destroy him for that cause alone.   A human being cannot be valued by silver and gold, and in consequence a nation can never be authorized to sacrifice or expose thousands of lives for the

mere recovery of property of which it has been spoiled.
To secure compensation for the past is very seldom a
sufficient object for war. The true end is security for
the future. An injury inflicted by one nation on another
may manifest a lawless, hostile spirit, from which, if
unresisted, future and increasing outrages are to be
feared, which would embolden other communities in
wrong-doing, and against which neither property, nor
life, nor liberty would be secure. To protect a state
from this spirit of violence and unprincipled aggression
is the duty of rulers; and protection may be found only
in war. Here is the legitimate occasion and the true end
of an appeal to arms. Let me ask you to apply this
rule of wisdom to a case the bearings of which will be
easily seen. Suppose, then, an injury to have been
inflicted on us by a foreign nation a quarter of a century
ago. Suppose it to have been inflicted by a government
which has fallen through its lawlessness, and which can
never be restored. Suppose this injury to have been
followed, during this long period, by not one hostile act
and not one sign of a hostile spirit. Suppose a disposition to repair it to be expressed by the head of the new
government of the injurious nation; and suppose, further, that our long endurance has not exposed us to a
single insult from any other power since the general
pacification of Europe. Under these circumstances, can
it be pretended, with any show of reason, that threatened wrong, or that future security, requires us to bring
upon ourselves and the other nation the horrors and
miseries of war? Does not wisdom join with humanity
in reprobating such a conflict?

I have said that the honor of a nation requires it to engage in a war for a wise end. I add, as a more important rule, that its dignity demands of it to engage in no conflict without a full consciousness of rectitude. It must not appeal to arms for doubtful rights. It must not think it enough to establish a probable claim. The true principle for a nation, as for an individual, is that it will suffer rather than do wrong. It should prefer being injured to the hazard of doing injury. To secure to itself this full consciousness of rectitude, a nation should always desire to refer its disputes to an impartial umpire. It cannot too much distrust its own judgment in its own cause. That same selfish partiality which blinds the individual to the claims of a rival or foe, and which has compelled society to substitute public and disinterested tribunals for private war, disqualifies nations, more or less, to determine their own rights, and should lead them to seek a more dispassionate decision. The great idea which should rise to the mind of a country on meditating war is rectitude. In declaring war it should listen only to the voice of duty. To resolve on the destruction of our fellow-creatures without a command from conscience — a commission from God — is to bring on a people a load of infamy and crime. A nation, in declaring war, should be lifted above its passions by the fearfulness and solemnity of the act. It should appeal with unfeigned confidence to heaven and earth for its uprightness of purpose. It should go forth as the champion of truth and justice, as the minister of God, to vindicate and sustain that great moral and national law, without which life has no security, and social improvements no defense. It should be inspired with invincible courage, not by its passions, but by the dignity and holiness of its cause. Nothing in the whole compass of legislation is so solemn as a declaration of war. By nothing do a people incur such tremendous responsibility. Unless justly waged, war involves a people in the guilt of murder. The state which, without the command of justice and God, sends out fleets and armies to slaughter fellow-creatures, must answer for the blood it sheds, as truly as the assassin for the death of his victim. Oh, how loudly does the voice of blood cry to heaven from the field of battle ! Undoubtedly the men whose names have come down to us with the loudest shouts of ages stand now before the tribunal of eternal justice condemned as murderers ; and the victories which have been thought to encircle a nation with glory have fixed the same brand on multitudes in the sight of the final and Almighty Judge. How essential is it to a nation's honor that it should engage in war with a full conviction of rectitude !

But there is one more condition of an honorable war. A nation should engage in it with unfeigned sorrow. It should beseech the throne of grace with earnest supplication that the dreadful office of destroying fellow-beings may not be imposed on it. War concentrates all the varieties of human misery, and a nation which can inflict these without sorrow contracts deeper infamy than from cowardice. It is essentially barbarous, and will be looked back upon by more enlightened and Christian ages with the horror with which we recall the atrocities of savage tribes. Let it be remembered that the calamities of war, its slaughter, famine, and desolation, instead of being confined to its criminal authors, fall chiefly on multitudes who have had no share in provoking and no voice in proclaiming it; and let not a nation talk of its honor which has no sympathy with these woes, which is steeled to the most terrible sufferings of humanity.

I have now spoken, my friends, of the sentiments with which war should be regarded. Is it so regarded? When recently the suggestion of war was thrown out to this people, what reception did it meet? Was it viewed at once in the light in which a Christian nation should immediately and most earnestly consider it? Was it received as a proposition to slaughter thousands of our fellow-creatures? Did we feel as if threatened with a calamity more fearful than earthquakes, famine, or pestilence? The blight which might fall on our prosperity drew attention; but the thought of devoting, as a people, our power and resources to the destruction of mankind, of those whom a common nature, whom reason, conscience, and Christianity command us to love and save, — did this thrill us with horror? Did the solemn inquiry break forth through our land, Is the dreadful necessity indeed laid upon us to send abroad death and woe? No. There was little manifestation of the sensibility with which men and Christians should look such an evil in the face. As a people we are still seared and blinded to the crimes and miseries of war. The principles of honor, to which the barbarism and infatuation of dark ages gave birth, prevail among us. The generous, merciful spirit of our religion is little understood.

The law of love preached from the cross and written in the blood of the Saviour is trampled on by public men. The true dignity of man, which consists in breathing and cherishing God's spirit of justice and philanthropy towards every human being, is counted folly in comparison with that spirit of vindictiveness and self-aggrandizement which turns our earth into an image of the abodes of the damned. How long will the friends of humanity, of religion, of Christ, silently, passively, uncomplainingly, suffer the men of this world, the ambitious, vindictive, and selfish, to array them against their brethren in conflicts which they condemn and abhor? Shall not truth, humanity, and the mild and holy spirit of Christianity find a voice to rebuke and awe the wickedness which precipitates nations into war, and to startle and awaken nations to their fearful responsibility in taking arms against the children of their Father in heaven? Prince of Peace! Saviour of men! speak in thine own voice of love, power, and fearful warning; and redeem the world for which thou hast died from lawless and cruel passions, from the spirit of rapine and murder, from the powers of darkness and hell!

LECTURE ON WAR

THIS lecture was delivered in the beginning of the last year (1838). It was prepared with a distinct knowledge of the little interest taken in the subject by the people at large, and was prepared on that very account. It is now published in consequence of fresh proofs of the insensibility of the mass of this community to the crimes and miseries of war. For a few weeks this calamity has been brought distinctly before us : we have been driven by one of the states into a hostile position towards a great European power; and the manner in which the subject has been treated in and out of Congress is a sad proof of the very general want of Christian and philanthropic views of the subject, as well as of strange blindness to our national and individual well-being. One would think that the suggestion of a war with England would call forth one strong, general burst of opposing feelings. Can a more calamitous event, with the exception of civil war, be imagined? What other nation can do us equal harm? With what other nation do we hold equally profitable connections? To what other are we bound by such strong and generous ties? We are of one blood. We speak one language. We have a common religion. We have the noble bond of free institutions; and to these two countries, above

72

all others, is the cause of freedom on earth intrusted
by Providence. A war with England would, to a great
extent, sweep our ships from the seas, cut off our intercourse with the world, shut up our great staples, palsy
the spirit of internal improvement, and smite with lan-
guor, if not death, our boldest enterprises. It would
turn to the destruction of our fellow-creatures vast
resources which are now working out for us unparalleled prosperity. It would load us with taxes and
public debts, and breed internal discontents, with which
a free government contends at fearful odds in the midst
of war. Instead of covering the ocean with the sails of
a beneficent commerce, we should scour it with priva-
teers, that is, as legalized pirates. Our great cities
would be threatened with invasion, and the din of
industry in the streets of this metropolis would be
stilled. And all this would come upon us at a moment
when the country is pressing forward to wealth, greatness, and every kind of improvement, with an impulse,
a free, joyous activity, which has no parallel in the
history of the world. And these immense sacrifices are
to be made for a tract of wild land, perhaps not worth
the money which it has cost us within a few weeks past,
if we take into account the expenses of Maine, and
the losses which the whole country has suffered by
interruption of trade.

But this is not all. We are not to suffer alone. We
should inflict in such a war deep wounds on England,
not only on her armed bands, on her rich merchants, on
her widespread interests, but on vast numbers of her
poor population, who owe subsistence to the employment

furnished by the friendly intercourse of the two countries. Thousands and ten thousands of her laborers
would be reduced to want and misery. Nor would it
be any mitigation of these evils to a man of humanity
that we were at war with the government of England.

And this is not all. A war between these countries
would be felt through the whole civilized world. The
present bears no resemblance to those half-barbarous
ages when nations stood apart, frowning on one another
in surly independence. Commerce is binding all nations
together, and of this golden chain England and America
are the chief links. The relations between these countries cannot become hostile without deranging more or
less the intercourse of all other communities, and bringing evils on the whole Christian world.

Nor is this all. War can hardly spring up between
two great countries without extending beyond them.
This fire naturally spreads. The peace of nations is
preserved by a kind of miracle. The addition of a new
cause of conflict is always to be dreaded; but never
more than at this moment, when communities are slowly
adjusting themselves to a new order of things. All
nations may be drawn into the conflict which we may
thoughtlessly begin; and if so, we shall have to answer
for wide and prolonged slaughters from which we should
recoil with horror could they be brought plainly before
our eyes.

And these evils would be brought on the world at
a moment of singular interest and promise to society;
after an unparalleled duration of peace; when a higher
civilization seems to be dawning on Christendom; when

nations are everywhere waking up to develop their own
resources; when the conquests of industry, art, and
science are taking the place of those of war; when new
facilities of intercourse are bringing countries from their
old unsocial distance into neighborhood; and when the
greatest of all social revolutions is going on, that is, the
elevation of the middling and laboring classes, of the
multitude of the human race.   To throw the firebrand
of war among the nations at this period would be treason against humanity and civilization, as foul as was ever
perpetrated.   The nation which does this must answer
to God and to society for every criminal resistance to
the progress of the race.   Every year, every day of
peace is a gain to mankind, for it adds some strength
to the cords which are drawing the nations together.
And yet, in the face of all these motives to peace, we
have made light of the present danger.   How few of
us seem to have felt the infinite interests which a war
would put in jeopardy!   Many have talked of national
honor, as duelists talk of their reputation; a few have
used language worthy of a mob making a ring to see
a fight.   Hardly anywhere has a tone worthy of the
solemnity of the subject been uttered.   National honor!
This has been on our lips; as if the true honor of a
nation did not consist in earnest, patient efforts for
peace, not only for its own sake, but for the sake of
humanity; as if this great country, after a long history
which has borne witness to its prowess, needed to rush
to battle to prove itself no coward!   Are we still in
the infancy of civilization?   Has Christianity no power
over us?   Can a people never learn the magnanimity

of sacrifices to peace and humanity? The vast majority of the community would shrink from this war were it to come nearer. But had we feelings worthy of Christians, should we wait for the evil to stand at our door before waking up to the use of every means for averting it?...

And here I am bound to express my gratitude to the present Chief Magistrate of the Union for his temperate and wise efforts for the preservation of peace. He will feel, I trust, that there. is a truer glory in saving a country from war than in winning a hundred battles. Much also is due to the beneficent influence of General Scott. To this distinguished man belongs the rare honor of uniting with military energy and daring the spirit of a philanthropist. His exploits in the field, which placed him in the first rank of our soldiers, have been obscured by the purer and more lasting glory of a pacificator and of a friend of mankind. In the whole history of the intercourse of civilized with barbarous or half-civilized communities we doubt whether a brighter page can be found than that which records his agency in the removal of the Cherokees. As far as the wrongs done to this race can be atoned for, General Scott has made the expiation. In his recent mission to the disturbed borders of our country he has succeeded, not so much by policy as by the nobleness and generosity of his character, by moral influences, by the earnest conviction with which he has enforced on all with whom he had to do the obligations of patriotism, justice, humanity, and religion. It would not be easy to find among us a man who has won a purer fame; and I am happy to offer this tribute, because I would do something, no matter how little, to hasten the time when the spirit of Christian humanity shall be accounted an essential attribute and the brightest ornament in a public man.

I close this preface with a topic which ought not to be set aside as an unmeaning commonplace. We have Christians among us not a few. Have they been true to themselves and their religion in the present agitation of the question of war? Have they spoken with strength and decision? Have they said, We will take no part in a rash, passionate, unnecessary war? Or have they sat still and left the country to parties and politicians? Will they always consent to be the passive tools of the ambitious or designing? Is the time never to come when they will plant themselves on their religion and resolve not to stir an inch in obedience to the policy or legislation of the men of this world? On this topic I have enlarged in the following discourse, and I respectfully ask for it the impartial attention of Christians.

LECTURE

In commencing this lecture on war my thoughts are irresistibly drawn to that exemplary servant of God, the late Noah Worcester, through whose labors, more than through any other cause, the attention of the community has been awakened to the guilt and misery of war. I feel my own obligation to him in this particular. In truth, it was not easy to know him and to escape wholly the influence of his character. So imbued was he with the spirit of peace that it spread itself around him like the fragrance of sweet flowers. Even those within his sphere, who listened at first with distrust or with a feeling approaching opposition, were not seldom overcome by the singular union in his conversation of gentleness, earnestness, and serene wisdom. He did not live in vain. One of my motives for taking part in this course of lectures is my respect for this venerated man. Another and a stronger motive is the fact that, notwithstanding the favorable impression made by his efforts, there is yet comparatively little interest in the subject of peace. It is a reason for setting forth great truths, that skeptics deride them and the multitude pass them by with unconcern. Dr. Worcester was not roused by the shouts of a crowd to lift up his voice in behalf of peace. He did not postpone his testimony to "a more convenient season." He was as "one crying in the wilderness." He began his ministry amidst the triumphs of the spirit of war. He took counsel not of men, but of the divine oracle in his own breast. The truth, which was burning as a fire within him, he could not but give forth. He had faith in it. He had faith in God, its inspirer. So ought we to trust. So ought we to bear a more fervent witness to truth, on the very ground that it is unpopular, neglected, despised.

In the following lecture I shall aim to set forth the chief evil of war, to set forth its great remedy, and then to point out some of the causes of the faint impression made by its woes and crimes.

Before entering on these topics I would offer one or two remarks. In speaking, as I propose to do, of the evils of war, I have no thought of denying that war has sometimes done good. There is no unmixed evil in the

universe. Providence brings good from everything,
from fearful sufferings, from atrocious crimes. But
sufferings and crimes are not therefore to be set down
among our blessings. Murder sometimes cuts short the
life and triumphs of a monster of guilt. Robbery may
throw into circulation the useless hoards of a miser.
Despotism may subdue an all-wasting anarchy. But we
do not therefore canonize despotism, robbery, and murder. In fierce ages, when common life is made up of
violence and borders on bloodshed, when piracy is an
honorable trade and a stranger is a foe, war, by accumulating force in the hands of an able chieftain, may
gather many petty tribes under one iron will, and thus
a state may be founded, and its rude organization may
prove a germ of social order. In later times war may
carry into less civilized regions the influences, knowledge, arts, and religion of more cultivated nations.
Above all, war may call forth, in those whom it assails,
an indignant patriotism, a fervent public spirit, a generous daring, and heroic sacrifices, which testify to the
inborn greatness of human nature; just as great vices,
by the horror with which they thrill us, and by the
reaction they awaken, often give strength to the moral
sentiments of a community. These, however, are the
incidental influences of war. Its necessary fruits are
crime and woe. To enthrone force above right is its
essential character; and order, freedom, civilization, are
its natural prey. Besides, the benefits of war, such as
they are, belong to unrefined ages, when the passions,
if not expended in public conflicts, would break out in
worse forms of rapine and lust, and when one nation

can act on another only by violence. Society, in its present stage, stands in need of war no more than of the ordeal, the rack, the inquisition, the baronial license of the middle ages. All these monuments and ministers of barbarism should be buried in one grave.

I. I now proceed to consider, first, as I proposed, the chief evil of war. The chief evil of war! What is it? What induces us to place war at the head of human calamities? In replying to these questions I shall not direct you to the physical sufferings of war, however great or terrible. Death in its most agonizing forms, the overthrow of proud cities, the devastation of fruit-ful fields, the impoverishing of nations, famine, pesti-lence, — these form the train of victorious war. But these are not the distinguishing evils of war. These are inflic-tions of other causes much more than of war. Other causes are wasting human life and joy more than battles. Millions, indeed, die by the sword, but these millions are as nothing compared with the countless multitudes who die by slow and painful disease. Cities are over-thrown by earthquakes as well as by armies, and more frequently swept by accidental conflagrations than by the flames of war. Hostile bands ravage the fields; but how much oftener do whirlwinds, storms, hurri-canes rush over land and sea, prostrating harvests and destroying the labors of years on a scale so vast as to reduce human devastations to a narrow extent! The truth is, that man is surrounded with mighty powers of nature which he cannot comprehend or withstand; and, amidst their beneficent operations, all of them inflict much suffering. What distinguishes war is not that man is slain, but that he is slain, spoiled, crushed by the cruelty, the injustice, the treachery, the murderous hand of man. The evil is moral evil. War is the concentration of all human crimes. Here is its distinguishing, accursed brand. Under its standard gather violence, malignity, rage, fraud, perfidy, rapacity, and lust. If it only slew men, it would do little. It turns man into a beast of prey. Here is the evil of war, that man, made to be the brother, becomes the deadly foe of his kind; that man, whose duty it is to mitigate suffering, makes the infliction of suffering his study and end ; that man, whose office it is to avert and heal the wounds which come from nature's powers, makes researches into nature's laws and arms himself with her most awful forces, that he may become the destroyer of his race. Nor is this all. There is also found in war a cold-hearted indifference to human miseries and wrongs, perhaps more shocking than the bad passions it calls forth. To my mind this contempt of human nature is singularly offensive. To hate expresses something like respect. But in war man treats his brother as nothing worth, sweeps away human multitudes as insects, tramples them down as grass, mocks at their rights, and does not deign a thought to their woes.

These remarks show us the great evil of war. It is moral evil. The field of battle is a theater, got up at immense cost, for the exhibition of crime on a grand scale. There the hell within the human breast blazes out fiercely and without disguise. A more fearful hell in any region of the universe cannot well be conceived. There the fiends hold their revels and spread their fury.

To many the physical evils of war are more striking
than the moral. The outward impresses multitudes more
than the inward. It is because they cannot look inward,
because they are too earthly and sensual to see and comprehend the deformity of a selfish, unjust, malignant
soul. The outward evils of life are emblems of the
inward, and are light when severed from these. The
saddest view of war is, that it is the breaking out of
the human heart, revealing there what is more awful
than the miseries which it inflicts. The death groan is
fearful; but how much more appalling the spirit of
murder which extorts it!

Suppose two multitudes of men, each composed of
thousands, meeting from different countries, but meeting not to destroy but to consult and labor for the good
of the race; and suppose them, in the midst of their
deliberations, to be smitten suddenly by some mysterious visitation of God, and their labors to be terminated
by immediate death. We should be awe-struck by this
strange, sudden, widespread ruin. But reflection would
teach us that this simultaneous extinction of life in so
many of our race was but an anticipation or peculiar
fulfillment of the sentence passed on all mankind; and
a tender reverence would spring up as we should think
of so many generous men coming together from so
many different regions, in the spirit of human brotherhood, to be wrapped in one pall, to sleep in one grave.
We should erect a monument on the solemn spot — but
chiefly to commemorate the holy purpose which had
gathered them from their scattered abodes; and we
should write on it, "To the memory of a glorious

company, suddenly taken from God's ministry on earth to enter again, a blessed brotherhood, on a higher ministry in heaven." Here you have death sweeping away hosts in a moment. But how different from death in a field of battle, where man meets man as a foe, where the countenance flashes rage and the arm is nerved for slaughter, where brother hews down brother, and where thousands are sent unprepared, in the moment of crime, to give their account! When nature's laws, fulfilling the mysterious will of God, inflict death on the good, we bow, we adore, we give thanks. How different is death from the murderous hand of man!

Allow me to make another supposition, which may bring out still more strongly the truth on which I now insist, that the great evil of war is inward, moral; that its physical woes, terrible as they may be, are light by the side of this. Suppose, then, that in traveling through a solitary region, you should catch the glimpse of a distant dwelling. You approach it eagerly in the hope of hearing a welcome after your weary journey. As you draw nigh, an ominous stillness damps your hope; and on entering, you see the inmates of the house, a numerous family, stretched out motionless and without life. A wasting pestilence has in one day made their dwelling a common tomb. At first you are thrilled with horror by the sight; but as you survey the silent forms you see on all their countenances, amidst traces of suffering, an expression of benignity. You see some of the dead lying side by side, with hands mutually entwined, showing that the last action of life was a grasp of affection, whilst some lie locked in one another's arms.

The mother's cold lips are still pressed to the cheek of
the child, and the child's arms still wind round the neck
of the mother. In the forms of others you see no
ambiguous proof that the spirit took its flight in the
act of prayer. As you look on these signs of love and
faith, stronger than the last agony, what a new feeling
steals over you! Your horror subsides. Your eyes
are suffused with tears, not of anguish, but of sympathy, affection, tender reverence. You feel the spot to
be consecrated. Death becomes lovely, like the sleep
of infancy. You say, Blessed family, death hath not
divided you!

With soothed and respectful sorrow you leave this
resting place of the good, and another dwelling, dimly
descried in the horizon, invites your steps. As you
approach it the same stillness is an augury of a like
desolation, and you enter it expecting to see another
family laid low by the same mysterious disease. But
you open the door, and the spectacle freezes your blood
and chains your steps to the threshold. On every face
you see the distortion of rage. Every man's hand grasps
a deadly weapon ; every breast is gored with wounds.
Here lies one, rived asunder by a sword. There two
are locked together, but in the death grapple of hatred,
not the embrace of love. Here lies woman, trampled
on and polluted, and there the child, weltering in his
own blood. You recoil with horror as soon as the sickness of the heart will suffer you to move. The deadly
steam of the apartment oppresses, overpowers you, as
if it were the suffocating air of hell. You are terror-
struck, as if through the opening earth you had sunk

into the abode of fiends; and when the time for reflection comes, and you recall the blessed habitation you had just before left, what a conviction rushes on you that nothing deserves the name of woe but that which crime inflicts! You feel that there is a sweetness, loveliness, sacredness in suffering and death when these are pervaded by holy affections; and that infinite wretchedness and despair gather over these when springing from unholy passion, when bearing the brand of crime.

In these remarks I do not mean to deny that the physical sufferings of war are great and should incite us to labor for its abolition. But sufferings, separate from crime, coming not through man's wickedness but from the laws of nature, are not unmixed evils. They have a ministry of love. God has ordained them, that they should bind men to one another, that they should touch and soften the human heart, that they should call forth mutual aid, solace, gratitude, and self-forgetting love. Sorrow is the chief cement of souls. Death, coming in the order of nature, gathers round the sufferer sympathizing, anxious friends, who watch day and night, with suffused eyes and heart-breathed prayer, to avert or mitigate the last agonies. It calls up tender recollections, inspires solemn thought, rebukes human pride, obscures the world's glories, and speaks of immortality. From the still deathbed, what softening, subduing, chastening, exalting influences proceed! But death in war, death from the hand of man, sears the heart and conscience, kills human sympathies, and scatters the thought of judgment to come. Man dying in battle, unsolaced, unpitied, and a victim to hatred, rapacity, and insatiable ambition, leaves behind him wrongs to be revenged. His blood does not speak peace or speak of heaven, but sends forth a maddening cry, and exasperates survivors to new struggles.

Thus war adds to suffering the unutterable weight of crime, and defeats the holy and blessed ministry which all suffering is intended to fulfill. When I look back on the ages of conflict through which the race has passed, what most moves me is not the awful amount of suffering which war has inflicted. This may be borne. The terrible thought is that this has been the work of crime ; that men, whose great law is love, have been one another's butchers ; that God's children have stained his beautiful earth, made beautiful for their home, with one another's blood ; that the shriek which comes to us from all regions and ages has been extorted by human cruelty; that man has been a demon and has turned earth into hell. All else may be borne. It is this which makes history so horrible a record to the benevolent mind.

II. I have now set before you what I deem the chief evil of war. It is moral evil. And from these views you will easily judge what I regard as the true remedy of war, as the means of removing it, which above all others we should employ. If the most terrible view of war be that it is the triumph and jubilee of selfish and malignant passions, then its true cure is to be sought in the diffusion of the principles of universal justice and love, in that spirit of Jesus Christ which expels the demons of selfishness and malignity from the heart. Even supposing that war could be abolished by processes which leave the human character unchanged,

that it could be terminated by the progress of a civilization
which, whilst softening manners, would not diminish the
selfishness, mercenariness, hard-heartedness, fraud, ambition of men, its worst evils would still remain, and society would reap in some other forms the fruits of its guilt.
God has ordained that the wickedness within us shall
always find its expression and punishment in outward
evil. War is nothing more than a reflection or image
of the soul. It is the fiend within coming out. Human
history is nothing more than the inward nature manifested in its native acts and issues. Let the soul continue unchanged; and should war cease, the inward
plague would still find its way to the surface. The
infernal fire at the center of our being, though it should
not break forth in the wasting volcano, would not slumber, but by other eruptions, more insensible yet not less
deadly, would lay waste human happiness. I do not
believe, however, that any remedy but the Christian
spirit can avail against war. The wild beast that has
gorged on millions of victims in every age is not to be
tamed by a polished or selfish civilization. Selfishness,
however drilled into courtesy, always tends to strife.
Man, as long as possessed by it, will sacrifice others to
his own interest and glory, and will grow angry and
fierce when others stand in his way.

War will never yield but to the principles of universal
justice and love; and these have no sure root but in the
religion of Jesus Christ. Christianity is the true remedy
for war, not Christianity in name, not such Christianity as
we see, not such as has grown up under arbitrary governments in church and state, not such as characterizes

any Christian sect at the present day, but Christianity
as it lived in the soul and came forth in the life of its
Founder; a religion that reveals man as the object of
God's infinite love, and which commends him to the
unbounded love of his brethren; a religion, the essence
of which is self-denial, self-sacrifice, in the cause of human
nature; a religion which proscribes, as among the worst
sins, the passion of man for rule and dominion over his
fellow-creatures; which knows nothing of rich or poor,
high or low, bond or free, and casts down all the walls of
partition which sever men from one another's sympathy
and respect.

Christian love alone can supplant war; and this love
is not a mere emotion, a tenderness awakened by human
suffering, but an intelligent, moral, spiritual love, a per-
ception and deep feeling of the sacredness of human
nature, a recognition of the inalienable rights, the solemn claims, of every human being. It protests fearlessly against all wrong, no matter how obscure the
victim. It desires to lift up each and all, no matter
how fallen. It is a sympathy with the spiritual principle dwelling under every human form. This is the
love which is to conquer war; and as yet this has been
but little diffused. The Quakers, indeed, have protested
against war as unchristian, but have done little towards
bringing into clear light, and sending forth with new
power, the spirit to which war is to yield. Cutting
themselves off by outward peculiarities from the community, secluding themselves from ordinary intercourse
through fear of moral infection, living almost as a separate race, they have been little felt in society; they

have done little to awaken that deep religious interest
in man as man, that sensibility to his rights, that hatred
of all wrong, that thirst for the elevation of every human
being, in which Christian love finds its truest manifestation.   Every sect has as yet been too imbued with the
spirit of sects, and has inherited too largely the exclusiveness of past ages, to understand or spread the true
spirit of human brotherhood.   The love which Christ
breathes, which looks through man's body to the immortal spirit, which sees something divine in the rational
and moral powers of the lowest human being, and which
challenges for the lowest the sympathy, respect, and fos-
tering aid of his race, —this has been rare; and yet it is
only by the gradual diffusion of this that the plague of
war can be stayed.   This reverence for humanity, could
it even prevail through a narrow sphere, could it bind
together but a small body of men, would send forth a
testimony against war which would break the slumber
of the Christian world, and which would strike awe
into many a contemner of his race.

I am aware that others are hoping for the abolition of
war by other causes; and other causes, I am aware, must
be brought into action.   I only say that, unless joined
with the spirit of Christianity, they give no assurance of
continued repose. This thought I would briefly illustrate.

The present unusual cessation of arms in the Christian
world is to some a promise of a happier era in human
affairs.   It is, indeed, a cheering fact, and may well
surprise us when we consider how many causes of war
have been in action, how many threatening clouds have
overcast the political sky during the pause of war.   But

if we examine the causes of this tranquillity we shall learn not to confide in it too strongly.

The first cause was the exhaustion in which Europe was left by the bloody conflicts of the French Revolution. The nations, worn out with struggles, wasted by successive invasions, and staggering under an unprecedented load of debt, yearned for repose. The strong man had bled too freely to fight more. For years poverty has kept the peace in Europe. One of the fruits of civilization is the increasing expensiveness of war, so that when the voice of humanity cannot be heard, the hollow sound of an empty treasury is a warning which cannot be slighted. This cause of peace is evidently temporary. Nations resting from exhaustion may be expected to renew their pernicious activity when their strength is renewed.

Another cause of the continuance of peace is undoubtedly the extension of new and profitable relations through the civilized world. Since the pacification of Europe in 1816, a new impulse has been given to industry. The discoveries of science have been applied with wonderful success to the useful arts. Nations have begun in earnest to develop their resources. Labor is discovered to be the grand conqueror, enriching and building up nations more surely than the proudest battles. As a necessary result of this new impulse, commerce has been wonderfully enlarged. Nations send the products of their soil and machinery where once they sent armies; and such a web of common interests has been woven that hostilities can spring up in no corner of the civilized world without deranging in a measure the order and industry of

every other state. Undoubtedly we have here a promise
of peace; but let us not be too sanguine. We have
just begun this career, and we know not its end. Let
wealth grow without a corresponding growth of the
temperate, just, and benevolent spirit of Christianity,
and I see few auguries but of evil. Wealth breeds
power, and power always tempts to wrong. Communities which at once grow rich and licentious breed desperate men, unprincipled adventurers, restless spirits,
who unsettle social order at home, who make freedom a
cloak and instrument of ambition, and find an interest in
embroiling their country with foreign foes. Another
consequence of growing prosperity is the rapid growth
of population; and this, in the absence of Christian
restraints and Christian principles, tends to pauperism
and crime, tends to make men cheap, and to destroy the
sacredness of human life; and communities are tempted
to throw off this dangerous load, this excess of numbers,
in foreign war. In truth, the vices which fester in the
bosom of a prosperous, licentious, over-peopled state are
hardly less fearful than those of war, and they naturally
seek and find their punishment in this awful calamity.
Let us not speak of industry, commerce, and wealth as
insuring peace. Is commerce never jealous and grasping? Have commercial states no collisions? Have commercial rights never drawn the sword in self-defense?
Are not such states a tempting prey? And have they
no desire to prey on others? Does trade cherish nothing
analogous to the spirit of war in ordinary pursuits? Is
there no fighting on the exchange? Is bargaining nothing but friendship and peace? Why, then, expect from

trade alone peace among nations? Nothing, nothing can bind nations together but Christian justice and love. I insist on this the more earnestly because it is the fashion now to trust for every good to commerce, industry, and the wonderful inventions which promise indefinite increase of wealth. But to improve man's outward condition is not to improve man himself, and this is the sole ground of hope. With all our ingenuity we can frame no machinery for manufacturing wisdom, virtue, peace. Railroads and steamboats cannot speed the soul to its perfection. This must come, if it come at all, from each man's action on himself, from putting forth our power on the soul and not over nature, from a sense of inward not outward miseries, from " hunger and thirst after righteousness," not after wealth. I should rejoice, like the prophet, " to bring glad tidings, to publish peace." But I do fear that, without some great spiritual revolution, without some new life and love breathed into the church, without some deep social reforms, men will turn against each other their new accumulations of power ; that their wealth and boasted inventions will be converted into weapons of destruction; that the growing prosperity of nations will become the nutriment of more wasteful wars, will become fuel for more devouring fires of ambition or revenge.

Another cause of the recent long cessation of foreign wars has been the dread of internal convulsions, of civil wars. The spirit of revolution has more or less penetrated the whole civilized world. The grand idea of human rights has found its way even into despotisms. Kings have less confidence in their subjects and soldiers.

They have felt their thrones totter, and have felt that a disastrous war would expose them to a force more terrible than that of victorious foes, — the force of burning discontent, exasperated opinion at home. It is understood that the next general war will be a war not of nations but of principles, that absolutism must measure swords with liberalism, despotism with free constitutions; and from this terrible encounter both parties recoil. We indeed believe that, with or without war, liberal principles and institutions are destined to advance, to make the conquest of Europe; and it is thought that these, being recognitions of human rights, will be less prodigal of human blood than absolute power. But can we hope that these, unsanctioned, unsustained by the Christian spirit, will insure peace? What teaches our own experience? Because free, have we no wars? What, indeed, is the free spirit of which we so much boast? Is it not much more a jealousy of our own rights than a reverence for the rights of all? Does it not consist with the inflictions of gross wrongs? Does it not spoil the Indian? Does it not enslave the African? Is it not anxious to spread bondage over new regions? Who can look on this free country, distracted by parties, rent by local jealousies, in some districts administering justice by mobs and silencing speech and the press by conflagration and bloodshed, — who can see this free country and say that liberal opinions and institutions are of themselves to banish war? Nowhere are the just, impartial, disinterested principles of Christianity so much needed as in a free state. Nowhere are there more elements of strife to be composed, more passions to be curbed, more threatened wrongs to be repressed. Freedom has its perils as well as inestimable blessings. In loosening outward restraints, it demands that justice and love be enthroned within man's soul. Without Christian principle, freedom may swell the tide of tumult and war.

One other cause will probably be assigned by some for the long cessation of hostilities in the civilized world; and that is the greater success of statesmen in securing that long-sought good among nations, the balance of power. Be it so. But how soon may this balance be disturbed? How does it tremble now? Europe has long been threatened by the disproportionate growth of Russia. In the north of Europe is silently growing up a power which, many fear, is one day to grasp at universal empire. The south, it is said, is to fulfill its old destiny, that is, to fall a prey to the north. All Europe is interested in setting bounds to this half-civilized despotism. But the great absolute powers, Prussia and Austria, dreading more the progress of liberal opinions than of Russian hordes, may rather throw themselves into her scale, and be found fighting with her the battles of legitimacy against free institutions. It is true that many wise men dismiss these fears as vain, and believe that the ill-cemented union of the provinces, or rather nations, which compose the colossal empire of the north, cannot endure or at least will admit no steady prosecution of schemes of domination. I presume not to read the future. My single object is to show the uncertainty of all means of abolishing war, unless joined with and governed by the spreading spirit of our disinterested faith. No calculations of interest, no schemes of policy can do the work of love, of the spirit of human brotherhood. There can be no peace without but through peace within. Society must be an expression of the souls of its members. Man's character molds his outward lot. His destiny is woven by the good or evil principles which bear rule in his breast. I indeed attach importance to all the causes of peace which I have now stated. They are far from powerless; but their power will be spent in vain unless aided by mightier and diviner energy, by the force of moral and religious principles, the strength of disinterested love.

III. I have now considered the great evil of war and the great remedy of this scourge of nations, and I proceed, as proposed, to point out some causes of that insensibility to its evils, so common in the world, and so common even among those from whom better things might be hoped; and this I do, not to gratify a love of speculation, but in the belief that this insensibility will be resisted and overcome, in proportion as its sources shall be explained.

Among its chief causes, one undoubtedly is the commonness of war. This hardens us to its evils. Its horrors are too familiar to move us unless they start up at our own door. How much more would they appall us were they rare? If the history of the race were, with one solitary exception, a history of peace, concord, brotherly love; if but one battle had been fought in the long succession of ages; if from the bosom of profound tranquillity two armies on one fatal day had sprung forth and rushed together for mutual destruction; if but one spot on earth had been drenched with human blood shed by human hands, — how different would be our apprehensions of war! What a fearful interest would gather round that spot! How would it remain deserted, dreaded, abhorred! With what terrible distinctness would the leaders of those armies stand out as monsters, not men! How should we confound them with Moloch and the fiercest fallen spirits! Should we not feel as if on that mysterious day the blessed influences of heaven had been intercepted, and a demoniacal frenzy had been let loose on the race? And has war in becoming common lost its horrors? Is it less terrible because its Molochs crowd every page of history and its woes and crimes darken all nations and all times? Do base or ferocious passions less degrade and destroy because their victims are unnumbered? If, indeed, the evils of war were only physical, and were inevitable, we should do well to resign ourselves to that kindly power of habit which takes the edge from oft-repeated pains. But moral evils, evils which may and ought to be shunned, which have their spring in human will, which our higher powers are given us to overcome, these it is a crime unresistingly to endure. The frequency and strength of these are more urgent reasons for abhorring and withstanding them. Reflection should be summoned to resist the paralyzing power of habit. From principle we should cherish a deeper horror of war, because its "sword devours forever."

I proceed to a second cause of insensibility to the evils of war, and one of immense power. I refer to the common and almost universal belief that the right of

war belongs to civil government.   Let us be just to
human nature.   The idea of "right" has always mixed
itself with war, and this has kept out of view the real
character of most of the conflicts of nations.   The sovereign, regarding the right of war as an essential attribute
of sovereignty, has on this ground ascribed a legitimacy to all national hostilities, and has never dreamed
that in most of his wars 'he was a murderer.   So the
subject has thought himself bound to obey his sovereign, and on this ground has acquitted himself of
'crime, has perhaps imputed to himself merit, in fighting
and slaughtering for the defense of the most iniquitous
claims.   Here lies the delusion which we should be
most anxious to remove.   It is the legality ascribed to
war, on account of its being waged by government, which
produces insensibility to its horrors and crimes.   When
a notorious robber, seized by Alexander, asked the conqueror of the world whether he were not a greater robber than himself, the spirit of the hero repelled the title
with indignation.   And why so?   Had he not, without
provocation and cause, spoiled cities and realms, whilst
the robber had only plundered individuals and single
dwellings?   Had he not slaughtered ten thousand innocent fellow-creatures for one victim who had fallen
under the robber's knife?   And why, then, did the
arch-robber disclaim the name, and seriously believe
that he could not justly be confounded with ruffians?
Because he was a king, the head of a state, and as
such authorized to make war.   Here was the shelter
for his conscience and his fame.   Had the robber, after
addressing his question to Alexander, turned to the

Macedonian soldier, and said to him, " Are you not, too, a greater robber than I? Have not your hands been busier in pillage? Are they not dyed more deeply in innocent blood?" The unconscious soldier, like his master, would have repelled the title. And why? "I am a subject," he would have replied, "and bound to obey my sovereign; and in fulfilling a duty I cannot be sunken to the level of fhe most hated criminal." Thus king and subject take refuge in the right of war which inheres in sovereignty, and thus the most terrible crimes are perpetrated with little reproach.

I need not tell you that there are Christians who, to strip war of this pretext or extenuation, deny that this right exists; who teach that Jesus Christ has wrested the sword from the magistrate as truly as from the private man. On this point I shall not now enter. I believe that more good may be done in the present instance by allowing to government the right of war. I still maintain that most wars bring the guilt of murder on the government by whom they are declared, and on the soldier by whom they are carried on, so that our sensibility ought in no degree to be impaired by the supposed legitimacy of national hostilities.

I will allow that government has the right of war. But a right has bounds, and when these are transgressed by us it ceases to exist; and we are as culpable as if it had never existed. The private citizen, it is generally acknowledged, has the right of taking life in self-defense; but if, under plea of this right, he should take life without cause, he would not stand absolved of murder. In like manner, though government be

authorized to make war in self-defense, it still contracts
the guilt of murder if it proclaim war from policy, ambition, or revenge.   By the Constitution of this country
various rights are conferred on Congress for the public
good; and should they extend these rights beyond the
limits prescribed by the national charter, for purposes
of cruelty, rapacity, and arbitrary power, they would be
as treacherous, as criminal, as if they had laid claim to
unconceded rights.   Now, stricter bounds are set to the
right of war than those which the Constitution has prescribed to the rulers.   A higher authority than man's
defines this terrible prerogative.   Woe! woe to him who
impatiently, selfishly spurns the restraints of God, and
who winks out of sight the crime of sending forth the
sword to destroy, because as a sovereign he has the
right of war.

From its very nature this right should be exercised
above all others anxiously, deliberately, fearfully.   It is
the right of passing sentence of death on thousands of
our fellow-creatures.   If any action on earth ought to
be performed with trembling, with deep prostration
before God, with the most solemn inquisition into
motives, with the most reverent consultation of conscience, it is a declaration of war.   This stands alone
among acts of legislation.   It has no parallel.   These
few words, " Let war be," have the power of desolation
which belongs to earthquakes and lightnings ; they
may stain the remotest seas with blood ; may wake the
echoes of another hemisphere with the thunders of artillery ; may carry anguish into a thousand human abodes.
No scheme of aggrandizement, no doubtful claims, no

uncertain fears, no anxiety to establish a balance of
power, will justify this act. It can find no justification
but in plain, stern necessity, in unquestionable justice,
in persevering wrongs, which all other and long-tried
means have failed to avert. Terrible is the responsibility, beyond that of all others, which falls on him who
involves nations in war. He has no excuse for rashness,
passion, or private ends. He ought at such a moment
to forget, to annihilate himself. The spirit of God and
justice should alone speak and act through him. To
commit this act rashly, passionately, selfishly, is to bring
on himself the damnation of a thousand murders. An
act of legislation, commanding fifty thousand men to be
assembled on yonder common, there to be shot, stabbed,
trampled under horses' feet until their shrieks and
agonies should end in death, would thrill us with horror:
and such an act is a declaration of war ; and a government which can perform it without the most solemn
sense of responsibility and the clearest admonitions of
duty deserves, in expiation of its crime, to endure the
whole amount of torture which it has inflicted on its
fellow-creatures.

I have said a declaration of war stands alone. There
is one act which approaches it, and which, indeed, is the
very precedent on which it is founded. I refer to the
signing of a death warrant by a chief magistrate. In
this case how anxious is society that the guilty only
should suffer ! The offender is first tried by his peers
and allowed the benefit of skillful counsel. The laws
are expounded and the evidence weighed by learned
and upright judges ; and when, after these protections

of innocence, the unhappy man is convicted, he is still allowed to appeal for mercy to the highest authority of the state, and to enforce his own cry by solicitations of friends and the people; and when all means of averting his doom fail, religion, through her ministers, enters his cell, to do what yet can be done for human nature in its most fallen, miserable state. Society does not cast from its bosom its most unworthy member without reluctance, without grief, without fear of doing wrong, without care for his happiness. But wars, by which thousands of the unoffending and worthiest perish, are continually proclaimed by rulers, in madness, through ambition, through infernal policy, from motives which should rank them with the captains of pirate ships or leaders of banditti.

It is time that the right of war should not shield governments from the infamy due to hostilities to which selfish, wicked passions give birth. Let rulers learn that for this right they are held to a fearful responsibility. Let a war not founded in plain justice and necessity never be named but as murder. Let the Christian give articulate voice to the blood that cries from the earth against rulers by whom it has been criminally shed. Let no soft terms be used. On this subject a new moral sense and a new language are needed throughout the whole civilized and Christian world; and just in proportion as the truth shall find a tongue war will cease.

But the right of war, which is said to belong to sovereignty, not only keeps out of sight the enormous guilt of rulers in almost all national conflicts; it also hides or extenuates the frequent guilt of subjects in taking part in the hostilities which their rulers declare. In this way much of the prevalent insensibility to the evils of war is induced, and perhaps on no point is light more needed. The ferocity and cruelty of armies impress us little, because we look on them as doing a work of duty. The subject or citizen, as we think, is bound to obey his rulers. In his worst deeds as a soldier he is discharging his obligations to the state; and thus murder and pillage, covered with a cloak of duty, excite no deep, unaffected reprobation and horror.

I know it will be asked: " And is not the citizen bound to fight at the call of his government? Does not his commission absolve him from the charge of murder or enormous crime? Is not obedience to the sovereign power the very foundation on which society rests?" I answer: " Has the duty of obeying government no bounds? Is the human sovereign a God? Is his sovereignty absolute? If he command you to slay a parent, must you obey? If he forbid you to worship God, must you obey? Have you no right to judge his acts? Have you no self-direction? Is there no unchangeable right which the ruler cannot touch? Is there no higher standard than human law?" These questions answer themselves. A declaration of war cannot sanction wrong or turn murder into a virtuous deed. Undoubtedly, as a general rule, the citizen is bound to obey the authorities under which he lives. No difference of opinion as to the mere expediency of measures will warrant opposition. Even in cases of doubtful right he may submit his judgment to the law. But when called to do what his conscience clearly pronounces wrong, he must not waver. No outward law is so sacred as the voice of God in his own breast. He cannot devolve on rulers an act so solemn as the destruction of fellow-beings convicted of no offense. For no act will more solemn inquisition be made at the bar of God.

I maintain that the citizen, before fighting, is bound to inquire into the justice of the cause which he is called to maintain with blood, and bound to withhold his hand if his conscience condemn the cause. On this point he is able to judge. No political question, indeed, can be determined so easily as this of war. War can be justified only by plain, palpable necessity; by unquestionable wrongs, which, as patient trial has proved, can in no other way be redressed; by the obstinate, persevering invasion of solemn and unquestionable rights. The justice of war is not a mystery for cabinets to solve. It is not a state secret which we must take on trust. It lies within our reach. We are bound to examine it.

We are especially bound to this examination because there is always a presumption against the justice of war; always reason to fear that it is condemned by impartial conscience and God. This solemn truth has peculiar claims on attention. It takes away the plea that we may innocently fight because our rulers have decreed war. It strips off the most specious disguise from the horrors and crimes of national hostilities. If hostilities were as a general rule necessary and just, if an unjust war were a solitary exception, then the citizen might extenuate his share in the atrocities of military life by urging his obligation to the state. But if there is always

reason to apprehend the existence of wrong on the part
of rulers, then he is bound to pause and ponder well his
path. Then he advances at his peril, and must answer
for the crimes of the unjust, unnecessary wars in which
he shares.

The presumption is always against the justice and
necessity of war. This we learn from the spirit of all
rulers and nations towards foreign states. It is partial,
unjust. Individuals may be disinterested, but nations
have no feeling of the tie of brotherhood to their race.
A base selfishness is the principle on which the affairs
of nations are commonly conducted. A statesman is
expected to take advantage of the weaknesses and wants
of other countries. How loose a morality governs the
intercourse of states ! What falsehoods and intrigues
are licensed diplomacy ! What nation regards another
with true friendship ? What nation makes sacrifices to
another's good ? What nation is as anxious to perform
its duties as to assert its rights ? What nation chooses
to suffer wrong rather than to inflict it ? What nation
lays down the everlasting law of right, casts itself fearlessly on its principles, and chooses to be poor or to
perish rather than to do wrong ? Can communities
so selfish, so unfriendly, so unprincipled, so unjust, be
expected to wage righteous wars ? Especially if with
this selfishness are joined national prejudices, antipathies,
and exasperated passions, what else can be expected in
the public policy but inhumanity and crime ? An individual, we know, cannot be trusted in his own cause to
measure his own claims, to avenge his own wrongs;
and the civil magistrate, an impartial umpire, has been

substituted as the only means of justice. But nations are even more unfit than individuals to judge in their own cause, more prone to push their rights to excess and to trample on the rights of others, because nations are crowds, and crowds are unawed by opinion and more easily inflamed by sympathy into madness. Is there not, then, always a presumption against the justice of war?

This presumption is increased when we consider the false notions of patriotism and honor which prevail in nations. Men think it a virtuous patriotism to throw a mantle, as they call it, over their country's infirmities, to wink at her errors, to assert her most doubtful rights, to look jealously and angrily on the prosperity of rival states ; and they place her honor not in unfaltering adherence to the right, but in a fiery spirit, in quick resentment, in martial courage, and especially in victory; and can a good man hold himself bound and stand prepared to engage in war at the dictate of such a state?

The citizen or subject, you say, may innocently fight at the call of his rulers ; and I ask, Who are his rulers? Perhaps an absolute sovereign, looking down on his people as another race, as created to toil for his pleasure, to fight for new provinces, to bleed for his renown. There are, indeed, republican governments. But were not the republics of antiquity as greedy of conquest, as prodigal of human life, as steeled against the cries of humanity, as any despots who ever lived? And if we come down to modern republics, are they to be trusted with our consciences? What does the Congress of these United States represent? Not so much the virtue of the

country as a vicious principle, the spirit of party. It
acts not so much for the people as for parties; and are
parties upright? Are parties merciful? Are the wars
to which party commits a country generally just?

Unhappily, public men under all governments are of
all moral guides the most unsafe, the last for a Christian
to follow. Public life is thought to absolve men from
the strict obligations of truth and justice. To wrong an
adverse party or another country is not reprobated as
are wrongs in private life. Thus duty is dethroned;
thus the majesty of virtue insulted in the administration
of nations. Public men are expected to think more of
their own elevation than of their country. Is the city
of Washington the most virtuous spot in this republic?
Is it the school of incorruptible men? The hall of Congress, disgraced by so many brawls, swayed by local
interest and party intrigues, in which the right of petition is trodden under foot, is this the oracle from which
the responses of justice come forth? Public bodies
want conscience. Men acting in masses shift off responsibility on one another. Multitudes never blush. If
these things be true, then I maintain that the Christian
has not a right to take part in war blindly, confidingly,
at the call of his rulers. To shed the blood of fellow-
creatures is too solemn a work to be engaged in lightly.
Let him not put himself, a tool, into wicked hands.
Let him not meet on the field his brother man, his
brother Christian, in a cause on which heaven frowns.
Let him bear witness against unholy wars, as his country's greatest crimes. If called to take part in them, let
him deliberately refuse. If martial law seize on him,

let him submit.   If hurried to prison, let him submit.
If brought thence to be shot, let him submit.   There
must be martyrs to peace as truly as to other principles
of our religion.   The first Christians chose to die rather
than obey the laws of the state which commanded them
to renounce their Lord.   " Death rather than crime," —
such is the good man's watchword, such the Christian's
vow.   Let him be faithful unto death.

Undoubtedly it will be objected that if one law of the
state may in any way be resisted, then all may be, and
so government must fall.   This is precisely the argument on which the doctrine of passive obedience to the
worst tyrannies rests.   The absolutist says: " If one
government may be overturned, none can stand.   Your
right of revolution is nothing but the right of anarchy,
of universal misrule."   The reply is in both instances
the same.   Extreme cases speak for themselves.   We
must put confidence in the common sense of men, and
suppose them capable of distinguishing between reasonable laws and those which require them to commit manifest crimes.   The objection which we are considering
rests on the supposition that a declaration of war is a
common act of legislation, bearing no strong marks of
distinction from other laws, and consequently to be
obeyed as implicitly as all.   But it is broadly distinguished.   A declaration of war sends us forth to destroy
our fellow-creatures, to carry fire, sword, famine, bereave-
ment, want, and woe into the fields and habitations of
our brethren ; whilst Christianity, conscience, and all the
pure affections of our nature call us to love our brethren, and to die, if need be, for their good.   And from

whence comes this declaration of war? From men who would rather die than engage in unjust or unnecessary conflict? Too probably from men to whom Christianity is a name, whose highest law is honor, who are used to avenge their private wrongs and defend their reputations by shedding blood, and who, in public as in private life, defy the laws of God. Whoever, at such men's dictation, engages in war without solemnly consulting conscience and inquiring into the justice of the cause, contracts great guilt; nor can the "right of war," which such men claim as rulers, absolve him from the crimes and woes of the conflict in which he shares.

I have thus considered the second cause of the prevalent insensibility to war, namely, the common vague belief that, as the right of war inheres in government, therefore murder and pillage in national conflicts change their nature or are broadly distinguished from the like crimes in common life. This topic has been so extended that I must pass over many which remain, and can take but a glance at one or two which ought not to be wholly overlooked. I observe then, thirdly, that men's sensibility to the evil of war has been very much blunted by the deceptive show, the costume, the splendor in which war is arrayed. Its horrors are hidden under its dazzling dress. To the multitude the senses are more convincing reasoners than the conscience. In youth — the period which so often receives impressions for life — we cannot detect, in the heart-stirring fife and drum, the true music of war, — the shriek of the newly wounded or the faint moan of the dying. Arms glittering in the sunbeam do not remind us of bayonets dripping with blood. To one who reflects there is something very shocking in these decorations of war. If men must fight, let them wear the badges which become their craft. It would shock us to see a hangman dressed out in scarf and epaulet and marching with merry music to the place of punishment. The soldier has a sadder work than the hangman. His office is not to dispatch occasionally a single criminal ; he goes to the slaughter of thousands as free from crime as himself. The sword is worn as an ornament; and yet its use is to pierce the heart of a fellow-creature. As well might the butcher parade before us his knife, or the executioner his ax or halter. Allow war to be necessary ; still it is a horrible necessity, a work to fill a good man with anguish of spirit. Shall it be turned into an occasion of pomp and merriment? To dash out men's brains, to stab them to the heart, to cover the body with gashes, to lop off the limbs, to crush men under the hoof of the war horse, to destroy husbands and fathers, to make widows and orphans, all this may be necessary ; but to attire men for this work with fantastic trappings, to surround this fearful occupation with all the circumstances of gayety and pomp, seems as barbarous as it would be to deck a gallows or to make a stage for dancing beneath the scaffold. I conceive that the military dress was not open to as much reproach in former times as now. It was then less dazzling and acted less on the imagination, because it formed less an exception to the habits of the times. The dress of Europe, not many centuries ago, was fashioned very much after what may be called the harlequin style. That is, it affected strong colors and strong contrasts. This taste belongs to rude ages and has passed away very much with the progress of civilization. The military dress alone has escaped the reform. The military man is the only harlequin left us from ancient times. It is time that his dazzling finery were gone, that it no longer corrupted the young, that it no longer threw a glare over his terrible vocation.

I close with assigning what appears to me to be the most powerful cause of the prevalent insensibility to war. It is our blindness to the dignity and claims of human nature. We know not the worth of a man. We know not *who* the victims are on whom war plants its foot, whom the conqueror leaves to the vulture on the field of battle or carries captive to grace his triumph. Oh! did we know what men are, did we see in them the spiritual, immortal children of God, what a voice should we lift against war! How indignantly, how sorrowfully should we invoke heaven and earth to right our insulted, injured brethren!

"Must the sword devour forever?" Is the kingdom of God, the reign of truth, duty, and love, never to prevail? Must the sacred name of brethren be only a name among men? Must the divinity in man's nature never be recognized with veneration? Is the earth always to steam with human blood shed by man's hands, and to echo with groans wrung from hearts which violence has pierced? Can you and I, my friends, do nothing, nothing to impress a different character on the future history of our race? You say we are weak; and why weak? It is from inward defect, not from outward necessity. We are inefficient abroad because faint within, — faint in love and trust and holy resolution. Inward power always comes forth and works without. Noah Worcester, enfeebled in body, was not weak. George Fox, poor and uneducated, was not weak. They had light and life within and therefore were strong abroad. Their spirits were stirred by Christ's truth and spirit, and so moved they spoke and were heard. We are dead and therefore cannot act. Perhaps we speak against war; but if we speak from tradition, if we echo what we hear, if peace be a cant on our lips, our words are unmeaning air. Our own souls must bleed when our brethren are slaughtered. We must feel the infinite wrong done to man by the brute force which treads him in the dust. We must see in the authors of unjust, selfish, ambitious, revengeful wars, monsters in human form, incarnations of the dread enemy of the human race. Under the inspiration of such feelings we shall speak, even the humblest of us, with something of prophetic force. This is the power which is to strike awe into the counselors and perpetrators of now licensed murder, which is to wither the laureled brow of now worshiped heroes. Deep moral convictions, unfeigned reverence and fervent love for man, and living faith in Christ are mightier than armies; mighty through God to the pulling down of the strongholds of oppression and war. Go forth, then, friends of mankind, peaceful soldiers of Christ! and in your various relations, at home and abroad, in private life, and if it may be in more public spheres, give faithful utterance to the principles of universal justice and love, give utterance to your deep, solemn, irreconcilable hatred of the spirit of war.

THE CITIZEN'S DUTY IN WAR WHICH HE CONDEMNS [1]

In all circumstances, at all times, war is to be deprecated. The evil passions which it excites, its ravages, its bloody conflicts, the distress and terror which it carries into domestic life, the tears which it draws from the widow and fatherless, all render war a tremendous scourge.

There are, indeed, conditions in which war is justifiable, is necessary. It may be the last and only method of repelling lawless ambition and of defending invaded liberty and essential rights. It may be the method which God's providence points out by furnishing the means of success. In these cases we must not shrink from war, though even in these we should deeply lament the necessity of shedding human blood. In such wars our country claims and deserves our prayers, our cheerful services, the sacrifice of wealth and even of life. In such wars we have one consolation when our friends fall on the field of battle: we know that they have fallen in a just cause. Such conflicts, which our hearts and consciences approve, are suited to call forth generous sentiments, to breathe patriotism and fortitude through a community. But what can we say when we are precipitated into a war which we cannot

[1] Extracts from various sermons.

112

justify and which promises not a benefit, that we can discover, to our country or to the world?

It becomes you to remember that government is a divine institution, essential to the improvement of our nature, the spring of industry and enterprise, the shield of property and life, the refuge of the weak and oppressed. It is to the security which laws afford that we owe the successful application of human powers. Government, though often perverted by ambition and other selfish passions, still holds a distinguished rank among those influences by which man has been rescued from barbarism and conducted through the ruder stages of society to the habits of order, the diversified employments and dependencies, the refined and softened manners, the intellectual, moral, and religious improvements of the age in which we live. We are bound to respect government as the great security for social happiness, and we should carefully cherish that habit of obedience to the laws without which the ends of government cannot be accomplished. All wanton opposition to the constituted authorities, all censures of rulers originating in a factious, aspiring, or envious spirit, all unwillingness to submit to laws which are directed to the welfare of the community should be rebuked and repressed by the frown of public indignation.

It is impossible that all the regulations of the wisest government should equally benefit every individual, and sometimes the general good will demand arrangements which will interfere with the interests of particular members or classes of the nation. In such circumstances the individual is bound to regard the inconveniences under which he suffers as inseparable from a social, connected state, as the result of the condition which God has appointed, and not as the fault of his rulers; and he should cheerfully submit, recollecting how much more he receives from the community than he is called to resign to it.　Disaffection towards a government which is administered with a view to the general welfare is a great crime; and such opposition, even to a bad government, as springs from and spreads a restless temper, an unwillingness to yield to wholesome and necessary restraint, deserves no better name.　In proportion as a people want a conscientious regard to the laws and are prepared to evade them by fraud or to arrest their operation by violence, — in that proportion they need and deserve an arbitrary government strong enough to crush at a blow every symptom of opposition.

But the citizen has rights as well as duties.　Government is instituted for one and a single end, — the benefit of the governed, the protection, peace, and welfare of society; and when it is perverted to other objects, to purposes of avarice, ambition, or party spirit, we are authorized and even bound to make such opposition as is suited to restore it to its proper end, to render it as pure as the imperfection of our nature and state will admit.

The Scriptures have sometimes been thought to enjoin an unqualified, unlimited subjection to the "higher powers"; but in the passages which seem so to teach it is supposed that these powers are "ministers of God for good," are a terror to evil-doers, and an encouragement to those that do well.　When a government wants this character, when it becomes an engine of oppression, the Scriptures enjoin subjection no longer. Expediency may make it our duty to obey, but the government has lost its rights; it can no longer urge its claims as an ordinance of God.

There have, indeed, been times when sovereigns have demanded subjection as an inalienable right, and when the superstition of subjects has surrounded them with a mysterious sanctity, with a majesty approaching the divine. But these days are past. Under the robe of office we, my hearers, have learned to see a man like ourselves. There is no such sacredness in rulers as forbids scrutiny into their motives or condemnation of their measures. In leaving the common walks of life they leave none of their imperfections behind them. Power has even a tendency to corrupt, to feed an irregular ambition, to harden the heart against the claims and sufferings of mankind. Rulers are not to be viewed with a malignant jealousy, but they ought to be inspected with a watchful, undazzled eye. Their virtues and services are to be rewarded with generous praise, and their crimes and arts and usurpations should be exposed with a fearless sincerity to the indignation of an injured people. We are not to be factious, and neither are we to be servile. With a sincere disposition to obey should be united a firm purpose not to be oppressed.

So far is an existing government from being clothed with an inviolable sanctity that the citizen, in particular circumstances, acquires the right not only of remonstrating but of employing force for its destruction.

This right accrues to him when a government wantonly disregards the ends of social union, when it threatens the subversion of national liberty and happiness, and when no relief but force remains to the suffering community. This, however, is a right which cannot be exercised with too much deliberation. Subjects should very slowly yield to the conviction that rulers have that settled hostility to their interests which authorizes violence. They must not indulge a spirit of complaint and suffer their passions to pronounce on their wrongs. They must remember that the best government will partake the imperfection of all human institutions, and that if the ends of the social compact are in any tolerable degree accomplished, they will be mad indeed to hazard the blessings they possess for the possibility of greater good.

Resistance of established power is so great an evil, civil commotion excites such destructive passions, the result is so tremendously uncertain, that every milder method of relief should first be tried, and fairly tried. The last dreadful resort is never justifiable until the injured members of the community are brought to despair of other relief, and are so far united in views and purposes as to be authorized in the hope of success. Civil commotion should be viewed as the worst of national evils, with the single exception of slavery. . . .

It becomes us to rejoice, my friends, that we live under a constitution one great design of which is to prevent the necessity of appealing to force, to give the people an opportunity of removing without violence those rulers from whom they suffer or apprehend an invasion of rights. This is one of the principal advantages of a republic over an absolute government. In a despotism there is no remedy for oppression but force. The subject cannot influence public affairs but by convulsing the state. With us rulers may be changed without the horrors of a revolution. A republican government secures to its subjects this immense privilege by confirming to them two most important rights, — the right of suffrage and the right of discussing with freedom the conduct of rulers. The value of these rights in affording a peaceful method of redressing public grievances cannot be expressed, and the duty of maintaining them, of never surrendering them, cannot be too strongly urged. Resign either of these, and no way of escape from oppression will be left you but civil commotion.

From the important place which these rights hold in a republican government you should consider yourselves bound to support every citizen in the lawful exercise of them, especially when an attempt is made to wrest them from any by violent means. It is particularly your duty to guard with jealousy the right of expressing with freedom your honest convictions respecting the measures of your rulers. Without this the right of election is not worth possessing. If public abuses may not be exposed, their authors will never be driven from power. Freedom of opinion, of speech, and of the press is our most valuable privilege, the very soul of republican institutions, the safeguard of all other rights. We may learn its value if we reflect that there is nothing which tyrants so much dread. They

anxiously fetter the press; they scatter spies through
society, that the murmurs, anguish, and indignation of
their oppressed subjects may be smothered in their own
breasts, that no generous sentiment may be nourished
by sympathy and mutual confidence.   Nothing awakens
and improves men so much as free communication of
thoughts and feelings.   Nothing can give to public
sentiment that correctness which is essential to the
prosperity of a commonwealth but the free circulation
of truth from the lips and pens of the wise and good.
If such men abandon the right of free discussion; if,
awed by threats, they suppress their convictions ; if
rulers succeed in silencing every voice but that which
approves them; if nothing reaches the people but what
would lend support to men in power, — farewell to
liberty.   The form of a free government may remain,
but the life, the soul, the substance is fled.

We have heard the strange doctrine that to expose
the measures of rulers is treason.   The cry has been
that, war being declared, all opposition should therefore be hushed.   A sentiment more unworthy of a free
country can hardly be propagated.   If this doctrine be
admitted, rulers have only to declare war, and they are
screened at once from scrutiny.   At the very time
when they have armies at command, when their patronage is most extended and their power most formidable,
not a word of warning, of censure, of alarm must be
heard.   The press, which is to expose inferior abuses,
must not utter one rebuke, one indignant complaint,
although our best interests and most valuable rights
are put to hazard by an unnecessary war !   Admit this

doctrine, let rulers once know that by placing the country in a state of war they place themselves beyond the only power they dread, — the power of free discussion, — and we may expect war without end. Our peace and all our interests require that a different sentiment should prevail. We should teach all rulers that there is no measure for which they must render so solemn an account to their constituents as for a declaration of war; that no measure will be so freely, so fully discussed; that no administration can succeed in persuading this people to exhaust their treasure and blood in supporting war unless it be palpably necessary and just. In war, then, as in peace, assert the freedom of speech and of the press. Cling to this as the bulwark of all your rights and privileges.

But I should not be faithful were I only to call you to hold fast this freedom. I would still more earnestly exhort you not to abuse it. Its abuse may be as fatal to our country as its relinquishment. If undirected, unrestrained by principle, the press, instead of enlightening, depraves the public mind, and by its licentiousness forges chains for itself and for the community. The right of free discussion is not the right of uttering what we please. Let nothing be spoken or written but truth. The influence of the press is exceedingly diminished by its gross and frequent misrepresentations. Each party listens with distrust to the statements of the other, and the consequence is that the progress of truth is slow and sometimes wholly obstructed. Whilst we encourage the free expression of opinion, let us unite in fixing the brand of infamy on falsehood and slander, wherever they originate, whatever be the cause they are designed to maintain.

But it is not enough that truth be told. It should be told for a good end, not to irritate but to convince, not to inflame the bad passions, but to sway the judgment and to awaken sentiments of patriotism. Unhappily the press seems now to be chiefly prized as an instrument of exasperation. Those who have embraced error are hardened in their principles by the reproachful epithets heaped on them by their adversaries. I do not mean by this that political discussion is to be conducted tamely, that no sensibility is to be expressed, no indignation to be poured forth on wicked men and wicked deeds. But this I mean, — that we shall deliberately inquire whether indignation be deserved before we express it; and the object of expressing it should ever be not to infuse ill-will, rancor, and fury into the minds of men, but to excite an enlightened and conscientious opposition to injurious measures.

Every good man must mourn that so much is continually published among us for no other apparent end than to gratify the malevolence of one party by wounding the feelings of the opposite. The consequence is that an alarming degree of irritation exists in our country. Fellow-citizens burn with mutual hatred, and some are evidently ripe for outrage and violence. In this feverish state of the public mind we are not to relinquish free discussion, but every man should feel the duty of speaking and writing with deliberation. It is the time to be firm without passion. No menace should be employed to provoke opponents, no defiance hurled, no language used which will in any measure justify the ferocious in appealing to force.

Let us hold fast the inheritance of our civil and religious liberties, which we have received from our fathers sealed and hallowed by their blood. That these blessings may not be lost, let us labor to improve public sentiment and to exalt men of wisdom and virtue to power. Let it be our labor to establish in ourselves and in our fellow-citizens the empire of true religion. Let us remember that there is no foundation of public liberty but public virtue, that there is no method of obtaining God's protection but adherence to his laws. . . .

We ought to remember that we live under a moral government which regards the character of communities as truly as of individuals. A nation has reason for fear in proportion to its guilt; and a virtuous nation, sensible of dependence on God and disposed to respect his laws, is assured of his protection. Every people must indeed be influenced in a measure by the general state of the world, by the changes and conflicts of other communities. When the ocean is in tumult every shore will feel the agitation. But a people faithful to God will never be forsaken. In addition to the direct and obvious tendency of national piety and virtue to national safety and exaltation, a virtuous community may expect peculiar interpositions of Providence for their defense and prosperity. They are not, indeed, to anticipate visible miracles. They are not to imagine that invading hosts will be annihilated, like Sennacherib's, by the arm of an angel. But God, we

must remember, can effect his purposes and preserve
the just without such stupendous interpositions. The
hearts of men are in his hand. The elements of nature
obey his word. He has winds to scatter the proudest
fleet, diseases to prostrate the strongest army. Consider how many events must conspire, how many secret
springs must act in concert, to accomplish the purposes
of the statesman or the plans of the warrior. How
often have the best concerted schemes been thwarted,
the most menacing preparations been defeated, the
proud boast of anticipated victory been put to shame,
by what we call casualty, by a slight and accidental
want of concert, by the error of a chief, or by neglect
in subordinate agents ! Let God determine the defeat
of an enemy, and we need not fear that means will be
wanting. He sends terror or blindness or mad presumption into the minds of leaders. Heaven, earth, and
sea are arrayed to oppose their progress. An unconquerable spirit is breathed into the invaded, and the
dreaded foe seeks his safety in dishonorable flight.

My friends, if God be for us, no matter who is against
us. Mere power ought not to intimidate us; he can
crush it in a moment. We live in a period when God's
supremacy has been remarkably evinced, when he has
signally confounded the powerful and delivered the
oppressed and endangered. At his word the forged
chain has been broken, mighty armies have been dis-
persed as chaff before the whirlwind, colossal thrones
have been shivered like the brittle clay. God is still
"wonderful in counsel and excellent in working," and
if he wills to deliver us we cannot be subdued. It is,

then, most important that we seek God's favor. And how is his favor to be obtained? I repeat it, — he is a moral governor, the friend of the righteous, the punisher of the wicked; and in proportion as piety, uprightness, temperance, and Christian virtue prevail among us, in that proportion we are assured of his favor and protection. A virtuous people, fighting in defense of their altars and firesides, may look to God with confidence. An invisible but almighty arm surrounds them, an impenetrable shield is their shadow and defense.

It becomes us, then, to inquire, How far have we sustained the character of a pious and virtuous people? And whose heart does not accuse him of many sins? Who can look around on his country and not see many proofs of ingratitude to God and of contempt of his laws? Do I speak to any who, having received success and innumerable blessings from God, have yet forgotten the Giver? to any who have converted abundance into the instrument of excess? to any who, having been instructed by the gospel, have yet refused to employ in well-doing the bounty of heaven? to any who are living in habits of intemperance, impurity, impiety, fraud, or any known sin? To such I would say, You are among the enemies of your country and, should she fall, among the authors of her ruin. We owe to ourselves and our country deep sorrow for our sins, and those sincere purposes of reformation which more than all things bring down blessings from heaven.

This is a time when we should all bring clearly and strongly to our minds our duties to our country, and should cherish a strong and ardent attachment to the public good. The claims of country have been felt and obeyed even in the rudest ages of society. The community to which we belong is commended by our very nature to our affection and service. Christianity, in enjoining a disinterested and benevolent spirit, admits and sanctions this sentiment of nature, this attachment to the land of our fathers, the land of our nativity. It only demands that our patriotism be purified from every mixture of injustice towards foreign nations. Within this limit we cannot too ardently attach ourselves to the welfare of our country. Especially in its perils we should fly to its rescue with filial zeal and affection, resolved to partake its sufferings and prepared to die in its defense. . . .

We should animate our patriotism by reflecting that we have a country which deserves every effort and sacrifice. . . . We have the deeds of our fathers, their piety and virtues, and their solicitude for the rights and happiness of their posterity, to awaken our emulation. How invaluable the inheritance they have left us, earned by their toils and defended by their blood! Our populous cities and cultivated fields, our schools, colleges, and churches, our equal laws, our uncorrupted tribunals of justice, our spirit of enterprise, and our habits of order and peace, all combine to form a commonwealth as rich in blessings and privileges as the history of the world records. Such a community deserves our affection, our honor, our zeal, and the devotion of our lives. If we look back to Sparta, Athens, and Rome, we shall find that in the institutions of this commonwealth we have sources of incomparably richer blessings than those republics conferred on their citizens in their proudest days; and yet Sparta and Rome and Athens inspired a love stronger than death. In the day of their danger every citizen offered his breast as a bulwark, every citizen felt himself the property of his country. It is true a base alloy mingled with the patriotism of ancient times, and God forbid that a sentiment so impure should burn in our breasts! God forbid that, like the Greek and the Roman, we should carry fire and slaughter into other countries to build up a false, fleeting glory at home! But, whilst we take warning by their excesses, let us catch a portion of their fervor, and learn to live not for ourselves but for that country whose honor and interest God has intrusted to our care. No enemy can finally injure us if we are true to God, to our country, and to mankind.

THE PASSION FOR DOMINION[1]

IT is true both of the brightest virtues and the blackest vices, though they seem to set apart their possessors from the rest of mankind, that the seeds of them are sown in every human breast. The man who attracts and awes us by his intellectual and moral grandeur is only an example and anticipation of the improvements for which every mind was endowed with reason and conscience; and the worst man has become such by the perversion and excess of desires and appetites which he shares with his whole race. Napoleon had no element of character which others do not possess. It was his misery and guilt that he was usurped and absorbed by one passion; that his whole mind shot up into one growth; that his singular strength of thought and will, which if consecrated to virtue would have enrolled him among the benefactors of mankind, was enslaved by one lust. He is not to be gazed on as a miracle. He was a manifestation of our own nature. He teaches on a large scale what thousands teach on a narrow one. He shows us the greatness of the ruin which is wrought when the order of the mind is subverted, conscience dethroned, and a strong passion left without restraint to turn every inward and outward resource to the accomplishment of a selfish purpose.

[1] From the second paper on Napoleon.

The influence of the *love of power* on human affairs is
so constant, unbounded, and tremendous that we think
this principle of our nature worthy of distinct consideration. The passion for power is one of the most universal; nor is it to be regarded as a crime in all its
forms. Sweeping censures on a natural sentiment cast
blame on the Creator. This principle shows itself in
the very dawn of our existence. The child never exults
and rejoices more than when it becomes conscious of
power by overcoming difficulties or compassing new
ends. All our desires and appetites lend aid and energy
to this passion, for all find increase of gratification in
proportion to the growth of our strength and influence.
We ought to add that this principle is fed from nobler
sources. Power is a chief element of all the commanding qualities of our nature. It enters into all the higher
virtues, such as magnanimity, fortitude, constancy. It
enters into intellectual eminence. It is power of thought
and utterance which immortalizes the products of genius. Is it strange that an attribute through which all
our passions reach their objects, and which characterizes
whatever is great or admirable in man, should awaken
intense desire and be sought as one of the chief goods
of life?

This principle, we have said, is not in all its forms
a crime. There are, indeed, various kinds of power
which it is our duty to covet, accumulate, and hold fast.
First, there is *inward* power, the most precious of all
possessions: power over ourselves; power to withstand
trial, to bear suffering, to front danger; power over
pleasure and pain; power to follow our convictions

however resisted by menace or scorn; the power of
calm reliance in seasons of darkness and storms.   Again,
there is a power over *outward* things: the power by
which the mind triumphs over matter, presses into its
service the subtlest and strongest elements, makes the
winds, fire, and steam its ministers, rears the city, opens
a path through the ocean, and makes the wilderness
blossom as the rose.   These forms of power, especially
the first, are glorious distinctions of our race, nor can
we prize them too highly.

There is another power, which is our principal concern in the present discussion.   We mean power over
our fellow-creatures.   It is this which ambition chiefly
covets, and which has instigated to more crime and
spread more misery than any other cause.   We are not,
however, to condemn even this universally.   There is a
truly noble sway of man over man, one which it is our
honor to seek and exert, which is earned by well-
doing, which is a chief recompense of virtue.   We
refer to the quickening influence of a good and great
mind over other minds, by which it brings them into
sympathy with itself.   Far from condemning this, we
are anxious to hold it forth as the purest glory which
virtuous ambition can propose.   The power of awakening, enlightening, elevating our fellow-creatures may
with peculiar fitness be called divine; for there is no
agency of God so beneficent and sublime as that which
he exerts on rational natures and by which he assimi-
lates them to himself.   This sway over other souls is the
surest test of greatness.   We admire indeed the energy
which subdues the material creation or develops the

physical resources of a state. But it is a nobler might
which calls forth the intellectual and moral resources of
a people, which communicates new impulses to society,
throws into circulation new and stirring thoughts, gives
the mind a new consciousness of its faculties, and rouses
and fortifies the will to an unconquerable purpose of
well-doing. This spiritual power is worth all other.
To improve man's outward condition is a secondary
agency and is chiefly important as it gives the means
of inward growth. The most glorious minister of God
on earth is he who speaks with a life-giving energy to
other minds, breathing into them the love of truth and
virtue, strengthening them to suffer in a good cause,
and lifting them above the senses and the world.

We know not a more exhilarating thought than that
this power is given to men; that we can not only
change the face of the outward world and by virtuous
discipline improve ourselves, but that we may become
springs of life and light to our fellow-beings. We are
thus admitted to a fellowship with Jesus Christ, whose
highest end was that he might act with a new and celestial energy on the human mind. We rejoice to think
that he did not come to monopolize this divine sway, to
enjoy a solitary grandeur, but to receive others, even all
who should obey his religion, into the partnership of
this honor and happiness. Every Christian, in proportion to his progress, acquires a measure of this divine
agency. In the humblest conditions a power goes forth
from a devout and disinterested spirit, calling forth
silently moral and religious sentiment, perhaps in a
child or some other friend, and teaching without the

aid of words the loveliness and peace of sincere and
single-hearted virtue.   In the more enlightened classes
individuals now and then rise up, who, through a singular force and elevation of soul, obtain a sway over
men's minds to which no limit can be prescribed.   They
speak with a voice which is heard by distant nations
and which goes down to future ages.   Their names are
repeated with veneration by millions ; and millions read
in their lives and writings a quickening testimony to
the greatness of the mind, to its moral strength, to the
reality of disinterested virtue.   These are the true sovereigns of the earth.   They share in the royalty of Jesus
Christ.   They have a greatness which will be more and
more felt.   The time is coming, its signs are visible,
when this long-mistaken attribute of greatness will be
seen to belong eminently, if not exclusively, to those
who by their characters, deeds, sufferings, writings,
leave imperishable and ennobling traces of themselves
on the human mind.   Among these legitimate sovereigns of the world will be ranked the philosopher
who penetrates the secrets of the universe and of the
soul ; who opens new fields to the intellect ; who gives
it a new consciousness of its own powers, rights, and
divine original ; who spreads enlarged and liberal habits
of thought ; and who helps men to understand that an
ever-growing knowledge is the patrimony destined for
them by the "Father of their spirits."   Among them
will be ranked the statesman who, escaping a vulgar
policy, rises to the discovery of the true interest of a
state ; who seeks without fear or favor the common
good ; who understands that a nation's mind is more

valuable than its soil; who inspirits a people's enterprise without making them the slaves of wealth; who
is mainly anxious to originate or give stability to institutions by which society may be carried forward; who
confides with a sublime constancy in justice and virtue
as the only foundation of a wise policy and of public
prosperity; and, above all, who has so drunk into the
spirit of Christ and of God as never to forget that his
particular country is a member of the great human
family, bound to all nations by a common nature, by a
common interest, and by indissoluble laws of equity and
charity.   Among these will be ranked, perhaps, on the
highest throne, the moral and religious reformer who
truly merits that name; who rises above his times; who
is moved by a holy impulse to assail vicious establishments sustained by fierce passions and inveterate prejudices; who rescues great truths from the corruptions of
ages; who, joining calm and deep thought to profound
feeling, secures to religion at once enlightened and
earnest conviction; who unfolds to men higher forms
of virtue than they have yet attained or conceived; who
gives brighter and more thrilling views of the perfection
for which they were framed, and inspires a victorious
faith in the perpetual progress of our nature.

There is one characteristic of this power which
belongs to truly great minds, particularly deserving
notice.   Far from enslaving, it makes more and more
free those on whom it is exercised; and in this respect
it differs wholly from the vulgar sway for which ambition thirsts.   It awakens a kindred power in others, calls
their faculties into new life, and particularly strengthens

them to follow their own deliberate convictions of truth
and duty.   It breathes conscious energy, self-respect,
moral independence, and a scorn of every foreign yoke.

There is another power over men very different from
this, — a power not to quicken and elevate, but to
crush and subdue ; a power which robs men of the free
use of their nature, takes them out of their own hands,
and compels them to bend to another's will.   This is
the sway which men grasp at most eagerly, and which
it is our great purpose to expose.   To reign, to give
laws, to clothe their own wills with omnipotence, to
annihilate all other wills, to spoil the individual of that
self-direction which is his most precious right, — this
has ever been deemed by multitudes the highest prize
for competition and conflict.   The most envied men are
those who have succeeded in prostrating multitudes, in
subjecting whole communities, to their single will.   It
is the love of this power, in all its forms, which we are
anxious to hold up to reprobation.   If any crime should
be placed by society beyond pardon, it is this.

This power has been exerted most conspicuously and
perniciously by two classes of men — the priest or minister of religion, and the civil ruler.   Both rely on the
same instrument, — that is, pain or terror ; the first
calling to his aid the fires and torments of the future
world, and practicing on the natural dread of invisible
powers, and the latter availing himself of chains, dun-
geons, and gibbets in the present life.   Through these
terrible applications man has, in all ages and in almost
every country, been made in a greater or less degree a
slave and machine ; been shackled in all his faculties

and degraded into a tool of others' wills and passions.
The influence of almost every political and religious
institution has been to make man abject in mind, fearful, servile, a mechanical repeater of opinions which he
dares not try, and a contributor of his toil, sweat, and
blood to governments which never dreamed of the general weal as their only legitimate end.   On the immense
majority of men thus wronged and enslaved the consciousness of their own nature has not yet dawned ; and
the doctrine that each has a mind worth more than
the material world, and framed to grow forever by a
self-forming, self-directing energy, is still a secret, a
mystery, notwithstanding the clear annunciation of it
ages ago by Jesus Christ.   We know not a stronger
proof of the intenseness and nefariousness of the love
of power than the fact of its having virtually abrogated
Christianity, and even turned into an engine of dominion
a revelation which breathes throughout the spirit of
freedom, proclaims the essential equality of the human
race, and directs its most solemn denunciations against
the passion for rule and empire.

That this power, which consists in force and compulsion in the imposition on the many of the will and judgment of one or a few, is of a low order when compared
with the quickening influence over others of which we
have before spoken, we need not stop to prove.   But
the remark is less obvious, though not less true, that it
is not only inferior in kind but in amount or degree.
This may not be so easily acknowledged.   He whose
will is passively obeyed by a nation, or whose creed is
implicitly adopted by a spreading sect, may not easily

believe that his power is exceeded, not only in kind or quality but in extent, by him who wields only the silent, subtle influence of moral and intellectual gifts. But the superiority of moral to arbitrary sway in this particular is proved by its effects. Moral power is creative; arbitrary power wastes away the spirit and force of those on whom it is exerted. And is it not a mightier work to create than to destroy? A higher energy is required to quicken than to crush, to elevate than to depress, to warm and expand than to chill and contract. Any hand, even the weakest, may take away life; another agency is required to kindle or restore it. A vulgar incendiary may destroy in an hour a magnificent structure, the labor of ages. Has he energy to be compared with the creative intellect in which this work had its origin? A fanatic of ordinary talent may send terror through a crowd; and by the craft which is so often joined with fanaticism may fasten on multitudes a debasing creed. Has he power to be compared with him who rescues from darkness one only of these enslaved minds, and quickens it to think justly and nobly in relation to God, duty, and immortality? The energies of a single soul, awakened by such an influence to the free and full use of its powers, may surpass in their progress the intellectual activity of a whole community enchained and debased by fanaticism or outward force. Arbitrary power, whether civil or religious, if tried by the only fair test, that is, by its effects, seems to have more affinity with weakness than strength. It enfeebles and narrows what it acts upon. Its efficiency resembles that of darkness and cold in the natural world. True power is vivifying, productive, builds up and gives strength. We have a noble type and manifestation of it in the sun, which calls forth and diffuses motion, life, energy, and beauty. He who succeeds in chaining men's understandings and breaking their wills may indeed number millions as his subjects. But a weak, puny race are the products of his sway, and they can only reach the stature and force of men by throwing off his yoke. He who by an intellectual and moral energy awakens kindred energy in others touches springs of infinite might, gives impulse to faculties to which no bounds can be prescribed, begins an action which will never end. One great and kindling thought from a retired and obscure man may live when thrones are fallen, and the memory of those who filled them obliterated, and like an undying fire may illuminate and quicken all future generations.

We have spoken of the inferiority and worthlessness of that dominion over others which has been coveted so greedily in all ages. We should rejoice could we convey some just idea of its moral turpitude. Of all injuries and crimes the most flagrant is chargeable on him who aims to establish dominion over his brethren. He wars with what is more precious than life. He would rob men of their chief prerogative and glory, — we mean, of self-dominion, of that empire which is given to a rational and moral being over his own soul and his own life. Such a being is framed to find honor and happiness in forming and swaying himself, in adopting as his supreme standard his convictions of truth and duty, in unfolding his powers by free

exertion, in acting from a principle within, from his
growing conscience. His proper and noblest attributes
are self-government, self-reverence, energy of thought,
energy in choosing the right and the good, energy in
casting off all other dominion. He was created for
empire in his own breast; and woe, woe to them who
would pluck from him this scepter! A mind, inspired
by God with reason and conscience, and capable through
these endowments of progress in truth and duty, is a
sacred thing; more sacred than temples made with
hands, or even than this outward universe. It is of
nobler lineage than that of which human aristocracy
makes its boast. It bears the lineaments of a divine
Parent. It has not only a physical but moral connection with the Supreme Being. Through its self-
determining power it is accountable for its deeds and
for whatever it becomes. Responsibility — that which
above all things makes existence solemn — is laid upon
it. Its great end is to conform itself, by its own energy
and by spiritual succors which its own prayers and
faithfulness secure, to that perfection of wisdom and
goodness of which God is the original and source, which
shines upon us from the whole outward world, but of
which the intelligent soul is a truer recipient and a
brighter image even than the sun with all his splendors.
From these views we learn that no outrage, no injury,
can equal that which is perpetrated by him who would
break down and subjugate the human mind; who would
rob men of self-reverence; who would bring them to
stand more in awe of outward authority than of reason
and conscience in their own souls; who would make

himself a standard and law for his race, and shape by force or terror the free spirits of others after his own judgment and will.

All excellence, whether intellectual or moral, involves, as its essential elements, freedom, energy, and moral independence; so that the invader of these, whether from the throne or the pulpit, invades the most sacred interest of the human race. Intellectual excellence implies and requires these. This does not consist in passive assent even to the highest truths; or in the most extensive stores of knowledge acquired by an implicit faith and lodged in the inert memory. It lies in force, freshness, and independence of thought; and is most conspicuously manifested by him who, loving truth supremely, seeks it resolutely, follows the light without fear, and modifies the views of others by the patient, strenuous exercise of his own faculties. To a man thus intellectually free, truth is not what it is to passive multitudes, a foreign substance, dormant, lifeless, fruitless, but penetrating, prolific, full of vitality, and ministering to the health and expansion of the soul. And what we have said of intellectual excellence is still more true of moral. This has its foundation and root in freedom, and cannot exist a moment without it. The very idea of virtue is that it is a free act, the product or result of the mind's self-determining power. It is not good feeling, infused by nature or caught by sympathy; nor is it good conduct into which we have slidden through imitation, or which has been forced upon us by another's will. We ourselves are its authors in a high and peculiar sense. We indeed depend on

God for virtue; for our capacity of moral action is
wholly his gift and inspiration, and without his perpetual aid this capacity would avail nothing. But his aid
is not compulsion. He respects, he cannot violate, that
moral freedom which is his richest gift. To the individual the decision of his own character is left. He
has more than kingly power in his own soul. Let him
never resign it. Let none dare to interfere with it.
Virtue is self-dominion, or, what is the same thing, it is
self-subjection to the principle of duty, that highest law
in the soul. If these views of intellectual and moral
excellence be just, then to invade men's freedom is to
aim the deadliest blow at their honor and happiness;
and their worst foe is he who fetters their reason, who
makes his will their law, who makes them tools, echoes,
copies of himself.

Perhaps it may be objected to the representation of
virtue as consisting in self-dominion, that the Scriptures
speak of it as consisting in obedience to God. But
these are perfectly compatible and harmonious views;
for genuine obedience to God is the free choice and
adoption of a law the great principles of which our
own minds approve and our own consciences bind on
us; which is not an arbitrary injunction, but an emana-
tion and expression of the Divine Mind; and which
is intended throughout to give energy, dignity, and
enlargement to our best powers. He, and he only,
obeys God virtuously and acceptably who reverences
right, not power; who has chosen rectitude as his
supreme rule; who sees and reveres in God the fullness
and brightness of moral excellence, and who sees in

obedience the progress and perfection of his own nature.
That subjection to the Deity, which we fear is too
common, in which the mind surrenders itself to mere
power and will, is anything but virtue. We fear that
it is disloyalty to that moral principle which is ever to
be reverenced as God's vicegerent in the rational soul.

Perhaps some may fear that in our zeal for the
freedom and independence of the individual mind we
unsettle government, and almost imply that it is a
wrong. Far from it. We hold government to be an
essential means of our intellectual and moral education,
and would strengthen it by pointing out its legitimate
functions. Government, as far as it is rightful, is the
guardian and friend of freedom, so that in exalting the
one we enforce the other. The highest aim of all
authority is to confer liberty. This is true of domestic
rule. The great, we may say the single, object of
parental government, of a wise and virtuous education,
is to give the child the fullest use of his own powers;
to give him inward force; to train him up to govern
himself. The same is true of the authority of Jesus
Christ. He came indeed to rule mankind; but to rule
them not by arbitrary statutes, not by force and menace,
not by mere will, but by setting before them, in precept
and life, those everlasting rules of rectitude which
heaven obeys and of which every soul contains the
living germs. He came to exert a moral power; to
reign by the manifestation of celestial virtues; to
awaken the energy of holy purpose in the free mind.
He came to publish liberty to the captives; to open the
prison door; to break the power of the passions; to

break the yoke of a ceremonial religion which had been imposed in the childhood of the race; to exalt us to a manly homage and obedience of our Creator. Of civil government, too, the great end is to secure freedom. Its proper and highest function is to watch over the liberties of each and all, and to open to a community the widest field for all its powers. Its very chains and prisons have the general freedom for their aim. They are just only when used to curb oppression and wrong; to disarm him who has a tyrant's heart if not a tyrant's power, who wars against others' rights, who by invading property or life would substitute force for the reign of equal laws. Freedom — we repeat it — is the end of government. To exalt men to self-rule is the end of all other rule; and he who would fasten on them his arbitrary will is their worst foe.

We have aimed to show the guilt of the love of power and dominion by showing the ruin which it brings on the mind, by enlarging on the preciousness of that inward freedom which it invades and destroys. To us this view is the most impressive; but the guilt of this passion may also be discerned, and by some more clearly, in its outward influences, — in the desolation, bloodshed, and woe of which it is the perpetual cause. We owe to it almost all the miseries of war. To spread the sway of one or a few, thousands and millions have been turned into machines under the name of soldiers, armed with instruments of destruction, and then sent to reduce others to their own lot by fear and pain, by fire and sword, by butchery and pillage. And is it light guilt to array man against his brother; to make murder the trade of thousands; to drench the earth with human blood; to turn it into a desert; to scatter families like chaff; to make mothers widows and children orphans; and to do all this for the purpose of spreading a still gloomier desolation, for the purpose of subjugating men's souls, turning them into base parasites, extorting from them a degrading homage, humbling them in their own eyes, and breaking them to servility as the chief duty of life?   When the passion for power succeeds, as it generally has done, in establishing despotism, it seems to make even civilization a doubtful good.   Whilst the monarch and his court are abandoned to a wasteful luxury, the peasantry, rooted to the soil and doomed to a perpetual round of labors, are raised but little above the brute. There are parts of Europe, Christian Europe, in which the peasant, through whose sweat kings and nobles riot in plenty, seems to enjoy less, on the whole, than the untamed Indian of our forests.   Chained to one spot; living on the cheapest vegetables; sometimes unable to buy salt to season his coarse fare; seldom or never tasting animal food; having for his shelter a mud-walled hut floored with earth or stone, and subjected equally with the brute to the rule of a superior, he seems to us to partake less of animal, intellectual, and moral pleasures than the free wanderer of the woods whose steps no man fetters; whose wigwam no tyrant violates; whose chief toil is hunting, that noblest of sports; who feasts on the deer, that most luxurious of viands; to whom streams as well as woods pay tribute; whose adventurous life gives sagacity; and in whom peril

nourishes courage and self-command. We are no advocates for savage life. We know that its boasted freedom is a delusion. The single fact that human nature
in this wild state makes no progress is proof enough
that it wants true liberty. We mean only to say that
man in the hands of despotism is sometimes degraded
below the savage; that it were better for him to be
lawless than to live under lawless sway.

It is the part of Christians to look on the passion for
power and dominion with strong abhorrence; for it is
singularly hostile to the genius of their religion. Jesus
Christ always condemned it. One of the striking marks
of his moral greatness and of the originality of his
character was that he held no fellowship and made no
compromise with this universal spirit of his age, but
withstood it in every form. He found the Jews intoxicating themselves with dreams of empire. Of the
prophecies relating to the Messiah the most familiar
and dear to them were those which announced him as a
conqueror, and which were construed by their worldliness into a promise of triumphs to the people from
whom he was to spring. Even the chosen disciples of
Jesus looked to him for this good. " To sit on his
right hand and on his left," or, in other words, to
hold the most commanding station in his kingdom, was
not only their lurking wish but their open and impor-
tunate request. But there was no passion on which
Jesus frowned more severely than on this. He taught
that to be great in his kingdom men must serve,
instead of ruling, their brethren. He placed among
them a child as an emblem of the humility of his

religion. His most terrible rebukes fell on the lordly, aspiring Pharisee. In his own person he was mild and condescending, exacting no personal service, living with his disciples as a friend, sharing their wants, sleeping in their fishing boat, and even washing their feet; and in all this he expressly proposed himself to them as a pattern, knowing well that the last triumph of disinterestedness is to forget our own superiority in our sympathy, solicitude, tenderness, respect, and self-denying zeal for those who are below us. We cannot indeed wonder that the lust of power should be encountered by the sternest rebukes and menace of Christianity, because it wages open war with the great end of this religion. No corruption of this religion is more palpable and more enormous than that which turns it into an instrument of dominion, and which makes it teach that man's primary duty is to give himself a passive material into the hands of his minister, priest, or king.

The subject which we now discuss is one in which all nations have an interest, and especially our own; and we should fail of our main purpose were we not to lead our readers to apply it to ourselves. The passion for ruling, though most completely developed in despotisms, is confined to no forms of government. It is the chief peril of free states, the natural enemy of free institutions. It agitates our own country, and still throws an uncertainty over the great experiment we are making here in behalf of liberty. We will try, then, in a few words, to expose its influences and dangers, and to abate that zeal with which a participation in office and power is sought among ourselves.

It is the distinction of republican institutions that, whilst they compel the passion for power to moderate its pretensions, and to satisfy itself with more limited gratifications, they tend to spread it more widely through the community, and to make it a universal principle. The doors of office being open to all, crowds burn to rush in. A thousand hands are stretched out to grasp the reins which are denied to none. Perhaps, in this boasted and boasting land of liberty, not a few, if called to state the chief good of a republic, would place it in this, that every man is eligible to every office, and that the highest places of power and trust are prizes for universal competition. The superiority attributed by many to our institutions is not that they secure the greatest freedom, but give every man a chance of ruling; not that they reduce the power of government within the narrowest limits which the safety of the state admits, but throw it into as many hands as possible. The despot's great crime is thought to be that he keeps the delight of dominion to himself, that he makes a monopoly of it, whilst our more generous institutions, by breaking it into parcels and inviting the multitude to scramble for it, spread this joy more widely. The result is that political ambition infects our country, and generates a feverish restlessness and discontent which to the monarchist may seem more than a balance for our forms of liberty. The spirit of intrigue, which in absolute governments is confined to courts, walks abroad through the land; and, as individuals can accomplish no political purposes single-handed, they band themselves into parties, ostensibly framed for public ends, but aiming only at the acquisition of power. The nominal sovereign, — that is, the people, — like all other sovereigns, is courted and flattered, and told that it can do no wrong. Its pride is pampered, its passions inflamed, its prejudices made inveterate. Such are the processes by which other republics have been subverted, and he must be blind who cannot trace them among ourselves. We mean not to exaggerate our dangers. We rejoice to know that the improvements of society oppose many checks to the love of power. But every wise man who sees its workings must dread it as our chief foe.

This passion derives strength and vehemence in our country from the common idea that political power is the highest prize which society has to offer. We know not a more general delusion, nor is it the least dangerous. Instilled as it is in our youth, it gives infinite excitement to political ambition. It turns the active talent of the country to public station as the supreme good, and makes it restless, intriguing, and unprincipled. It calls out hosts of selfish competitors for comparatively few places, and encourages a bold, unblushing pursuit of personal elevation which a just moral sense and self-respect in the community would frown upon and cover with shame. This prejudice has come down from past ages, and is one of their worst bequests. To govern others has always been thought the highest function on earth. We have a remarkable proof of the strength and pernicious influence of this persuasion in the manner in which history has been written. Who fill the page of history?

Political and military leaders, who have lived for
one end, — to subdue and govern their fellow-beings.
These occupy the foreground, and the people, the
human race, dwindle into insignificance, and are
almost lost behind their masters.   The proper and
noblest object of history is to record the vicissitudes
of society, its spirit in different ages, the causes which
have determined its' progress and decline, and especially
the manifestations and growth of its highest attributes
and interests of intelligence, of the religious principle,
of moral sentiment, of the elegant and useful arts, of
the triumphs of man over nature and himself.   Instead
of this, we have records of men in power, often weak,
oftener wicked, who did little or nothing for the
advancement of their age, who were in no sense its
representatives, whom the accident of birth perhaps
raised to influence.   We have the quarrels of courtiers,
the intrigues of cabinets, sieges and battles, royal births
and deaths, and the secrets of a palace, that sink of
lewdness and corruption.   These are the staples of
history.   The inventions of printing, of gunpowder,
and the mariner's compass, were too mean affairs for
history to trace.   She was bowing before kings and
warriors.   She had volumes for the plots and quarrels
of Leicester and Essex in the reign of Elizabeth, but
not a page for Shakespeare; and if Bacon had not
filled an office she would hardly have recorded his
name, in her anxiety to preserve the deeds and sayings
of that Solomon of his age, James the First.

We have spoken of the supreme importance which
is attached to rulers and government, as a prejudice;

and we think that something may be done towards
abating the passion for power by placing this thought
in a clearer light. It seems to us not very difficult to
show that to govern men is not as high a sphere of
action as has been commonly supposed, and that those
who have obtained this dignity have usurped a place
beyond their due in history and men's minds. We
apprehend indeed that we are not alone in this opinion; that a change of sentiment on this subject has
commenced and must go on; that men are learning
that there are higher sources of happiness and more
important agents in human affairs than political rule.
It is one mark of the progress of society that it brings
down the public man and raises the private one. It
throws power into the hands of untitled individuals
and spreads it through all orders of the community.
It multiplies and distributes freely means of extensive
influence, and opens new channels by which the gifted
mind, in whatever rank or condition, may communicate
itself far and wide. Through the diffusion of education and printing a private man may now speak to
multitudes incomparably more numerous than ancient
or modern eloquence ever electrified in the popular
assembly or the hall of legislation. By these instruments truth is asserting her sovereignty over nations,
and her faithful ministers will become more and more
the lawgivers of the world. . . .

Virtue and intelligence are the great interests of a
community, including all others and worth all others,
and the noblest agency is that by which they are
advanced. Now we apprehend that political power is

not the most effectual instrument for their promotion, and accordingly we doubt whether government is the only or highest sphere for superior minds. Virtue from its very nature cannot be a product of what may be called the direct operation of government, that is, of legislation. Laws may repress crime. Their office is to erect prisons for violence and fraud. But moral and religious worth, dignity of character, loftiness of sentiment, — all that makes man a blessing to himself and society, — lie beyond their province. Virtue is of the soul, where laws cannot penetrate. Excellence is something too refined, spiritual, celestial to be produced by the coarse machinery of government. Human legislation addresses itself to self-love, and works by outward force. Its chief instrument is punishment. It cannot touch the springs of virtuous feelings, of great and good deeds. Accordingly, rulers, with all their imagined omnipotence, do not dream of enjoining by statute philanthropy, gratitude, devout sentiment, magnanimity, and purity of thought. Virtue is too high a concern for government. It is an inspiration of God, not a creature of law ; and the agents whom God chiefly honors in its promotion are those who, through experience as well as meditation, have risen to generous conceptions of it, and who show it forth not in empty eulogies but in the language of deep conviction and in lives of purity. . . .

We fear that here as elsewhere political power is of corrupting tendency ; and that, generally speaking, public men are not the most effectual teachers of truth, disinterestedness, and incorruptible integrity to the people.

A deeply rooted error prevails in relation to political concerns, — the growth of ages. We refer to the belief that public men are absolved in a measure from the everlasting and immutable obligations of morality; that political power is a prize which justifies arts and compliances that would be scorned in private life; that management, intrigue, hollow pretensions, and appeals to base passions deserve slight rebuke when employed to compass political ends. Accordingly, the laws of truth, justice, and philanthropy have seldom been applied to public as to private concerns. Even those individuals who have come to frown indignantly on the machinations, the office-seeking, and the sacrifices to popularity which disgrace our internal condition are disposed to acquiesce in a crooked or ungenerous policy towards foreign nations, by which great advantages may accrue to their own country. Now, the great truth on which the cause of virtue rests is that rectitude is an eternal, unalterable, and universal law, binding at once heaven and earth, the perfection of God's character and the harmony and happiness of the rational creation; and in proportion as political institutions unsettle this great conviction — in proportion as they teach that truth, justice, and philanthropy are local, partial obligations, claiming homage from the weak but shrinking before the powerful; in proportion as they thus insult the awful and inviolable majesty of the eternal law — in the same proportion they undermine the very foundation of a people's virtue.

In regard to the other great interest of the community, its intelligence, government may do much good by a direct influence; that is, by instituting schools or appropriating revenue for the instruction of the poorer classes. Whether it would do wisely in assuming to itself or in taking from individuals the provision and care of higher literary institutions is a question not easily determined. But no one will doubt that it is a noble function to assist and develop the intellect in those classes of the community whose hard condition exposes them to a merely animal existence. Still, the agency of government in regard to knowledge is necessarily superficial and narrow. The great sources of intellectual power and progress to a people are its strong and original thinkers, be they found where they may. . . . It is true that great men at the head of affairs may and often do contribute much to the growth of a nation's mind. But it too often happens that their station obstructs rather than aids their usefulness. Their connection with a party, and the habit of viewing subjects in reference to personal aggrandizement, too often obscure the noblest intellects and convert into patrons of narrow views and temporary interests those who in other conditions would have been the lights of their age and the propagators of everlasting truth. From these views of the limited influence of government on the most precious interests of society, we learn that political power is not the noblest power, and that in the progress of intelligence it will cease to be coveted as the chief and most honorable distinction on earth.

If we pass now to the consideration of that interest over which government is expected chiefly to watch, and on which it is most competent to act with power,

we shall not arrive at a result very different from that
which we have just expressed. We refer to property, or
wealth. That the influence of political institutions on
this great concern is important, inestimable, we mean
not to deny. But, as we have already suggested, it is
chiefly negative. Government enriches a people by
removing obstructions to their powers, by defending
them from wrong, and thus giving them opportunity to
enrich themselves. Government is not the spring of
the wealth of nations, but their own sagacity, industry,
enterprise, and force of character. To leave a people
to themselves is generally the best service their rulers
can render. Time was when sovereigns fixed prices
and wages, regulated industry and expense, and imagined that a nation would starve and perish if it were
not guided and guarded like an infant. But we have
learned that men are their own best guardians, that
property is safest under its owner's care, and that,
generally speaking, even great enterprises can better
be accomplished by the voluntary association of individuals than by the state. Indeed, we are met at every
stage of this discussion by the truth that political
power is a weak engine compared with individual
intelligence, virtue, and effort; and we are the more
anxious to enforce this truth because through an
extravagant estimate of government men are apt to
expect from it what they must do for themselves, and
to throw upon it the blame which belongs to their own
feebleness and improvidence. The great hope of society
is individual character. Civilization and political institutions are themselves sources of not a few evils, which

nothing but the intellectual and moral energy of the
private citizen can avert or relieve. . . . The great
lesson for men to learn is that their happiness is in
their own hands ; that it is to be wrought out by their
own faithfulness to God and conscience; that no outward institutions can supply the place of inward principle, of moral energy, whilst this can go far to supply
the place of almost every outward aid. . . .

In the remarks which we have now submitted to our
readers we have treated of great topics, if not worthily
yet we trust with a pure purpose. We have aimed to
expose the passion for dominion, the desire of ruling
mankind. We have labored to show the superiority of
moral power and influence to that sway which has for
ages been seized with eager and bloody hands. We
have labored to hold up to unmeasured reprobation him
who would establish an empire of brute force over
rational beings. We have labored to hold forth as the
enemy of his race the man who in any way would
fetter the human mind and subject other wills to his
own. In a word, we have desired to awaken others
and ourselves to a just self-reverence, to the free use
and expansion of our highest powers, and especially to
that moral force, that energy of holy, virtuous purpose,
without which we are slaves amidst the freest institutions. Better gifts than these we cannot supplicate
from God; nor can we consecrate our lives to nobler
acquisitions.

LESSONS FROM THE LIFE OF NAPOLEON BONAPARTE [1]

THERE has always existed, and still exists, a mournful obtuseness of moral feeling in regard to the crimes of military and political life. The wrong-doing of public men on a large scale has never drawn upon them that sincere, hearty abhorrence which visits private vice. Nations have seemed to court aggression and bondage by their stupid, insane admiration of successful tyrants. The wrongs from which men have suffered most in body and mind are yet unpunished. True, Christianity has put into our lips censures on the aspiring and the usurping; but these reproaches are as yet little more than sounds and unmeaning commonplaces. They are repeated for form's sake. When we read or hear them, we feel that they want depth and strength. They are not inward, solemn, burning convictions, breaking from the indignant soul with a tone of reality, before which guilt would cower. The true moral feeling in regard to the crimes of public men is almost to be created. . . .

We have no desire to withhold our admiration from the energies which war often awakens. Great powers, even in their perversion, attest a glorious nature, and we may feel their grandeur whilst we condemn with

[1] From the first paper on Napoleon, first published in the *Christian Examiner*.

our whole strength of moral feeling the evil passions by which they are depraved. We are willing to grant that war, abhor it as we may, often develops and places in strong light a force of intellect and purpose which raises our conceptions of the human soul. There is perhaps no moment in life in which the mind is brought into such intense action, in which the will is so strenuous, and in which irrepressible excitement is so tempered with self-possession, as in the hour of battle. Still, the greatness of the warrior is poor and low compared with the magnanimity of virtue. It vanishes before the greatness of principle. The martyr to humanity, to freedom, or religion ; the unshrinking adherent of despised and deserted truth, who, alone, unsupported and scorned, with no crowd to infuse into him courage, no variety of objects to draw his thoughts from himself, no opportunity of effort or resistance to rouse and nourish energy, still yields himself calmly, resolutely, with invincible philanthropy, to bear prolonged and exquisite suffering which one retracting word might remove, — such a man is as superior to the warrior as the tranquil and boundless heavens above us to the low earth we tread beneath our feet.

We have spoken of the energies of mind called forth by war. We would observe that military talent, even of the highest order, is far from holding the first place among intellectual endowments. It is one of the lower forms of genius ; for it is not conversant with the highest and richest objects of thought. We grant that a mind which takes in a wide country at a glance, and understands almost by intuition the positions it affords for a successful campaign, is a comprehensive and vigorous one. The general who disposes his forces so as to counteract a greater force, who supplies by skill, science, and invention the want of numbers, who dives into the counsels of his enemy, and who gives unity, energy, and success to a vast variety of operations in the midst of casualties and obstructions which no wisdom could foresee, manifests great power. But still the chief work of a general is to apply physical force, to remove physical obstructions, to avail himself of physical aids and advantages, to act on matter, to overcome rivers, ramparts, mountains, and human muscles — and these are not the highest objects of mind, nor do they demand intelligence of the highest order; and accordingly nothing is more common than to find men eminent in this department who are wanting in the noblest energies of the soul, in habits of profound and liberal thinking, in imagination and taste, in the capacity of enjoying works of genius, and in large and original views of human nature and society. The office of a great general does not differ widely from that of a great mechanician, whose business it is to frame new combinations of physical forces, to adapt them to new circumstances, and to remove new obstructions. Accordingly great generals, away from the camp, are often no greater men than the mechanician taken from his workshop. In conversation they are often dull. Deep and refined reasonings they cannot comprehend. We know that there are splendid exceptions. Such was Cæsar, at once the greatest soldier and the most sagacious statesman of his age, whilst in eloquence and literature he

left behind him almost all who had devoted themselves
exclusively to these pursuits.   But such cases are rare.
The conqueror of Napoleon, the hero of Waterloo,
possesses undoubtedly great military talents, but we do
not understand that his most partial admirers claim for
him a place in the highest class of minds.   We will
not go down for illustration to such men as Nelson, a
man great on the deck but debased by gross vices, and
who never pretended to enlargement of intellect.   To
institute a comparison in point of talent and genius
between such men and Milton, Bacon, and Shakespeare
is almost an insult on these illustrious names.   Who
can think of these truly great intelligences, — of the
range of their minds through heaven and earth; of
their deep intuition into the soul; of their new and
glowing combinations of thought; of the energy with
which they grasped and subjected to their main purpose the infinite materials of illustration which nature
and life afford, — who can think of the forms of
transcendent beauty and grandeur which they created
or which were rather emanations of their own minds;
of the calm wisdom and fervid imagination which they
conjoined; of the voice of power in which "though
dead, they still speak," and awaken intellect, sensibility,
and genius in both hemispheres, — who can think of
such men and not feel the immense inferiority of
the most gifted warrior, whose elements of thought
are physical forces and physical obstructions, and
whose employment is the combination of the lowest
class of objects on which a powerful mind can be
employed? . . .

All must concede to Napoleon a sublime power of action, an energy equal to great effects. We are not disposed, however, to consider him as preëminent even in this order of greatness. War was his chief sphere. He gained his ascendency in Europe by the sword. But war is not the field for the highest active talent, and Napoleon, we suspect, was conscious of this truth. The glory of being the greatest general of his age would not have satisfied him. He would have scorned to take his place by the side of Marlborough or Turenne. It was as the founder of an empire, which threatened for a time to comprehend the world, and which demanded other talents besides that of war, that he challenged unrivaled fame. And here we question his claim. Here we cannot award him supremacy. The project of universal empire, however imposing, was not original — the revolutionary governments of France had adopted it before; nor can we consider it as a sure indication of greatness when we remember that the weak and vain mind of Louis the Fourteenth was large enough to cherish it. The question is, Did Napoleon bring to this design the capacity of advancing it by bold and original conceptions, adapted to an age of civilization and of singular intellectual and moral excitement? Did he discover new foundations of power? Did he frame new bonds of union for subjugated nations? Did he discover or originate some common interests by which his empire might be held together? Did he breathe a spirit which could supplant the old national attachments, or did he invent any substitutes for those vulgar instruments of force and corruption

which any and every usurper would have used? Never
in the records of time did the world furnish such materials to work with, such means of modeling nations
afresh, of building up a new power, of introducing a
new era, as did Europe at the period of the French
Revolution. Never was the human mind so capable of
new impulses. And did Napoleon prove himself equal
to the condition of the world? Do we detect one
original conception in his means of universal empire?
Did he seize on the enthusiasm of his age, that powerful principle, more efficient than arms or policy, and
bend it to his purpose? What did he do but follow
the beaten track, — but apply force and fraud in
their very coarsest forms? Napoleon showed a vulgar
mind when he assumed self-interest as the sole spring
of human action. With the sword in one hand
and bribes in the other, he imagined himself absolute
master of the human mind. The strength of moral,
national, and domestic feeling he could not comprehend. The finest and, after all, the most powerful
elements in human nature hardly entered into his
conceptions of it; and how, then, could he have established a durable power over the human race? We
want little more to show his want of originality and
comprehensiveness, as the founder of an empire, than
the simple fact that he chose as his chief counselors
Talleyrand and Fouché, names which speak for themselves. We may judge of the greatness of the master
spirit from the minds which he found most congenial
with his own. In war Bonaparte was great, for he
was bold, original, and creative. Beyond the camp he

indeed showed talent, but not superior to that of other eminent men.

There have been two circumstances which have done much to disarm or weaken the strong moral reprobation with which Bonaparte ought to have been regarded, and which we deem worthy of notice. We refer to the wrongs which he is supposed to have suffered at St. Helena, and to the unworthy use which the Allied Powers have made of their triumph over Napoleon. First, his supposed wrongs at St. Helena have excited a sympathy in his behalf which has thrown a veil over his crimes. We are not disposed to deny that an unwarrantable, because unnecessary, severity was exercised towards Bonàparte. We think it not very creditable to the British government that it tortured a sensitive captive by refusing him a title which he had long worn. We think that not only religion and humanity but self-respect forbids us to inflict a single useless pang on a fallen foe. But we should be weak indeed if the moral judgments and feelings with which Napoleon's career ought to be reviewed should give place to sympathy with the sufferings by which it was closed. With regard to the scruples which not a few have expressed as to the right of banishing him to St. Helena, we can only say that our consciences are not yet refined to such exquisite delicacy as to be at all sensitive on this particular. We admire nothing more in Bonaparte than the effrontery with which he claimed protection from the laws of nations. That a man who had set these laws at open defiance should fly to them for shelter, that the oppressor of the world should claim its sympathy as an oppressed man, and that his claim should find advocates, — these things are to be set down among the extraordinary events of this extraordinary age. Truly the human race is in a pitiable state. It may be trampled on, spoiled, loaded like a beast of burden, made the prey of rapacity, insolence, and the sword, but it must not touch a hair or disturb the pillow of one of its oppressors unless it can find chapter and verse in the code of national law to authorize its rudeness towards the privileged offender. For ourselves we should rejoice to see every tyrant, whether a usurper or hereditary prince, fastened to a lonely rock in the ocean. Whoever gives clear, undoubted proof that he is prepared and sternly resolved to make the earth a slaughterhouse, and to crush every will adverse to his own, ought to be caged like a wild beast, and to require mankind to proceed against him according to written laws and precedents, as if he were a private citizen in a quiet court of justice, is just as rational as to require a man in imminent peril from an assassin to wait and prosecute his murderer according to the most protracted forms of law. There are great, solemn rights of nature which precede laws and on which law is founded. There are great exigencies in human affairs which speak for themselves and need no precedent to teach the right path. There are awful periods in the history of our race which do not belong to its ordinary state, and which are not to be governed and judged by ordinary rules. Such a period was that when Bonaparte, by infraction of solemn engagements, had thrown himself into France and convulsed all Europe; and they who confound this with the ordinary events of history, and see in Bonaparte but an ordinary foe to the peace and independence of nations, have certainly very different intellects from our own.

We confess, too, that we are not only unable to see the wrong done to Napoleon in sending him to St. Helena, but that we cannot muster up much sympathy for the inconveniences and privations which he endured there. Our sympathies in this particular are wayward and untractable. When we would carry them to that solitary island, and fasten them on the illustrious victim of British cruelty, they will not tarry there, but take their flight across the Mediterranean to Jaffa, and across the Atlantic to the platform where the Duke d'Enghien was shot, to the prison of Toussaint, and to fields of battle where thousands at his bidding lay weltering in blood. When we strive to fix our thoughts upon the sufferings of the injured hero, other and more terrible sufferings, of which he was the cause, rush upon us; and his complaints, however loud and angry, are drowned by groans and execrations, which fill our ears from every region which he traversed. We have no tears to spare for fallen greatness when that greatness was founded in crime, and reared by force and perfidy. We reserve them for those on whose ruin it rose. We keep our sympathies for our race, for human nature in its humbler forms, for the impoverished peasant, the widowed mother, the violated virgin; and are even perverse enough to rejoice that the ocean has a prison-house where the author of those miseries may be safely lodged. Bonaparte's history is to us too solemn, the wrongs for which humanity and freedom arraign him are too flagrant, to allow us to play the part of sentimentalists around his grave at St. Helena. We leave this to the more refined age in which we live; and we do so in the hope that an age is coming of less tender mold, but of loftier, sterner feeling, and of deeper sympathy with the whole human race. Should our humble page then live, we trust with an undoubting faith that the uncompromising indignation with which we plead the cause of our oppressed and insulted nature will not be set down to the account of vindictiveness and hardness of heart.

We observed that the moral indignation of many towards Bonaparte had been impaired or turned away not only by his supposed wrongs but by the unworthy use which his conquerors made of their triumph. We are told that, bad as was his despotism, the Holy Alliance is a worse one; and that Napoleon was less a scourge than the present coalition of the continental monarchs, framed for the systematic suppression of freedom. By such reasoning his crimes are cloaked, and his fall is made a theme of lamentation. It is not one of the smallest errors and sins of the Allied Sovereigns that they have contrived, by their base policy, to turn the resentments and moral displeasure of men from the usurper upon themselves. For these sovereigns we have no defense to offer. We yield to none in detestation of the Holy Alliance, profanely so called. To us its doctrines are as false and pestilent as any broached by Jacobinism. The Allied Monarchs are adding to the other wrongs of despots that of flagrant ingratitude; of ingratitude to the generous and brave nations to whom

they owe their thrones, whose spirit of independence
and patriotism, and whose hatred of the oppressor, contributed more than standing armies to raise up the fallen
and to strengthen the falling monarchies of Europe. Be
it never forgotten in the records of despotism, let history
record it on her most durable tablet, that the first use
made by the principal continental sovereigns of their
regained or confirmed power was to conspire against
the hopes and rights of the nations by whom they had
been saved; to combine the military power of Europe
against free institutions, against the press, against the
spirit of liberty and patriotism which had sprung up in
the glorious struggle with Napoleon, against the right
of the people to exert an influence on the governments
by which their dearest interests were to be controlled.
Never be it forgotten that such was the honor of sovereigns, such their requital for the blood which had been
shed freely in their defense. Freedom and humanity
send up a solemn and prevailing cry against them to
that tribunal where kings and subjects are soon to stand
as equals.

But still we should be strangely blind if we were not
to feel that the fall of Napoleon was a blessing to the
world. Who can look, for example, at France, and not
see there a degree of freedom which could never have
grown up under the terrible frown of the usurper?
True, Bonaparte's life, though it seemed a charmed one,
must at length have ended; and we are told that then
his empire would have been broken, and that the general
crash, by some inexplicable process, would have given
birth to a more extensive and durable liberty than can

now be hoped.   But such anticipations seem to us to be built on a strange inattention to the nature and inevitable consequences of Napoleon's power.   It was wholly a military power.   He was literally turning Europe into a camp, and drawing its best talent into one occupation, — war.   Thus Europe was retracing its steps to those ages of calamity and darkness when the only law was the sword.   The progress of centuries, which had consisted chiefly in the substitution of intelligence, public opinion, and other mild and rational influences for brutal force, was to be reversed.   At Bonaparte's death his empire must indeed have been dissolved; but military chiefs, like Alexander's lieutenants, would have divided it.   The sword alone would have shaped its future communities; and, after years of desolation and bloodshed, Europe would have found not repose, but a respite, an armed truce, under warriors whose only title to empire would have been their own good blades, and the weight of whose thrones would have been upheld by military force alone.   Amidst such convulsions, during which the press would have been everywhere fettered, and the military spirit would have triumphed over and swallowed up the spirit and glory of letters and liberal arts, we greatly fear that the human intellect would have lost its present impulse, its thirst for progress, and would have fallen back towards barbarism.   Let not the friends of freedom bring dishonor on themselves or desert their cause by instituting comparisons between Napoleon and legitimate sovereigns which may be construed into eulogies on the former.   For ourselves, we have no sympathy with tyranny, whether it bear the name of usurpation or

legitimacy. We are not pleading the cause of the Allied
Sovereigns. In our judgment, they have contracted the
very guilt against which they have pretended to combine. In our apprehension a conspiracy against the
rights of the human race is as foul a crime as rebellion
against the rights of sovereigns; nor is there less of
treason in warring against public freedom than in assailing royal power. Still we are bound in truth to confess that the Allied Sovereigns are not to be ranked
with Bonaparte, whose design against the independence
of nations and the liberties of the world, in this age
of civilization, liberal thinking, and Christian knowledge, is in our estimation the most nefarious enterprise
recorded in history.

The series of events which it has been our province
to review offers subjects of profound thought and solemn
instruction to the moralist and politician. We have
retraced it with many painful feelings. It shows us a
great people, who had caught some indistinct glimpses
of freedom and of a nobler and a happier political constitution, betrayed by their leaders, and brought back
by a military despot to heavier chains than they had
broken. We see with indignation one man — a man
like ourselves — subjecting whole nations to his absolute rule. It is this wrong and insult to our race which
has chiefly moved us. Had a storm of God's ordination passed over Europe, prostrating its capitals, sweeping off its villages, burying millions in ruins, we should
have wept, we should have trembled. But in this there
would have been only wretchedness. Now we also see
debasement. To us there is something radically and

increasingly shocking in the thought of one man's will
becoming a law to his race; in the thought of multitudes, of vast communities, surrendering conscience,
intellect, their affections, their rights, their interests, to
the stern mandate of a fellow-creature. When we see
one word of a frail man on the throne of France tearing
a hundred thousand sons from their homes, breaking
asunder the sacred ties of domestic life, sentencing
myriads of the young to make murder their calling and
rapacity their means of support, and extorting from
nations their treasures to extend this ruinous sway, we
are ready to ask ourselves, Is not this a dream? And
when the sad reality comes home to us, we blush for a
race which can stoop to such an abject lot. At length,
indeed, we see the tyrant humbled, stripped of power;
but stripped by those who in the main are not unwilling to play the despot on a narrower scale, and to break
down the spirit of nations under the same iron sway.

How is it that tyranny has thus triumphed? that the
hopes with which we greeted the French Revolution
have been crushed? that a usurper plucked up the last
roots of the tree of liberty, and planted despotism in its
place? The chief cause is not far to seek, nor can it
be too often urged on the friends of freedom. France
failed through the want of that moral preparation for
liberty without which the blessing cannot be secured.
She was not ripe for the good she sought. She was too
corrupt for freedom. France had indeed to contend
with great political ignorance; but had not ignorance
been reenforced by deep moral defect she might have
won her way to free institutions. Her character forbade

her to be free; and it now seems strange that we could
ever have expected her to secure this boon. How
could we believe that a liberty of which that heartless
scoffer, Voltaire, was a chief apostle, could have triumphed? Most of the preachers of French liberty had
thrown off all the convictions which ennoble the mind.
Man's connection with God they broke, for they declared
that there was no God in whom to trust in the great
struggle for liberty. Human immortality — that truth
which is the seed of all greatness — they derided. To
their philosophy, man was a creature of chance, a com-
pound of matter, an ephemeron, a worm, who was soon
to rot and perish forever. What insanity was it to
expect that such men were to work out the emancipation of their race! that in such hands the hopes and
dearest rights of humanity were secure! Liberty was
tainted by their touch, polluted by their breath; and
yet we trusted that it was to rise in health and glory
from their embrace. We looked to men who openly
founded morality on private interests for the sacrifices,
the devotion, the heroic virtue, which Freedom always
demands from her assertors.

The great cause of the discomfiture of the late European
struggle for liberty is easily understood by an American,
who recurs to the history of his own revolution. This
issued prosperously, because it was begun and was conducted under the auspices of private and public virtue.
Our liberty did not come to us by accident, nor was it
the gift of a few leaders; but its seeds were sown plen-
tifully in the minds of the whole people. It was rooted
in the conscience and reason of the nation. It was the

growth of deliberate convictions and generous principles liberally diffused. We had no Paris, no metropolis, which a few leaders swayed, and which sent forth its influences, like "a mighty heart," through dependent and subservient provinces. The country was all heart. The living principle pervaded the community, and every village added strength to the solemn purpose of being free. We have here an explanation of a striking fact in the history of our revolution, — we mean the want or absence of that description of great men whom we meet in other countries; men who, by their distinct and single agency, and by their splendid deeds, determine a nation's fate. There was too much greatness in the American people to admit this overshadowing greatness of leaders. Accordingly, the United States had no liberator, no political saviour. Washington, indeed, conferred on us great blessings; but Washington was not a hero in the common sense of that word. We never spoke of him as the French did of Bonaparte, never talked of his eagle-eyed, irresistible genius, as if this were to work out our safety. We never lost our self-respect. We felt that, under God, we were to be free through our own courage, energy, and wisdom, under the animating and guiding influences of this great and good mind. Washington served us chiefly by his sublime moral qualities. To him belonged the proud distinction of being the leader in a revolution without awakening one doubt or solicitude as to the spotless purity of his purpose. His was the glory of being the brightest manifestation of the spirit which reigned in his country; and in this way he became a source of energy, a bond of union, the center of an enlightened people's confidence. In such a revolution as that of France, Washington would have been nothing; for that sympathy which subsisted between him and his fellow-citizens, and which was the secret of his power, would have been wanting. By an instinct which is unerring, we call Washington, with grateful reverence, the father of his country, but not its saviour. A people which wants a saviour, which does not possess an earnest and pledge of freedom in its own heart, is not yet ready to be free.

Let the friends of freedom in Europe especially teach that great truth, which is the seminal principle of a virtuous freedom, and the very foundation of morals and religion, — we mean the doctrine that conscience, the voice of God in every heart, is to be listened to above all other guides and lords; that there is a sovereign within us, clothed with more awful powers and rights than any outward king; and that he alone is worthy the name of a man who gives himself up solemnly, deliberately, to obey this internal guide through peril and in death. This is the spirit of freedom; for no man is wholly and immutably free but he who has broken every outward yoke, that he may obey his own deliberate conscience. This is the lesson to be taught alike in republics and despotisms. As yet it has but dawned on the world. Its full application remains to be developed. They who have been baptized, by a true experience, into this vital and all-comprehending truth must everywhere be its propagators; and he who makes one convert of it near a despot's throne has broken one link of that despot's chain. It is chiefly in the diffusion

of this loftiness of moral sentiment that we place our
hope of freedom; and we have a hope, because we
know that there are those who have drunk into this
truth, and are ready, when God calls, to be its martyrs.
We do not despair, for there is a contagion — we would
rather say, a divine power — in sublime moral principle.
This is our chief trust.   We have less and less hope
from force and bloodshed, as the instruments of working
out man's redemption from slavery.   History shows us
not a few princes who have gained or strengthened
thrones by assassination or war.   But freedom, which
is another name for justice, honor, and benevolence,
scorns to use the private dagger, and wields with trembling the public sword.   The true conspiracy before
which tyranny is to fall is that of virtuous, elevated
minds, which shall consecrate themselves to the work
of awakening in men a consciousness of the rights,
powers, purposes, and greatness of human nature; which
shall oppose to force the heroism of intellect and conscience, and the spirit of self-sacrifice.   Let the friends
of freedom not stain their sacred cause by one cruel
deed, by the infliction of one needless pang, by shedding
without cause one drop of human blood.

THE FOUNDER OF THE PEACE SOCIETY

A Tribute to the Memory of the Rev. Noah Worcester, Boston, November 12, 1837.

A new commandment I give unto you, That ye love one another; as I have loved you, that ye also love one another. — *John* xiii. 34.

It was the great purpose of Christ to create the world anew, to make a deep, broad, enduring change in human beings. He came to breathe his own soul into men, to bring them through faith into a connection and sympathy with himself, by which they would receive his divine virtue as the branches receive quickening influences from the vine in which they abide, and the limbs from the head to which they are vitally bound.

It was especially the purpose of Jesus Christ to redeem men from the slavery of selfishness, to raise them to a divine, disinterested love. By this he intended that his followers should be known, that his religion should be broadly divided from all former institutions. He meant that this should be worn as a frontlet on the brow, should beam as a light from the countenance, should shed a grace over the manners, should give tones of sympathy to the voice, and especially should give energy to the will, energy to do and suffer for others' good. Here is one of the grand distinctions of Christianity, incomparably grander than all the mysteries which have borne its name. Our knowledge of Christianity is to be measured not by the laboriousness with which we have dived into the depths of theological systems, but by our comprehension of the nature, extent, energy, and glory of that disinterested principle which Christ enjoined as our likeness to God, and as the perfection of human nature.

This disinterestedness of Christianity is to be learned from Christ himself and from no other. It had dawned on the world before in illustrious men, in prophets, sages, and legislators. But its full orb rose at Bethlehem. All the preceding history of the world gives but broken hints of the love which shone forth from Christ. Nor can this be learned from his precepts alone. We must go to his life, especially to his cross. His cross was the throne of his love. There it reigned, there it triumphed. On the countenance of the crucified Saviour there was one expression stronger than of dying agony, — the expression of calm, meek, unconquered, boundless love. I repeat it, the cross alone can teach us the energy and grandeur of the love which Christ came to impart. There we see its illimitableness, for he died for the whole world. There we learn its inexhaustible placability, for he died for the very enemies whose hands were reeking with his blood. There we learn its self-immolating strength, for he resigned every good of life, and endured intensest pains in the cause of our race. There we learn its spiritual elevation, for he died not to enrich men with outward and worldly goods but to breathe new life, health, purity into the soul. There we learn its far-reaching aim, for he died to give immortality of happiness. There we learn its tenderness and sympathy, for amidst his cares for the world his heart overflowed with gratitude and love for his honored mother. There, in a word, we learn its divinity, for he suffered through his participation of the spirit and his devotion to the purposes of God, through unity of heart and will with his heavenly Father.

It is one of our chief privileges as Christians that we have in Jesus Christ a revelation of perfect love. This great idea comes forth to us from his life and teaching as a distinct and bright reality. To understand this is to understand Christianity. To call forth in us a corresponding energy of disinterested affection is the mission which Christianity has to accomplish on the earth.

There is one characteristic of the love of Christ to which the Christian world is now waking up as from long sleep, and which is to do more than all things for the renovation of the world. He loved individual man. Before his time the most admired form of goodness was patriotism. Men loved their country, but cared nothing for their fellow-creatures beyond the limits of country, and cared little for the individual within those limits, devoting themselves to public interests and especially to what was called the glory of the state. The legislator seeking by his institutions to exalt his country above its rivals and the warrior fastening its yoke on its foes and crowning it with bloody laurels were the great names of earlier times. Christ loved man, not masses of men; loved each and all, and not a particular country and class. The human being was dear to him for his own sake, not for the spot of earth on which he lived, not for the language he spoke, not for his rank in life; but for his humanity, for his spiritual nature, for the image of God in which he was made. Nothing outward in human condition engrossed the notice or narrowed the sympathies of Jesus. He looked to the human soul. That he loved. That divine spark he desired to cherish, no matter where it dwelt, no matter how it was dimmed. He loved man for his own sake, and all men without exclusion or exception. His ministry was not confined to a church, a chosen congregation. On the Mount he opened his mouth and spake to the promiscuous multitude. From the bosom of the lake he delivered his parables to the throng which lined its shores. His church was nature, the unconfined air and earth, and his truths, like the blessed influences of nature's sunshine and rain, fell on each and all. He lived in the highway, the street, the places of concourse, and welcomed the eager crowds which gathered round him from every sphere and rank of life. Nor was it to crowds that his sympathy was confined. He did not need a multitude to excite him. The humblest individual drew his regards. He took the little child into his arms and blessed it, he heard the beggar crying to him by the wayside where he sat for alms, and in the anguish of death he administered consolation to a malefactor expiring at his side. In this shone forth the divine wisdom as well as love of Jesus, that he understood the worth of a human being. So truly did he comprehend it that, as I think, he would have counted himself repaid for all his teachings and mighty works, for all his toils and sufferings and bitter death, by the redemption of a single soul. His love to every

human being surpassed that of a parent to an only
child.   Jesus was great in all things, but in nothing
greater than in his comprehension of the worth of a
human spirit.   Before his time no one dreamed of it.
The many had been sacrificed to the few.   The mass
of men had been trodden under foot.   History had
been but a record of struggles and institutions which
breathed nothing so strongly as contempt of the human
race.

Jesus was the first philanthropist.   He brought with
him a new era, the era of philanthropy, and from his
time a new spirit has moved over the troubled waters
of society, and will move until it has brought order and
beauty out of darkness and confusion.   The men whom
he trained and into whom he had poured most largely
his own spirit were signs, proofs that a new kingdom
had come.   They consecrated themselves to a work at
that time without precedent, wholly original, such as
had not entered human thought.   They left home, possessions, country; went abroad into strange lands, and
not only put life in peril but laid it down, to spread the
truth which they had received from their Lord to make
the true God, even the Father, known to his blinded
children, to make the Saviour known to the sinner, to
make life and immortality known to the dying, to give
a new impulse to the human soul.   We read of the
mission of the Apostles as if it were a thing of course.
The thought perhaps never comes to us that they
entered on a sphere of action until that time wholly
unexplored; that not a track had previously marked
their path; that the great conception which inspired

them of converting a world had never dawned on the
sublimest intellect; that the spiritual love for every
human being which carried them over oceans and
through deserts, amid scourgings and fastings and
imprisonments and death, was a new light from heaven,
breaking out on earth, a new revelation of the divinity
in human nature. Then it was that man began to
yearn for man with a godlike love. Then a new voice
was heard on earth, the voice of prayer for the recovery,
pardon, happiness of a world. It was most strange, it
was a miracle more worthy of admiration than the raising of the dead, that from Judea, the most exclusive,
narrow country under heaven, which hated and scorned
all other nations, and shrank from their touch as pollu-
tion, should go forth men to proclaim the doctrine of
human brotherhood; to give to every human being,
however fallen or despised, assurances of God's infinite
love; to break down the barriers of nation and rank; to
pour out their blood like water in the work of diffusing
the spirit of universal love. Thus mightily did the
character of Jesus act on the spirits of the men with
whom he had lived. Since that time the civilized
world has been overwhelmed by floods of barbarians,
and ages of darkness have passed. But some rays of
this divine light break on us through the thickest
darkness. The new impulse given by Christianity was
never wholly spent. The rude sculpture of the dark
ages represented Jesus hanging from his cross; and
however this image was abused to purposes of superstition, it still spoke to men of a philanthropy stronger
than death, which felt and suffered for every human

being, and a softening, humanizing virtue went from it
which even the barbarian could not wholly resist. In
our own times the character of Jesus is exerting more
conspicuously its true and glorious power. We have
indeed little cause for boasting. The great features of
society are still hard and selfish. The worth of a
human being is a mystery still hid from an immense
majority, and the most enlightened among us have not
looked beneath the surface of this great truth. Still
there is at this moment an interest in human nature, a
sympathy with human suffering, a sensibility to the
abuses and evils which deform society, a faith in man's
capacity of progress, a desire of human progress, a desire
to carry to every human being the means of rising to
a better condition and a higher virtue, such as has
never been witnessed before. Amidst the mercenariness which would degrade men into tools and the ambition which would tread them down in its march toward
power, there is still a respect for man as man, a recognition of his rights, a thirst for his elevation, which is
the surest proof of a higher comprehension of Jesus
Christ, and the surest augury of a happier state of
human affairs. Humanity and justice are crying out
in more and more piercing tones for the suffering, the
enslaved, the ignorant, the poor, the prisoner, the
orphan, the long-neglected seaman, the benighted heathen. I do not refer merely to new institutions for
humanity, for these are not the most unambiguous proofs
of progress. We see in the common consciousness of
society, in the general feelings of individuals, traces of
a more generous recognition of what man owes to man.

The glare of outward distinction is somewhat dimmed. The prejudices of caste and rank are abated. A man is seen to be worth more than his wardrobe or his title. It begins to be understood that a Christian is to be a philanthropist, and that, in truth, the essence of Christianity is a spirit of martyrdom in the cause of mankind.

This subject has been brought to my mind at the present moment by an event in this vicinity which has drawn little attention, but which I could not without self-reproach suffer to pass unnoticed. Within a few days a great and good man, a singular example of the philanthropy which Jesus Christ came to breathe into the world, has been taken away; and as it was my happiness to know him more intimately than most among us, I feel as if I were called to bear a testimony to his rare goodness and to hold up his example as a manifestation of what Christianity can accomplish in the human mind. I refer to the Rev. Noah Worcester, who has been justly called the apostle of peace, who finished his course at Brighton during the last week. His great age—for he was almost eighty—and the long and entire seclusion to which debility had compelled him have probably made his name a strange one to some who hear me. In truth, it is common in the present age for eminent men to be forgotten during their lives, if their lives are much prolonged. Society is now a quick-shifting pageant. New actors hurry the old ones from the stage. The former stability of things is strikingly impaired. The authority which gathered round the aged has declined. The young seize impatiently the prizes of life. The hurried, bustling, tumultuous,

feverish present swallows up men's thoughts, so that
he who retires from active pursuits is as little known
to the rising generation as if he were dead. It is
not wonderful, then, that Dr. Worcester was so far
forgotten by his contemporaries. But the future will
redress the wrongs of the present, and in the progress of civilization history will guard more and more
sacredly the memories of men who have advanced before
their age and devoted themselves to great but neglected
interests of humanity.

Dr. Worcester's efforts in relation to war or in the
cause of peace made him eminently a public man, and
constitute his chief claim to public consideration; and
these were not founded on accidental circumstances or
foreign influences, but wholly on the strong and peculiar tendencies of his mind. He was distinguished
above all whom I have known by his comprehension
and deep feeling of the spirit of Christianity, by the
sympathy with which he seized on the character of
Jesus Christ as a manifestation of perfect love, by the
honor in which he held the mild, humble, forgiving,
disinterested virtues of our religion. This distinguishing trait of his mind was embodied and brought out
in his whole life and conduct. He especially expressed
it in his labors for the promotion of universal peace on
earth. He was struck, as no other man within my
acquaintance has been, with the monstrous incongruity
between the spirit of Christianity and the spirit of
Christian communities, between Christ's teaching of
peace, mercy, forgiveness and the wars which divide
and desolate the church and the world. Every man

has particular impressions which rule over and give a hue to his mind. Every man is struck by some evils rather than others. The excellent individual of whom I speak was shocked, heart-smitten by nothing so much as by seeing that man hates man, that man destroys his brother, that man has drenched the earth with his brother's blood, that man in his insanity has crowned the murderer of his race with the highest honors; and, still worse, that Christian hates Christian, that church wars against church, that differences of forms and opinions array against each other those whom Christ died to join together in closest brotherhood, and that Christian zeal is spent in building up sects, rather than in spreading the spirit of Christ and enlarging and binding together the universal church. The great evil on which his mind and heart fixed was war, discord, intolerance, the substitution of force for reason and love. To spread peace on earth became the object of his life. Under this impulse he gave birth and impulse to peace societies. This new movement is to be traced to him above all other men, and his name, I doubt not, will be handed down to future time with increasing veneration as the "Friend of Peace," as having given new force to the principles which are gradually to abate the horrors and ultimately extinguish the spirit of war.

The history of the good man, as far as I have learned it, is singularly instructive and encouraging. He was self-taught, self-formed. He was born in narrow circumstances, and, to the age of twenty-one, was a laborious farmer, not only deprived of a collegiate education, but of the advantages which may be enjoyed in a more prosperous family. An early marriage brought on him the cares of a growing family. Still he found, or rather made, time for sufficient improvements to introduce him into the ministry before his thirtieth year. He was first settled in a parish too poor to give him even a scanty support; and he was compelled to take a farm, on which he toiled by day, whilst in the evening he was often obliged to use a mechanical art for the benefit of his family. He made their shoes, — an occupation of which Coleridge has somewhere remarked that it has been followed by a greater number of eminent men than any other trade. By the side of his workbench he kept ink and paper, that he might write down the interesting thoughts which he traced out or which rushed on him amidst his humble labors. I take pleasure in stating this part of his history. The prejudice against manual labor, as inconsistent with personal dignity, is one of the most irrational and pernicious, especially in a free country. It shows how little we comprehend the spirit of our institutions and how deeply we are tainted with the narrow maxims of the old aristocracies of Europe. Here was a man uniting great intellectual improvement with refinement of manners, who had been trained under unusual severity of toil. This country has lost much physical and moral strength, and its prosperity is at this moment depressed by the common propensity to forsake the plow for less manly pursuits, which are thought, however, to promise greater dignity as well as ease.

His first book was a series of letters to a Baptist minister; and in this he gave promise of the direction

which the efforts of his life were to assume. The great
object of these letters was not to settle the controversies about baptism, about the mode of administering it,
whether by immersion or sprinkling, or about the proper
subjects of it, whether children or adults alone. His
aim was to show that these were inferior questions, that
differences about these ought not to divide Christians,
that the "close communion," as it is called, of the
Baptists was inconsistent with the liberal spirit of
Christianity, and that this obstruction to Christian
unity ought to be removed.

His next publication was what brought him into
notice and gave him an important place in our theological history. It was a publication on the Trinity; and
it preceded the animated controversy on that point which
a few years after agitated this city and commonwealth.
. . . The work drew much attention, and its calm, benignant spirit had no small influence in disarming prejudice
and unkindness. He found, however, that his defection
from his original faith had exposed him to much suspicion and reproach; and he became at length so pain-
fully impressed with the intolerance which his work
had excited that he published another shorter work, a
work breathing the very spirit of Jesus, intended to
teach that diversities of opinion on subjects the most
mysterious and perplexing ought not to sever friends,
to dissolve the Christian tie, to divide the church, to
fasten on the dissenter from the common faith the
charge of heresy, to array the disciples of the Prince
of Peace in hostile bands. These works obtained such
favor that he was solicited to leave the obscure town

in which he ministered, and to take charge in this place
of a periodical called at first the *Christian Disciple*,
and now better known as the *Christian Examiner*.
At that time (about twenty-five years ago) I first saw
him. Long and severe toil and a most painful disease
had left their traces on his once athletic frame, but his
countenance beamed with a benignity which at once
attracted confidence and affection. For several years
he consulted me habitually in the conduct of the work
which he edited. I recollect with admiration the gentleness, humility, and sweetness of temper with which
he endured freedoms, corrections, retrenchments, some
of which I feel now to have been unwarranted, and
which no other man would so kindly have borne. This
work was commenced very much for doctrinal discus-
sions, but his spirit could not brook such limitations,
and he used its pages more and more for the dissemina-
tion of his principles of philanthropy and peace. At
length he gave these principles to the world in a form
which did much to decide his future career. He published a pamphlet, called "A Solemn Review of the
Custom of War." It bore no name and appeared without recommendation, but it immediately seized on attention. It was read by multitudes in this country, then
published in England, and translated, as I have heard,
into several languages of Europe. Such was the impression made by this work that a new association called
the Peace Society of Massachusetts was instituted in
this place. I well recollect the day of its formation in
yonder house, then the parsonage of this parish; and if
there was a happy man that day on earth, it was the

founder of this institution. This society gave birth to
all the kindred ones in this country, and its influence
was felt abroad. Dr. Worcester assumed the charge of
its periodical and devoted himself for years to this
cause with unabating faith and zeal; and it may be
doubted whether any man who ever lived contributed
more than he to spread just sentiments on the subject
of war and to hasten the era of universal peace. He
began his efforts in the darkest day, when the whole
civilized world was shaken by conflict, and threatened
with military despotism. He lived to see more than
twenty years of general peace, and to see through these
years a multiplication of national ties, an extension of
commercial communications, an establishment of new
connections between Christians and learned men through
the world, and a growing reciprocity of friendly and
beneficent influence among different states, — all giving
aid to the principles of peace and encouraging hopes
which a century ago would have been deemed insane.

The abolition of war, to which this good man devoted
himself, is no longer to be set down as a creation of
fancy, a dream of enthusiastic philanthropy. War rests
on opinion, and opinion is more and more withdrawing
its support. War rests on contempt of human nature,
on the long, mournful habit of regarding the mass of
human beings as machines, or as animals having no
higher use than to be shot at and murdered for the
glory of a chief, for the seating of this or that family
on a throne, for the petty interests or selfish rivalries
which have inflamed states to conflict. Let the worth
of a human being be felt, let the mass of a people be

elevated, let it be understood that a man was made to enjoy inalienable rights, to improve lofty powers, to secure a vast happiness, and a main pillar of war will fall. And is it not plain that these views are taking place of the contempt in which man has so long been held? War finds another support in the prejudices and partialities of a narrow patriotism. Let the great Christian principle of human brotherhood be comprehended, let the Christian spirit of universal love gain ground, and just so fast the custom of war, so long the pride of men, will become their abhorrence and execration. It is encouraging to see how outward events are concurring with the influences of Christianity in promoting peace; how an exclusive nationality is yielding to growing intercourse; how different nations, by mutual visits, by the interchange of thoughts and products, by studying one another's language and literature, by union of efforts in the cause of religion and humanity, are growing up to the consciousness of belonging to one great family. Every railroad connecting distant regions may be regarded as accomplishing a ministry of peace. Every year which passes without war, by interweaving more various ties of interest and friendship, is a pledge of coming years of peace. The prophetic faith with which Dr. Worcester, in the midst of universal war, looked forward to a happier era, and which was smiled at as enthusiasm or credulity, has already received a sanction beyond his fondest hopes by the wonderful progress of human affairs.

On the subject of war Dr. Worcester adopted opinions which are thought by some to be extreme. He

interpreted literally the precept, "Resist not evil," and
he believed that nations as well as individuals would
find safety, as well as "fulfill righteousness," in yielding
it literal obedience.   One of the most striking traits of
his character was his confidence in the power of love,
I might say in its omnipotence.   He believed that the
surest way to subdue a foe was to become his friend;
that a true benevolence was a surer defense than
swords, or artillery, or walls of adamant.   He believed
that no mightier man ever trod the soil of America than
William Penn when entering the wilderness unarmed,
and stretching out to the savage a hand which refused
all earthly weapons, in token of brotherhood and peace.
There was something grand in the calm confidence with
which he expressed his conviction of the superiority of
moral to physical force.   Armies, fiery passions, quick
resentments, and the spirit of vengeance, miscalled
honor, seemed to him weak, low instruments, inviting
and often hastening the ruin which they are used to
avert.   Many will think him in error; but if so, it was
a grand thought which led him astray.

At the age of seventy he felt as if he had discharged
his mission as a preacher of peace, and resigned his
office as secretary to the society, to which he had given
the strength of many years.   He did not, however, retire
to unfruitful repose.   Bodily infirmity had increased,
so that he was very much confined to his house; but he
returned with zeal to the studies of his early life, and
produced two theological works, one on the Atonement,
the other on Human Depravity, or the moral state of
man by nature, which I regard as among the most

useful books on these long-agitated subjects. These
writings, particularly the last, have failed of the popularity which they merit, in consequence of a defect of
style, which may be traced to his defective education
and which naturally increased with years. I refer to his
diffusiveness — to his inability to condense his thoughts.
His writings, however, are not wanting in merits of
style. They are simple and clear. They abound to a
remarkable degree in ingenious illustration, and they
have often the charm which original thinking always
gives to composition. He was truly an original writer,
not in the sense of making great discoveries, but in the
sense of writing from his own mind, and not from books
or tradition. What he wrote had perhaps been written
before, but in consequence of his limited reading it was
new to himself, and came to him with the freshness of
discovery. Sometimes great thoughts flashed on his
mind as if they had been inspirations, and in writing
his last book he seems to have felt as if some extraordinary light had been imparted from above. After
his seventy-fifth year he ceased to write books, but his
mind lost nothing of its activity. He was so enfeebled
by a distressing disease that he could converse but for
a few moments at a time, yet he entered into all the
great movements of the age with an interest distinguished from the fervor of youth only by its mildness
and its serene trust. The attempts made in some of
our cities to propagate atheistical principles gave him
much concern, and he applied himself to fresh inquiries
into the proofs of the existence and perfections of God,
hoping to turn his labors to the account of his erring

fellow-creatures. With this view he entered on the study of nature as a glorious testimony to its almighty Author. I shall never forget the delight which illumined his countenance a short time ago as he told me that he had just been reading the history of the coral, the insect which raises islands in the sea. "How wonderfully," he exclaimed, "is God's providence revealed in these little creatures!" The last subject to which he devoted his thoughts was slavery. His mild spirit could never reconcile itself to the methods in which this evil is often assailed; but the greatness of the evil he deeply felt, and he left several essays on this as on the preceding subject, which, if they should be found unfit for publication, will still bear witness to the intense, unfaltering interest with which he bound himself to the cause of mankind.

I have thus given a sketch of the history of a good man who lived and died the lover of his kind and the admiration of his friends. Two views of him particularly impressed me. The first was the unity, the harmony of his character. He had no jarring elements. His whole nature had been blended and melted into one strong, serene love. His mission was to preach peace, and he preached it not on set occasions or by separate efforts, but in his whole life. It breathed in his tones. It beamed from his venerable countenance. He carried it where it is least apt to be found, into the religious controversies which raged around him with great vehemence, but which never excited him to a word of anger or intolerance. All my impressions of him are harmonious. I recollect no discord in his

beautiful life.   And this serenity was not the result of
torpidness or tameness, for his whole life was a conflict
with what he thought error.   He made no compromise
with the world, and yet he loved it as deeply and constantly as if it had responded in shouts to all his views
and feelings.

The next great impression which I received from
him was that of the sufficiency of the mind to its own
happiness, or of its independence on outward things.
He was for years debilitated, and often a great sufferer,
and his circumstances were very narrow, compelling
him to so strict an economy that he was sometimes
represented, though falsely, as wanting the common
comforts of life.   In this tried and narrow condition
he was among the most contented of men.   He spoke
of his old age as among the happiest portions, if not
the very happiest, in his life.   In conversation his religion manifested itself in gratitude more frequently than
in any other form.   When I have visited him in his
last years, and looked on his serene countenance, and
heard his cheerful voice, and seen the youthful earnestness with which he was reading a variety of books and
studying the great interests of humanity, I have felt
how little of this outward world is needed to our happiness.   I have felt the greatness of the human spirit
which could create to itself such joy from its own
resources.   I have felt the folly, the insanity of that
prevailing worldliness which in accumulating outward
good neglects the imperishable soul.   On leaving his
house and turning my face toward this city I have
said to myself, How much richer is this poor man than

the richest who dwell yonder! I have been ashamed of my own dependence on outward good. I am always happy to express my obligations to the benefactors of my mind; and I owe it to Dr. Worcester to say that my acquaintance with him gave me clearer comprehension of the spirit of Christ and of the dignity of a man.

And he has gone to his reward. He has gone to that world of which he carried in his own breast so rich an earnest and pledge, to a world of peace. He has gone to Jesus Christ, whose spirit he so deeply comprehended and so freely imbibed; and to God, whose universal, all-suffering, all-embracing love he adored and in a humble measure made manifest in his own life. But he is not wholly gone; not gone in heart, for I am sure that a better world has heightened, not extinguished, his affection for his race; and not gone in influence, for his thoughts remain in his works, and his memory is laid up as a sacred treasure in many minds. A spirit so beautiful ought to multiply itself in those to whom it is made known. May we all be incited by it to a more grateful, cheerful love of God, and a serener, gentler, nobler love of our fellow-creatures!

NATIONAL DESTINY IN NATIONAL CHARACTER

FROM THE LETTER ON THE ANNEXATION OF TEXAS

THE real and great causes of the present trouble in Texas are matters of notoriety, so as to need no minute exposition. The first great cause was the unbounded, unprincipled spirit of land speculation, which so tempting a prize as Texas easily kindled in multitudes in the United States, where this mode of gambling is too common a vice. Large grants of land in Texas were originally made to individuals, chiefly citizens of our country, who in many cases transferred their claims to joint-stock companies in some of our cities. A quotation will illustrate the nature of these grants and the frauds and speculations to which they gave birth: "The nominal grantee is called the *empresario*. He is considered, by the terms of the contract, merely as a trustee of the government, having no title himself to the land within the limits of his future colony, except upon condition of settling a number of families within a given time. The settlers themselves receive a title for each family for a league square, upon the express condition of settlement and cultivation and the payment of certain very moderate charges within a limited period. It is believed that these conditions were by

the colonization laws of Mexico the basis of all the
land titles in Texas, together with the further condition that all right and title should be forfeited if the
grantee or new settler should abandon the country or
sell his land before having cultivated it. An inspec-
tion of the various maps of Texas will show how numerous have been these privileges conceded to various
empresarios. The face of the province from Nueces
to Red River, and from the Gulf to the mountains, is
nearly covered by them. It became at last a matter
of greedy speculation; and it is a notorious fact that
many of the *empresarios*, forgetting the contingent
character of their own rights to the soil, and the
conditions upon which their future colonists were to
receive allotments of land, proceeded at once to make
out scrip, which has been sold in the United States to
an incalculable amount. . . ."

Texas, indeed, has been regarded as a prey for land
speculators within its own borders and in the United
States. To show the scale on which this kind of plunder has been carried on, it may be stated that the legislature of Coahuila and Texas, in open violation of the
laws of Mexico, was induced " by a company of land
speculators, never distinctly known, to grant them, in
consideration of twenty thousand dollars, the extent of
four hundred square leagues of the public land. This
transaction was disavowed and the grant annulled by
the Mexican government, and led to the dispersion of
the legislature and the imprisonment of the governor,
Viesca. And yet this unauthorized and perhaps corrupt grant of public lands formed the basis of new

speculation and frauds. A new scrip was formed and, according to the best information we have been able to obtain, four hundred leagues became in the hands of speculators as many thousands. The extent of these frauds is yet to be ascertained, for such is the blindness of cupidity that anything which looks fair on paper passes without scrutiny for a land title in Texas." The indignation excited in the Mexican government by this enormous grant, and the attempt to seize the legislators who perpetrated it, were among the immediate excitements to the revolt.   In consequence of these lawless proceedings great numbers in this country and Texas have nominal titles to land which can only be substantiated by setting aside the authority of the General Congress of Mexico, and are in consequence directly and strongly interested in severing this province from the Mexican confederacy.   Texan independence can alone legalize the mighty frauds of the land speculator.   Texas must be wrested from the country to which she owes allegiance, that her soil may pass into the hands of cheating and cheated foreigners. We have here one explanation of the zeal with which the Texan cause was embraced in the United States. From this country the great impulse has been given to the Texan revolution, and a principal motive has been the unappeasable hunger for Texan land.   An interest in that soil, whether real or fictitious, has been spread over our country. Thus "the generous zeal for freedom" which has stirred and armed so many of our citizens to fight for Texas turns out to be a passion for unrighteous spoil.

I proceed to another cause of the revolt, and this
was the resolution to throw Texas open to slaveholders
and slaves.   Mexico, at the moment of throwing off the
Spanish yoke, gave a noble testimony of her loyalty to
free principles by decreeing " that no person thereafter
should be born a slave or introduced as such into the
Mexican states; that all slaves then held should receive
stipulated wages, and be subject to no punishment but
on trial and judgment by the magistrate."   The subsequent acts of the government carried out fully these
constitutional provisions.   It is matter of deep grief
and humiliation that the emigrants from this country,
whilst boasting of superior civilization, refused to second
this honorable policy, intended to set limits to one of
the greatest social evils.   Slaves were brought into
Texas with their masters from the neighboring states
of this country.   One mode of evading the laws was
to introduce slaves under formal indentures for long
periods, in some cases it is said for ninety-nine years.
By a decree of the state legislature of Coahuila and
Texas, all indentures for a longer period than ten years
were annulled, and provision was made for the freedom
of children born during this apprenticeship.   This settled, invincible purpose of Mexico to exclude slavery
from her limits created as strong a purpose to annihilate her authority in Texas.   By this prohibition Texas
was virtually shut against emigration from the southern
and western portions of this country; and it is well
known that the eyes of the South and West had for
some time been turned to this province as a new market for slaves, as a new field for slave labor, and as a

vast accession of political power to the slaveholding states. That such views were prevalent we know; for, nefarious as they are, they found their way into the public prints. The project of dismembering a neighboring republic that slaveholders and slaves might overspread a region which had been consecrated to a free population was discussed in newspapers as coolly as if it were a matter of obvious right and unquestionable humanity. A powerful interest was thus created for severing from Mexico her distant province. We have here a powerful incitement to the Texan revolt, and another explanation of the eagerness with which men and money were thrown from the United States into that region to carry on the war of revolution. . . .

The great motives to revolt on which I have insisted are so notorious that it is wonderful that any among us could be cheated into sympathy with the Texan cause as the cause of freedom. Slavery and fraud lay at its very foundation. It is notorious that land speculators, slaveholders, and selfish adventurers were among the foremost to proclaim and engage in the crusade for " Texan liberties." From the hands of these we are invited to receive a province torn from a country to which we have given pledges of amity and peace. In these remarks I do not, of course, intend to say that every invader of Texas was carried thither by selfish motives. Some, I doubt not, were impelled by a generous interest in what bore the name of liberty, and more by that natural sympathy which incites a man to take part with his countrymen against a stranger without stopping to ask whether they are right or wrong. But the motives which rallied the great efficient majority round the standard of Texas were such as have been exposed, and should awaken any sentiment but respect.

Having considered the motives of the revolution, I proceed to inquire, How was it accomplished? The answer to this question will show more fully the criminality of the enterprise. The Texans, we have seen, were a few thousands, as unfit for sovereignty as one of our towns, and if left to themselves must have utterly despaired of achieving independence. They looked abroad; and to whom did they look? To any foreign state? To the government under which they had formerly lived? No; their whole reliance was placed on selfish individuals in a neighboring republic at peace with Mexico. They looked wholly to private individuals, to citizens of this country, to such among us as, defying the laws of the land and hungry for sudden gain, should be lured by the scent of this mighty prey and should be ready to stain their hands with blood for spoil. They held out a country as a prize to the reckless, lawless, daring, and avaricious, and trusted to the excitements of intoxicated imagination and insatiable cupidity to supply them with partners in their scheme of violence.

By whom has Texas been conquered? By the colonists? By the hands which raised the standard of revolt? By foreign governments espousing their cause? No; it has been conquered by your and my countrymen, by citizens of the United States, in violation of our laws and of the laws of nations. We, we have filled the ranks which have wrested Texas from Mexico.

In the army of eight hundred men who won the victory which scattered the Mexican force and made its chief a prisoner, "not more than fifty were citizens of Texas having grievances of their own to seek relief from on that field." The Texans in this warfare are little more than a name, a cover, under which selfish adventurers from another country have prosecuted their work of plunder.

Some crimes by their magnitude have a touch of the sublime, and to this dignity the seizure of Texas by our citizens is entitled. Modern times furnish no example of individual rapine on so grand a scale. It is nothing less than the robbery of a realm. The pirate seizes a ship. The colonists and their coadjutors can satisfy themselves with nothing short of an empire. They have left their Anglo-Saxon ancestors behind them. Those barbarians conformed to the maxims of their age, to the rude code of nations in time of thickest heathen darkness. They invaded England under their sovereigns, and with the sanction of the gloomy religion of the North. But it is in a civilized age and amidst refinements of manners, it is amidst the lights of science and the teachings of Christianity, amidst expositions of the law of nations and enforcements of the law of universal love, amidst institutions of religion, learning, and humanity, that the robbery of Texas has found its instruments. It is from a free, well-ordered, enlightened Christian country that hordes have gone forth in open day to perpetrate this mighty wrong. . . .

The United States have not discharged the obligations of a neutral state. They have suffered by a culpable negligence the violation of the Mexican territory by their citizens; and if now, in the midst of the conflict, whilst Mexico yet threatens to enforce her claims, they should proceed to incorporate Texas with themselves, they would involve themselves before all nations in the whole infamy of the revolt. The United States have not been just to Mexico. Our citizens did not steal singly, silently, in disguise, into that land. Their purpose of dismembering Mexico and attaching her distant province to this country was not wrapped in mystery. It was proclaimed in our public prints. Expeditions were openly fitted out within our borders for the Texan war. Troops were organized, equipped, and marched for the scene of action. Advertisements for volunteers to be enrolled and conducted to Texas at the expense of that territory were inserted in our newspapers. The government, indeed, issued its proclamation, forbidding these hostile preparations, but this was a dead letter. Military companies, with officers and standards, in defiance of proclamations and in the face of day, directed their steps to the revolted province. We had indeed an army near the frontiers of Mexico. Did it turn back these invaders of a land with which we were at peace? On the contrary, did not its presence give confidence to the revolters? After this what construction of our conduct shall we force on the world if we proceed, especially at this moment, to receive into our Union the territory which through our neglect has fallen a prey to lawless invasion? Are we willing to take our place among robber states? As a people have we no self-respect? Have we no reverence for national morality? Have we no feeling of responsibility to other nations and to Him by whom the fates of nations are disposed?

I proceed to a second very solemn consideration, namely, that by this act our country will enter on a career of encroachment, war, and crime, and will merit and incur the punishment and woe of aggravated wrong-doing. The seizure of Texas will not stand alone. It will darken our future history. It will be linked by an iron necessity to long-continued deeds of rapine and blood. Ages may not see the catastrophe of the tragedy the first scene of which we are so ready to enact. It is strange that nations should be so much more rash than individuals, and this in the face of experience, which has been teaching from the beginning of society that of all precipitate and criminal deeds those perpetrated by nations are the most fruitful of misery.

Did this country know itself or were it disposed to profit by self-knowledge, it would feel the necessity of laying an immediate curb on its passion for extended territory. It would not trust itself to new acquisitions. It would shrink from the temptation to conquest. We are a restless people, prone to encroachment, impatient of the ordinary laws of progress, less anxious to consolidate and perfect than to extend our institutions, more ambitious of spreading ourselves over a wide space than of diffusing beauty and fruitfulness over a narrower field. We boast of our rapid growth, forgetting that throughout nature noble growths are slow. Our people throw themselves beyond the bounds of civilization, and expose themselves to relapses into a semi-barbarous state, under the impulse of wild imagination and for the name of great possessions. Perhaps there is no people on earth on whom the ties of local attachment sit so loosely. Even the wandering tribes of Scythia are bound to one spot, the graves of their fathers; but the homes and graves of our fathers detain us feebly. The known and familiar is often abandoned for the distant and untrodden; and sometimes the untrodden is not the less eagerly desired because belonging to others. We owe this spirit in a measure to our descent from men who left the Old World for the New, the seats of ancient cultivation for a wilderness, and who advanced by driving before them the old occupants of the soil. To this spirit we have sacrificed justice and humanity, and through its ascendency the records of this young nation are stained with atrocities at which communities grown gray in corruption might blush.

It is full time that we should lay on ourselves serious, resolute restraint. Possessed of a domain vast enough for the growth of ages, it is time for us to stop in the career of acquisition and conquest. Already endangered by our greatness, we cannot advance without imminent peril to our institutions, union, prosperity, virtue, and peace. Our former additions of territory have been justified by the necessity of obtaining outlets for the population of the South and the West. No such pretext exists for the occupation of Texas. We cannot seize upon or join to ourselves that territory without manifesting and strengthening the purpose of setting no limits to our empire. We give ourselves an impulse which will and must precipitate us into new invasions of our neighbors' soil. Is it by pressing forward in this course that we are to learn self-restraint? Is cupidity to be appeased by gratification? Is it by unrighteous grasping that an impatient people will be instructed how to hem themselves within the rigid bounds of justice?

Texas is a country conquered by our citizens, and the annexation of it to our Union will be the beginning of conquests which unless arrested and beaten back by a just and kind Providence will stop only at the Isthmus of Darien. Henceforth we must cease to cry, Peace, peace. Our Eagle will whet, not gorge, its appetite on its first victim; and will snuff a more tempting quarry, more alluring blood, in every new region which opens southward. To annex Texas is to declare perpetual war with Mexico. That word " Mexico," associated in men's minds with boundless wealth, has already awakened rapacity. Already it has been proclaimed that the Anglo-Saxon race is destined to the sway of this magnificent realm, that the rude form of society which Spain established there is to yield and vanish before a higher civilization. Without this exposure of plans of rapine and subjugation, the result, as far as our will can determine it, is plain. Texas is the first step to Mexico. The moment we plant our authority on Texas, the boundaries of those two countries will become nominal, will be little more than lines on the sand of the seashore. In the fact that portions of the southern and western states are already threatened with devastation, through the impatience of multitudes

to precipitate themselves into the Texan land of promise, we have a pledge and earnest of the flood which
will pour itself still farther south when Texas shall
be but partially overrun.

Can Mexico look without alarm on the approaches
of this ever-growing tide? Is she prepared to be a
passive prey? to shrink and surrender without a struggle? Is she not strong in her hatred if not in her
fortresses or skill? strong enough to make war a
dear and bloody game? . . .

Even were the dispositions of our government most
pacific and opposed to encroachment, the annexation of
Texas would almost certainly embroil us with Mexico.
This territory would be overrun by adventurers, and the
most unprincipled of these — the proscribed, the disgraced, the outcasts of society — would, of course, keep
always in advance of the better population. These
would represent our republic on the borders of the Mexican states. The history of the connection of such men
with the Indians forewarns us of the outrages which
would attend their contact with the border inhabitants of our southern neighbor. Texas, from its remote-
ness from the seat of government, would be feebly
restrained by the authorities of the nation to which it
would belong. Its whole early history would be a
lesson of scorn for Mexico, an education for invasion
of her soil. Its legislature would find in its position
some color for stretching to the utmost the doctrine of
state sovereignty. It would not hear unmoved the cries
for protection and vengeance which would break from
the frontier, — from the very men whose lawlessness

would provoke the cruelties so indignantly denounced; nor would it sift very anxiously the question on which side the wrong began. To the wisdom, moderation, and tender mercies of the back settlers and lawgivers of Texas the peace of this country would be committed.

Have we counted the cost of establishing and making perpetual these hostile relations with Mexico? Will wars begun in rapacity, carried on so far from the center of the confederation, and of consequence little checked or controlled by Congress, add strength to our institutions or cement our union or exert a healthy moral influence on rulers or people? What limits can be set to the atrocities of such conflicts? What limits to the treasures which must be lavished on such distant borders? What limits to the patronage and power which such distant expeditions must accumulate in the hands of the Executive? Are the blood and hard-earned wealth of the older states to be poured out like water to protect and revenge a new people whose character and condition will plunge them into perpetual wrongs?

Is the time never to come when the neighborhood of a more powerful and civilized people will prove a blessing, instead of a curse, to an inferior community? It was my hope, when the Spanish colonies of this continent separated themselves from the mother country and, in admiration of the United States, adopted republican institutions, that they were to find in us friends to their freedom, helpers to their civilization. If ever a people were placed by Providence in a condition to do good to a neighboring state, we of this country sustained such relation to Mexico. That nation, inferior in science, arts, agriculture, and legislation, looked to us with a generous trust. She opened her ports and territories to our farmers, mechanics, and merchants. We might have conquered her by the only honorable arms, — by the force of superior intelligence, industry, and morality. We might silently have poured in upon her our improvements, and by the infusion of our population have assimilated her to ourselves. Justice, good will, and profitable intercourse might have cemented a lasting friendship. And what is now the case? A deadly hatred burns in Mexico towards this country. No stronger national sentiment now binds her scattered provinces together than dread and detestation of republican America. She is ready to attach herself to Europe for defense from the United States. All the moral power which we might have gained over Mexico we have thrown away, and suspicion, dread, and abhorrence have supplanted respect and trust.

I am aware that these remarks are met by a vicious reasoning which discredits a people among whom it finds favor. It is sometimes said that nations are swayed by laws as unfailing as those which govern matter; that they have their destinies; that their character and position carry them forward irresistibly to their goal; that the stationary Turk must sink under the progressive civilization of Russia as inevitably as the crumbling edifice falls to the earth; that by a like necessity the Indians have melted before the white man, and the mixed, degraded race of Mexico must melt before the Anglo-Saxon. Away with this vile sophistry! There is no necessity for crime. There is no fate to justify rapacious nations, any more than to justify gamblers and robbers in plunder. We boast of the progress of society, and this progress consists in the substitution of reason and moral principle for the sway of brute force. It is true that more civilized must always exert a great power over less civilized communities in their neighborhood. But it may and should be a power to enlighten and improve, not to crush and destroy. We talk of accomplishing our destiny. So did the late conqueror of Europe; and destiny consigned him to a lonely rock in the ocean, the prey of an ambition which destroyed no peace but his own. . . .

It is of great and manifest importance that we should use every just means to separate this continent from the politics of Europe; that we should prevent, as far as possible, all connection except commercial between the Old and the New World; that we should give to foreign states no occasion or pretext for insinuating themselves into our affairs. For this end we should maintain towards our sister republics a more liberal policy than was ever adopted by nation towards nation. We should strive to appease their internal divisions and to reconcile them to each other. We should even make sacrifices to build up their strength. Weak and divided, they cannot but lean upon foreign support. No pains should be spared to prevent or allay the jealousies which the great superiority of this country is suited to awaken. By an opposite policy we shall favor foreign interference. By encroaching on Mexico we shall throw her into the arms of European states, shall compel her to seek defense in transatlantic alliance.

How plain is it that alliance with Mexico will be hostility to the United States; that her defenders will repay themselves by making her subservient to their views; that they will thus strike root in her soil, monopolize her trade, and control her resources.   And with what face can we resist the aggressions of others on our neighbor if we give an example of aggression? . . .

Is war the policy by which this country is to flourish? Was it for interminable conflicts that we formed our Union?   Is it blood, shed for plunder, which is to consolidate our institutions?   Is it by collision with the greatest maritime power that our commerce is to gain strength?   Is it by arming against ourselves the moral sentiments of the world that we are to build up national honor?   Must we of the North buckle on our armor to fight the battles of slavery; to fight for a possession which our moral principles and just jealousy forbid us to incorporate with our confederacy?   In attaching Texas to ourselves we provoke hostilities and at the same time expose new points of attack to our foes.   Vulnerable at so many points, we shall need a vast military force. Great armies will require great revenues and raise up great chieftains.   Are we tired of freedom, that we are prepared to place it under such guardians?   Is the republic bent on dying by its own hands?   Does not every man feel that with war for our habit our institutions cannot be preserved?   If ever a country were bound to peace, it is this.   Peace is our great interest. In peace our resources are to be developed, the true interpretation of the constitution to be established, and the interfering claims of liberty and order to be adjusted.

In peace we are to discharge our great debt to the human race, and to diffuse freedom by manifesting its fruits. A country has no right to adopt a policy, however gainful, which, as it may foresee, will determine it to a career of war. A nation, like an individual, is bound to seek, even by sacrifices, a position which will favor peace, justice, and the exercise of a beneficent influence on the world. A nation provoking war by cupidity, by encroachment, and, above all, by efforts to propagate the curse of slavery, is alike false to itself, to God, and to the human race.

I proceed now to a consideration of what is to me the strongest argument against annexing Texas to the United States. This measure will extend and perpetuate slavery. I have necessarily glanced at this topic in the preceding pages, but it deserves to be brought out distinctly. I shall speak calmly, but I must speak earnestly. . . . The annexation of Texas will extend and perpetuate slavery. It is fitted and, still more, intended to do so. On this point there can be no doubt. As far back as the year 1829 the annexation of Texas was agitated in the southern and western states, and it was urged on the ground of the strength and extension it would give the slaveholding interest. In a series of essays ascribed to a gentleman now a senator in Congress it was maintained that five or six slaveholding states would by this measure be added to the Union, and he even intimated that as many as nine states as large as Kentucky might be formed within the limits of Texas. In Virginia, about the same time, calculations were made as to the increased value which would thus be given to slaves, and it was even said that this acquisition would raise the price fifty per cent. Of late the language on this subject is most explicit. The great argument for annexing Texas is that it will strengthen " the peculiar institutions " of the South and open a new and vast field for slavery.

By this act slavery will be spread over regions to which it is now impossible to set limits. Texas, I repeat it, is but the first step of aggressions. I trust, indeed, that Providence will beat back and humble our cupidity and ambition. But one guilty success is often suffered to be crowned, as men call it, with greater, in order that a more awful retribution may at length vindicate the justice of God and the rights of the oppressed. Texas, smitten with slavery, will spread the infection beyond herself. We know that the tropical regions have been found most propitious to this pestilence; nor can we promise ourselves that its expulsion from them for a season forbids its return. By annexing Texas we may send this scourge to a distance which if now revealed would appall us, and through these vast regions every cry of the injured will invoke wrath on our heads.

By this act slavery will be perpetuated in the old states as well as spread over new. It is well known that the soil of some of the old states has become exhausted by slave cultivation. Their neighborhood to communities which are flourishing under free labor forces on them perpetual arguments for adopting this better system. They now adhere to slavery not on account of the wealth which it extracts from the soil, but because it furnishes men and women to be sold in newly settled and more southern districts. It is by slave-breeding and slave-selling that these states subsist. Take away from them a foreign market and slavery would die. Consequently, by opening a new market it is prolonged and invigorated. By annexing Texas we shall not only create it where it does not exist, but breathe new life into it where its end seemed to be near. States which might and ought to throw it off will make the multiplication of slaves their great aim and chief resource.

Nor is the worst told. As I have before intimated, — and it cannot be too often repeated, — we shall not only quicken the domestic slave trade; we shall give a new impulse to the foreign. This indeed we have pronounced in our laws to be felony; but we make our laws cobwebs when we offer to rapacious men strong motives for their violation. Open a market for slaves in an unsettled country with a sweep of seacoast and at such a distance from the seat of government that laws may be evaded with impunity, and how can you exclude slaves from Africa? It is well known that cargoes have been landed in Louisiana. What is to drive them from Texas? In incorporating this region with the Union to make it a slave country we send the kidnapper to prowl through the jungles, and to dart like a beast of prey on the defenseless villages of Africa; we chain the helpless, despairing victims; crowd them into the fetid, pestilential slave ship; expose them to the unutterable cruelties of the middle passage, and, if they survive it, crush them with perpetual bondage.

I now ask whether as a people we are prepared to seize on a neighboring territory for the end of extending

slavery. I ask whether as a people we can stand forth
in the sight of God, in the sight of the nations, and
adopt this atrocious policy. Sooner perish ! Sooner
be our name blotted out from the record of nations ! . . .
Is it within the bounds of credibility that a people boasting of freedom, of civilization, of Christianity, should
systematically strive to spread this calamity over the
earth?

To perpetuate and extend slavery is not now in a
moral point of view what it once was. We cannot shelter ourselves under the errors and usages of our times.
We do not belong to the dark ages or to heathenism.
We have not grown up under prejudices of a blinding,
crushing tyranny. We live under free institutions
and under the broad light of Christianity. Every principle of our government and religion condemns slavery. The spirit of our age condemns it. The decree
of the civilized world has gone out against it. England
has abolished it. France and Denmark meditate its
abolition. The chain is falling from the serf in Russia.
In the whole circuit of civilized nations, with the single
exception of the United States, not a voice is lifted up
in defense of slavery. All the great names in legislation and religion are against it. The most enduring
reputations of our times have been won by resisting it.
Recall the great men of this and the last generation,
and, be they philosophers, philanthropists, poets, econo-
mists, statesmen, jurists, all swell the reprobation of slavery. The leaders of opposing religious sects — Wesley,
the patriarch of Methodism, Edwards and Hopkins,
pillars of Calvinism — join as brothers in one solemn

testimony against slavery. And is this an age in which
a free and Christian people shall deliberately resolve to
extend and perpetuate the evil?   In so doing we cut
ourselves off from the communion of the nations; we
sink below the civilization of our age; we invite the
scorn, indignation, and abhorrence of the world. . . .

What is the tendency of all governments in the
Christian world?   To secure more and more to every
man his rights, be his condition what it may.   Even in
despotisms, where political rights are denied, private
rights are held more and more sacred.   The absolute
monarch is more and more anxious to improve the laws
of the state and to extend their protection and restraints
over all classes and individuals without distinction.
Equality before the law is the maxim of the civilized
world.   To place the rights of a large part of the community beyond the protection of law, to place half a
people under private, irresponsible power, is to oppose
one of the most characteristic and glorious tendencies
of modern times.   Who has the courage to set down
this reverence for private rights among the fashions and
caprices of the day?   Is it not founded in everlasting
truth?   And dare we, in the face of it, extend and perpetuate an institution the grand feature of which is that
it tramples private rights in the dust?

Whoever studies modern history with any care must
discern in it a steady, growing movement towards one
most interesting result, — I mean towards the elevation
of the laboring class of society.   This is not a recent,
accidental turn of human affairs.   We can trace its
beginning in the feudal times, and its slow advances in

subsequent periods, until it has become the master movement of our age. Is it not plain that those who toil
with their hands, and whose productive industry is the
spring of all wealth, are rising from the condition of
beasts of burden, to which they were once reduced, to
the consciousness, intelligence, self-respect, and proper
happiness of men? Is it not the strong tendency of our
times to diffuse among the many the improvements once
confined to the few? He who overlooks this has no
comprehension of the great work of Providence or of
the most signal feature of his times. And is this an age
for efforts to extend and perpetuate an institution the
very object of which is to keep down the laborer and to
make him a machine for another's gratification?

I know it has been said in reply to such views that,
do what we will with the laborer, call him what we will,
he is and must be in reality a slave. The doctrine has
been published at the South that nature has made two
classes, the rich and the poor; the employer and the
employed, the capitalist and the operative, and that
the class who work are to all intents slaves to those in
whose service they are engaged. In a report on the
mail recently offered to the Senate of the United States
an effort was made to establish resemblances between
slavery and the condition of free laborers, for the obvious
purpose of showing that the shades of difference between
them are not very strong. Is it possible that such
reasonings escaped from a man who has trod the soil
of New England and was educated at one of her colleges? Whom did he meet at that college? The sons
of her laborers, — young men whose hands had been

hardened at the plow.   Does he not know that the
families of laborers have furnished every department in
life among us with illustrious men, have furnished our
heroes in war, our statesmen in council, our orators in
the pulpit and at the bar, our merchants whose enterprises embrace the whole earth?   What! the laborer of
the free state a slave and to be ranked with the despised
negro whom the lash drives to toil and whose dearest
rights are at the mercy of irresponsible power?   If there
be a firm, independent spirit on earth, it is to be found
in the man who tills the fields of the free states and
moistens them with the sweat of his brow. . . . It is
true that much remains to be done for the laboring class
in the most favored regions; but the intelligence already
spread through this class is an earnest of a brighter day,
of the most glorious revolution in history, of the elevation of the mass of men to the dignity of human beings.

It is the great mission of this country to forward this
revolution, and never was a sublimer work committed
to a nation.   Our mission is to elevate society through
all its conditions; to secure to every human being the
means of progress; to substitute the government of
equal laws for that of irresponsible individuals; to prove
that under popular institutions the people may be carried
forward, that the multitude who toil are capable of
enjoying the noblest blessings of the social state.   The
prejudice that labor is a degradation, one of the worst
prejudices handed down from barbarous ages, is to receive
here a practical refutation.   The power of liberty to raise
up the whole people, this is the great idea on which our
institutions rest, and which is to be wrought out in our

history.   Shall a nation having such a mission abjure it and even fight against the progress which it is specially called to promote ?

The annexation of Texas, if it should be accomplished, would do much to determine the future history and character of this country.   It is one of those measures which call a nation to pause, reflect, look forward, because their force is not soon exhausted.   Many acts of government intensely exciting at the moment are yet of little importance because their influence is too transient to leave a trace on history.   A bad administration may impoverish a people at home or cripple its energies abroad for a year or more.   But such wounds heal soon. A young people soon recruits its powers and starts forward with increased impulse after the momentary suspension of its activity.   The chief interest of a people lies in measures which, making perhaps little noise, go far to fix its character, to determine its policy and fate for ages, to decide its rank among nations.   A fearful responsibility rests on those who originate or control these pregnant acts.   The destiny of millions is in their hands.   The execration of millions may fall on their heads.   Long after present excitements shall have passed away, long after they and their generation shall have vanished from the earth, the fruits of their agency will be reaped.   Such a measure is that of which I now write.   It will commit us to a degrading policy the issues of which lie beyond human foresight.   In opening to ourselves vast regions through which we may spread slavery, and in spreading it for this among other ends, that the slaveholding states may bear rule in the national councils, we make slavery the predominant interest of the state. We make it the basis of power, the spring or guide of public measures, the object for which the revenues, strength, and wealth of the country are to be exhausted. Slavery will be branded on our front as the great idea, the prominent feature of the country. We shall renounce our high calling as a people and accomplish the lowest destiny to which a nation can be bound.

And are we prepared for this degradation? Are we prepared to couple with the name of our country the infamy of deliberately spreading slavery, and especially of spreading it through regions from which the wise and humane legislation of a neighboring republic had excluded it? We call Mexico a semi-barbarous people, and yet we talk of planting slavery where Mexico would not suffer it to live. What American will not blush to lift his head in Europe if this disgrace shall be fastened on his country? Let other calamities, if God so will, come on us. Let us be steeped in poverty. Let pestilence stalk through our land. Let famine thin our population. Let the world join hands against our free institutions and deluge our shores with blood. All this can be endured. A few years of industry and peace will recruit our wasted numbers and spread fruitfulness over our desolated fields. But a nation devoting itself to the work of spreading and perpetuating slavery stamps itself with a guilt and shame which generations may not be able to efface. The plea on which we have rested, that slavery was not our choice but a sad necessity bequeathed us by our fathers, will avail us no longer. The whole guilt will be assumed by ourselves. . . .

I wish not to be understood as having the slightest doubt as to the approaching fall of slavery. It may be prolonged, to our reproach and greater ultimate suffering. But fall it will and must. This many of us know, and this we rejoice to know. The advocates of slavery must not imagine that to carry a vote is to sustain their cause. With all their power they cannot withstand the providence of God, the principles of human nature, the destinies of the race. To succeed they must roll back time to the dark ages, must send back Luther to the cell of his monastery, must extinguish the growing light of Christianity and moral science, must blot out the declaration of American independence. The fall of slavery is as sure as the descent of the Ohio. Moral laws are as irresistible as physical. In the most enlightened countries of Europe a man would forfeit his place in society by vindicating slavery. The slaveholder must not imagine that he has nothing to do but fight with a few societies. These of themselves are nothing. He should not waste on them one fear. They are strong only as representing the spirit of the Christian and civilized world. His battle is with the laws of human nature and the irresistible tendencies of human affairs. These are not to be withstood by artful strokes of policy or by daring crimes. The world is against him, and the world's Maker. Every day the sympathies of the world are forsaking him. Can he hope to sustain slavery against the moral feeling, the solemn sentence of the human race ? . . .

I suppose that I shall be charged with unfriendly feelings towards the South.   All such I disclaim.   Strange
as it may seem, if I have partialities they are rather for
the South.   I spent a part of my early life in that
region, when manners probably retained more of their
primitive character than they now do ; and to a young
man unaccustomed to life and its perils there was something singularly captivating in the unbounded hospi-
tality, the impulsive generosity, the carelessness of the
future, the frank, open manners, the buoyant spirit and
courage which marked the people ; and, though I have
since learned to interpret more wisely what I then saw,
still the impressions which I then received and the
friendships formed at a yet earlier age with the youth
of the South have always given me a leaning towards
that part of the country.   I am unconscious of local
prejudices.   My interest in the South strengthens my
desire to avert the annexation of Texas to the Union.
That act I feel will fix an indelible stain on the South.
It will conflict with the generous elements of character
which I take pleasure in recollecting there.   The South
will cease to be what it was.   In the period to which I
have referred slavery was acknowledged there to be a
great evil.   I heard it spoken of freely with abhorrence.
The moral sentiment of the community on this point
was not corrupt.   The principles of Mr. Jefferson in
relation to it found a wide response.   The doctrine that
slavery is a good, if spread by the seizure of Texas, will
work a moral revolution, the most disastrous which can
befall the South.   It will paralyze every effort for escape
from this enormous evil.   A deadly sophistry will weigh

on men's consciences and hearts, until terrible convulsions — God's just judgments — will hasten the deliverance which human justice and benevolence were bound to accomplish. . . .

Next to liberty, union is our great political interest; and this cannot but be loosened — it may be dissolved — by the proposed extension of our territory. I will not say that every extension must be pernicious, that our government cannot hold together even our present confederacy, that the central heart cannot send its influences to the remote states which are to spring up within our present borders. Old theories must be cautiously applied to the institutions of this country. If the federal government will abstain from minute legislation and rigidly confine itself within constitutional bounds, it may be a bond of union to more extensive communities than were ever comprehended under one sway. Undoubtedly there is peril in extending ourselves, and yet the chief benefit of the Union, which is the preservation of peaceful relations among neighboring states, is so vast that some risk should be taken to secure it in the greatest possible degree. The objection to the annexation of Texas drawn from the unwieldiness it would give to the country, though very serious, is not decisive. A far more serious objection is that it is to be annexed to us for the avowed purpose of multiplying slaveholding states and thus giving political power. This can not, ought not to be borne. It will justify, it will at length demand the separation of the states. . . .

The annexation of Texas will give new violence and passion to the agitation of the question of slavery. It

is well known that a majority at the North have discouraged the discussion of this topic on the ground
that slavery was imposed on the South by necessity,
that its continuance was not of choice, and that the
states in which it subsists, if left to themselves, would
find a remedy in their own way. Let slavery be systematically proposed as the policy of these states, let it
bind them together in efforts to establish political power,
and a new feeling will burst forth through the whole
North. It will be a concentration of moral, religious,
political, and patriotic feelings. The fire, now smothered, will blaze out, and in consequence new jealousies
and exasperations will be kindled at the South. The
annexation of Texas would stir up an open, uncompromising hostility to slavery, of which we have seen no
example, and which would produce a reaction very
dangerous to union. . . .

I am but one of a nation of fifteen millions, and as
such may seem too insignificant to protest against a
public measure. But in this country every man, even the
obscurest, participates in the sovereignty, and is responsible for public acts, unless by some mode of opposition proportioned to his sense of the evil he absolves
himself from the guilt. I shrink from an act which is
to pledge us as a people to robbery and war, to the work
of upholding and extending slavery without limitation
or end. On this point the decree of the world has
gone forth, and no protests or clamors can drown the
deep, solemn voice of humanity, gathering strength with
every new generation. A community acknowledging
the evils of slavery and continuing it only because the

first law of nature, self-preservation, seems to require gradual processes of change, may retain the respect of those who deem their fears unfounded. But a community wedding itself to slavery inseparably, with choice and affection, and with the purpose of spreading the plague far and wide, must become a byword among the nations, and the friend of humanity will shake off the dust of his feet against it in testimony of his reprobation.

The cause of liberty, of free institutions, — a cause more sacred than union, — forbids the annexation of Texas. It is plain from the whole preceding discussion that this measure will exert a disastrous influence on the moral sentiments and principles of this country by sanctioning plunder, by inflaming cupidity, by encouraging lawless speculation, by bringing into the confederacy a community whose whole history and circumstances are adverse to moral order and wholesome restraint, by violating national faith, by proposing immoral and inhuman ends, by placing us as a people in opposition to the efforts of philanthropy and the advancing movements of the civilized world. It will spread a moral corruption already too rife among us, and in so doing it will shake the foundations of freedom at home and bring reproach on it abroad. It will be treachery to the great cause which has been confided to this above all nations.

The dependence of freedom on morals is an old subject, and I have no thought of enlarging on the general truth. I wish only to say that it is one which needs to be brought home to us at the present moment and that it cannot be trifled with but to our great peril. There are symptoms of corruption amongst us which show us that we cannot enter on a new career of crime without peculiar hazard. I cannot do justice to this topic without speaking freely of our country, as freely as I should of any other; and, unhappily, we are so accustomed as a people to receive incense, to be soothed by flattery, and to account reputation as a more important interest than morality, that my freedom may be construed into a kind of disloyalty. But it would be wrong to make concessions to this dangerous weakness. I believe that morality is the first interest of a people, and that this requires self-knowledge in nations as truly as in individuals. He who helps a community to comprehend itself and to apply to itself a higher rule of action is the truest patriot and contributes most to its enduring fame.

I have said that we shall expose our freedom to great peril by entering on a new career of crime. We are corrupt enough already. In one respect our institutions have disappointed us all. They have not wrought out for us that elevation of character which is the most precious and in truth the only substantial blessing of liberty. Our progress in prosperity has indeed been the wonder of the world; but this prosperity has done much to counteract the ennobling influence of free institutions. The peculiar circumstances of the country and of our times have poured in upon us a torrent of wealth, and human nature has not been strong enough for the assault of such severe temptation. Prosperity has become dearer than freedom. Government is regarded

more as a means of enriching the country than of securing private rights. We have become wedded to gain
as our chief good. That under the predominance of this
degrading passion the higher virtues, the moral independence, the simplicity of manners, the stern uprightness, the self-reverence, the respect for man as man,
which are the ornaments and safeguards of a republic,
should wither and give place to selfish calculation and
indulgence, to show and extravagance, to anxious, envious, discontented strivings, to wild adventure, and to
the gambling spirit of speculation, will surprise no one
who has studied human nature. The invasion of Texas
by our citizens is a mournful comment on our national
morality. Whether, without some fiery trial, some signal prostration of our prosperity, we can rise to the force
and self-denial of freemen, is a question not easily
solved.

There are other alarming views. A spirit of lawlessness pervades the community, which if not repressed
threatens the dissolution of our present forms of society.
Even in the old states mobs are taking the government
into their hands, and a profligate newspaper finds little
difficulty in stirring up multitudes to violence. When
we look at the parts of the country nearest Texas we
see the arm of the law paralyzed by the passions of the
individual. Men take under their own protection the
rights which it is the very office of government to
secure. The citizen wearing arms as means of defense
carries with him perpetual proofs of the weakness of
the authorities under which he lives. The substitution
of self-constituted tribunals for the regular course of

justice, and the infliction of immediate punishment in the moment of popular frenzy, are symptoms of a people half reclaimed from barbarism. I know not that any civilized country on earth has exhibited during the last year a spectacle so atrocious as the burning of a colored man by a slow fire in the neighborhood of St. Louis; and this infernal sacrifice was offered not by a few fiends selected from the whole country, but by a crowd gathered from a single spot. Add to all this the invasions of the rights of speech and of the press by lawless force, the extent and toleration of which oblige us to believe that a considerable portion of our citizens have no comprehension of the first principles of liberty.

It is an undeniable fact that, in consequence of these and other symptoms, the confidence of many reflecting men in our free institutions is very much impaired. Some despair. That main pillar of public liberty, mutual trust among citizens, is shaken. That we must seek security for property and life in a stronger government is a spreading conviction. Men who in public talk of the stability of our institutions whisper their doubts (perhaps their scorn) in private. So common are these apprehensions that the knowledge of them has reached Europe. Not long ago I received a letter from an enlightened and fervent friend of liberty in Great Britain beseeching me to inform him how far he was to rely on the representations of one of his countrymen just returned from the United States, who had reported to him that in the most respectable society he had again and again been told that the experiment of freedom here was a failure and that faith in our

institutions was gone.   That the traveler misinterpreted
in a measure what he heard we shall all acknowledge.
But is the old enthusiasm of liberty unchilled among us?
Is the old jealousy of power as keen and uncompromising?   Do not parties more unscrupulously encroach on
the constitution and on the rights of minorities?   In
one respect we must all admit a change.   When you
and I grew up, what a deep interest pervaded this
country in the success of free institutions abroad!
With what throbbing hearts did we follow the struggles
of the oppressed!   How many among us were ready
to lay down their lives for the cause of liberty on the
earth!   And now who cares for free institutions abroad?
How seldom does the topic pass men's lips!   Multitudes, discouraged by the licentiousness at home, doubt
the value of popular institutions, especially in less
enlightened countries; whilst greater numbers, locked
up in gain, can spare no thought for the struggles of
liberty, and, provided they can drive a prosperous trade
with foreign nations, care little whether they are bond
or free.

I may be thought inclined to draw a dark picture of
our moral condition.   But at home I am set down
among those who hope against hope; and I have never
ceased to condemn as a crime the despondence of those
who, lamenting the corruption of the times, do not
lift a finger to withstand it.   I am far, very far from
despair.   I have no fears but such as belong to a friend
of freedom.   Among dark omens I see favorable influences, remedial processes, counteracting agencies.   I
well know that the vicious part of our system makes

more noise and show than the sound. I know that the prophets of ruin to our institutions are to be found most frequently in the party out of power, and that many dark auguries must be set down to the account of disappointment and irritation. I am sure, too, that imminent peril would wake up the spirit of our fathers in many who slumber in these days of ease and security. It is also true that, with all our defects, there is a wider diffusion of intelligence, moral restraint, and self-respect among us than through any other community. Still I am compelled to acknowledge an extent of corruption among us which menaces freedom and our dearest interests; and a policy which will give new and enduring impulse to corruption, which will multiply indefinitely public and private crime, ought to be reprobated as the sorest calamity we can incur. Freedom is fighting her battles in the world with sufficient odds against her. Let us not give new chances to her foes.

That the cause of republicanism is suffering abroad through the defects and crimes of our countrymen is as true as that it is regarded with increased skepticism among ourselves. Abroad republicanism is identified with the United States, and it is certain that the American name has not risen of late in the world. It so happens that whilst writing I have received a newspaper from England in which lynch law is as familiarly associated with our country as if it were one of our establishments. We are quoted as monuments of the degrading tendencies of popular institutions. When I visited England fifteen years ago, republican sentiments were freely expressed to me. I should probably hear none now. Men's minds seem to be returning to severer principles of government, and this country is responsible for a part of this change. It is believed abroad that property is less secure among us, order less stable, law less revered, social ties more easily broken, religion less enforced, life held less sacred, than in other countries. Undoubtedly the prejudices of foreign nations, the interests of foreign governments, have led to gross exaggeration of evils here. The least civilized parts of the country are made to represent the whole, and occasional atrocities are construed into habits. But who does not feel that we have given cause of reproach? And shall we fix this reproach and exasperate it into indignation and hatred by adopting a policy against which the moral sentiments of the Christian world revolt? . . .

When we look forward to the probable growth of this country; when we think of the millions of human beings who are to spread over our present territory; of the career of improvement and glory opened to this new people; of the impulse which free institutions if prosperous may be expected to give to philosophy, religion, science, literature, and arts; of the vast field in which the experiment is to be made of what the unfettered powers of man may achieve; of the bright page of history which our fathers have filled, and of the advantages under which their toils and virtues have placed us for carrying on their work, — when we think of all this can we help for a moment surrendering ourselves to bright visions of our country's glory before which all the glories of the past are to fade away? Is it presumption to say that, if just to ourselves and all nations, we shall be felt through this whole continent, that we shall spread our language, institutions, and civilization through a wider space than any nation has yet filled with a like beneficent influence?   And are we prepared to barter these hopes, this sublime moral empire, for conquests by force?   Are we prepared to sink to the level of unprincipled nations, to content ourselves with a vulgar, guilty greatness, to adopt in our youth maxims and ends which must brand our future with sordidness, oppression, and shame?   This country cannot without peculiar infamy run the common race of national rapacity.   Our origin, institutions, and position are peculiar, and all favor an upright, honorable course.   We have not the apologies of nations hemmed in by narrow bounds, or threatened by the overshadowing power of ambitious neighbors.   If we surrender ourselves to a selfish policy we shall sin almost without temptation, and forfeit opportunities of greatness vouchsafed to no other people, for a prize below contempt.

I have alluded to the want of wisdom with which we are accustomed to speak of our destiny as a people. We are *destined* (that is the word) to overspread North America, and, intoxicated with the idea, it matters little to us how we accomplish our fate.   To spread, to supplant others, to cover a boundless space, this seems our ambition, no matter what influence we spread with us.   Why cannot we rise to noble conceptions of our destiny?   Why do we not feel that our work as a nation is to carry freedom, religion, science, and a nobler

form of human nature over this continent? and why do
we not remember that to diffuse these blessings we
must first cherish them in our own borders, and that
whatever deeply and permanently corrupts us will
make our spreading influence a curse, not a blessing,
to this New World? It is a common idea in Europe
that we are destined to spread an inferior civilization
over North America; that our slavery and our absorp-
tion in gain and outward interests mark us out as fated
to fall behind the Old World in the higher improvements of human nature, in the philosophy, the refinements, the enthusiasm of literature and the arts, which
throw a luster round other countries. I am not prophet
enough to read our fate. I believe, indeed, that we are
to make our futurity for ourselves. I believe that a
nation's destiny lies in its character, in the principles
which govern its policy and bear rule in the hearts of
its citizens. I take my stand on God's moral and
eternal law. A nation renouncing and defying this
cannot be free, cannot be great.

Religious men in this community—and they are many
— are peculiarly bound to read the future history of their
country not in the flattering promises of politicians, but
in the warnings of conscience and in the declaration of
God's word. They know, and should make it known,
that nations cannot consolidate free institutions and
secure a lasting prosperity by crime. They know that
retribution awaits communities as well as individuals;
and they should tremble amidst their hopes when with
this solemn truth on their minds they look round on
their country. . . . Men buried in themselves and in

outward interests, atheists in heart and life, may scoff at the doctrine of national retribution because they do not see God's hand stretched out to destroy guilty communities.   But does not all history teach that the unlicensed passions of a guilty people are more terrible ministers of punishment than miraculous inflictions?   To chastise and destroy, God need not interfere by supernatural judgments.   In every community there are elements of discord, revolution, and ruin pent up in the human soul which need only to be quickened and set free by a new order of events to shake and convulse the whole social fabric.   Never were the causes of disastrous change in human affairs more active than at the present moment. Society heaves and trembles from the struggle of opposing principles as the earth quakes through the force of central fires.   This is not the time for presumption, for defying Heaven by new crimes, for giving a new range to cupidity and ambition.   Men who fear God must fear for their country in this "day of provocation," and they will be false to their country if they look on passively and see without remonstrance the consummation of a great national crime which cannot fail to bring down awful retribution.